Woman In Politics

Woman In Politics

Emma Guy Cromwell

Edited by Diana J. Taylor

Published by the Kentucky Commission on Women

Acknowledgements

The editor gratefully acknowledges for their assistance, advice, and encouragement: Marsha Weinstein, Leslie Bishop, Lindsay Campbell, and Virginia Woodward of the Kentucky Commission on Women; Kentucky historian Dr. Thomas D. Clark; Dr. Ann Butler, director of the Center of Excellence for the Study of Kentucky African Americans at Kentucky State University; Dr. Richard Taylor, professor of English at Kentucky State University; the Kentucky Department of Libraries and Archives, particularly Joe Horton; the Legislative Research Commission Library, particularly John McKee; grammarian and proofreader Linda Sherrard and journalist/writer Fran Ellers.

Foreword

When Emma Guy Cromwell died in July of 1952, she left a legacy of public service and historical precedents for the Commonwealth of Kentucky. Minimal, if any, notice has been given to her accomplishments, however, in the textbooks and writings that have educated countless Kentuckians about the people and events which shaped their state. This re-publication of Mrs. Cromwell's 1939 autobiography represents an effort by the Kentucky Commission on Women to provide a more complete picture of the state's history and the people who pioneered its social and political development.

Preface

Emma Guy Cromwell became the first woman elected to statewide office in Kentucky when she won a race for Secretary of State in 1923 — the first statewide campaign after enactment of the woman's suffrage amendment in 1920. It was a time when advertisements for women's dresses consumed much of the space on newspapers' front pages, while stories about "first woman" accomplishments were frequently found in the pages designated for society and other news of "interest to women." Regardless of the placement, however, the stories conveyed important messages about the changing role of women.

On the day after the 1923 Democratic primary, for example, *The Courier-Journal* carried a huge feature on "Aunty Rose" Barrett of Warrenton, Oregon, the first woman city manager in the United States. A day or so later, a brief story noted that three women were among the fifty-eight people who passed the state bar examination that July. Democratic gubernatorial nominee J.C. Cantrill, in a post-primary statement, expressed special appreciation to "the thousands of good women in the state who gave me their loyal support." (This was particularly noteworthy in view of Mr. Cantrill's opposition to woman's suffrage as a state representative.)[1] Another newspaper item recorded the election of Lois Roach as Graves County sheriff by the largest majority ever recorded in a sheriff's race in that Western Kentucky county. Mrs. Roach had been appointed earlier to finish out her deceased husband's term — an historically frequent route for Kentucky women into public office.

Mrs. Cromwell followed a different path, winning election in her own right from the outset of her political career. But the written record she left leads a reader to conclude that her status as a widow whose only son had died in young adulthood contributed significantly to her decision to enter politics. Indeed, she wrote that her married life "held the only true contentment I have ever known." Whether a stable home and family life would have kept Emma Guy Cromwell out of politics remains, of course, an unknown. But her writing makes it clear that she was a woman of ambition. And the aspirations and apprehensions evident in her autobiography are those shared by many women in public life today.

Mrs. Cromwell credited her initial experience in politics with teaching her several lessons that served her well throughout her public career, including an introduction to the fondness of some adults for a childhood game of "finger crossing." Her diplomatic description notwithstanding, she apparently gained an early understanding of and appreciation for the realities of politics. Kentucky historian Dr. Thomas D. Clark, who knew Mrs. Cromwell, and whom she praises as a supporter of libraries in her book, described her as someone who "knew a great deal about the people around her...what the politicians were up to, and she was able to play that game."[2]

Her political initiation preceded her first statewide race by more than two decades and came in a successful bid for state librarian, a post that in 1896 was determined by the vote of the Kentucky legislature. She came to Frankfort that year from her home town of Scottsville in Allen County and never moved away from the capital city. A year after her arrival, she married Frankfort attorney William F. Cromwell, who served as clerk of the Kentucky Senate for several terms. They had one son, William Foree Cromwell. The elder Cromwell died in 1909. The son, who served in the Army during World War I and became a businessman, was killed in an accident in early adulthood.

Mrs. Cromwell, who served as enrolling clerk for the House of Representatives in 1916 and 1918, paid tribute in her book to several women active in the suffrage movement, but her own level of activity was undocumented. She was subsequently described in newspaper accounts as "one of the first women to emerge after suffrage."[3] That emergence came in the 1923 race for Secretary of State, when both Republicans and Democrats were receptive to the idea of including a woman candidate on their tickets. Her first announced opponent was another woman, Mary Elliott Flannery of Catlettsburg, who later became the first woman elected to the Kentucky General Assembly. Two men completed the primary field.

While Mrs. Cromwell wrote that she learned of her victory within a matter of hours after the polls closed, newspaper accounts about the results being in question stretched through more than a week before the final tally was known. She subsequently defeated her Republican opponent, Eleanor Wickliffe of Bardstown, in the general election and was sworn in on January 10, 1924, as the first woman elected statewide in the Commonwealth.

The campaign issues of 1923 included pari-mutuel wagering,

teaching evolution in schools, and prohibition. The overriding issue for Mrs. Cromwell, however, was the propriety of women seeking a position that had always been held by men. The arguments against a woman came from both men and women, described by Mrs. Cromwell as "the stand-patters."

She decided while still Secretary of State to make a bid for Treasurer in 1927 and considered her race for that office to be less arduous in terms of "trail blazing," stating at one point that people had become more accustomed to seeing a woman run for public office. The challenge was still gender-specific, however, as she focused her efforts on convincing voters that a woman could handle the state's funds efficiently; she defeated two men in the primary and another in the general election. Kentucky's Constitution at the time prohibited statewide officials from succeeding themselves in office. They could, however, return to an office after a four-year break. Mrs. Cromwell's effort to return as Secretary of State following her term as Treasurer failed when she lost the Democratic Party's nomination to Sara W. Mahan of Danville at a state convention.[4]

She did not leave the public arena, however. Governor Ruby Laffoon appointed her State Park Director in 1932, and it was during this time that she found herself in the midst of controversy. A pair of newspaper articles offered an intriguing prelude to the events. On April 12, 1935, a *Courier-Journal* story noted that Mrs. Cromwell, in Louisville for a Kentucky Education Association meeting, said she was considering another race for treasurer. Just under one month later, on May 5, 1935, another article said she was ready to announce for the office but had changed her plans "suddenly." This story cited reports among her friends that Mrs. Cromwell was in line for a National Park Service position.

By the end of June, however, another possibility emerged. A June 29, 1935, article said Mrs. Cromwell was under fire from federal parks officials for her management of federal funds in connection with joint federal-state parks projects. As Mrs. Cromwell wrote in her autobiography, Kentucky was receiving federal assistance on a number of park improvement projects. She served as Federal Procurement Officer for those purposes in addition to her role as State Park Director — a customary arrangement in most states. Federal officials, however, felt that certain requirements were not being met in the expenditure of federal funds, according to the newspaper account. Mrs. Cromwell subsequently resigned as Federal Procurement Officer and retained her Park Director position; both Governor Laffoon and federal officials said they were not displeased with her work and that the change resulted from Mrs. Cromwell's being overburdened with responsibilities. Mrs. Cromwell, meanwhile, said her records were open for public inspection.

An appointment in September, 1937, by Governor Albert B. Chandler returned Mrs. Cromwell to the state library system, this time as Director of the Department of Library and Archives. The post was created under Governor Chandler's 1936 Reorganization Act but had never been filled. Mrs. Ethel Gist Cantrill had served in the elected state librarian position since 1924, winning the post the year after her husband, J.C. Cantrill, died. (His death came shortly after he won the Democratic gubernatorial nomination; his successor as nominee and eventual governor was William Fields, under whom Mrs. Cromwell served as Secretary of State.)

Here, again, emerged a small controversy. The Reorganization Act specified qualifications for the state librarian, and some questioned whether Mrs. Cromwell's experience was sufficient for the position. Particularly critical of her in this and other circumstances was the *Courier-Journal*'s J. Howard Henderson, who wrote a regular column from the state capital. Despite the criticism, Mrs. Cromwell remained in the post until she was replaced in 1940 by an appointee of Governor Keen Johnson.

Two years later, Mr. Henderson and others took aim at Mrs. Cromwell for a job she held as an adult education consultant under an appointment from Superintendent of Public Instruction John W. Brooker. State Attorney General Hubert Meredith called for her dismissal, maintaining that public school funds could not be used to pay her salary because they must be used exclusively for the schools. The *Courier-Journal* columnist described Mr. Brooker's description of Mrs. Cromwell's role as "blather."

For his part, the superintendent maintained that Mrs. Cromwell's salary was paid from an appropriation for the operation of his office, not from the public school funds.

A newspaper article about the dispute noted: "Mrs. Cromwell is known rather widely for the multiplicity of public jobs she has held, as well as for her tenacious efforts to find a new one when the old one runs out."[5]

As her public life continued, Mrs. Cromwell authored her autobiography, garnering a favorable review in the June 11, 1939, *Cou-*

rier-Journal. Under the headline "A Woman Who Did," reviewer Rosamond Milner wrote: "For the honor of women who hold offices they were once thought incompetent to fill, she tells of some of her achievements, but without egotism. And her book is remarkable for the absence of one rancorous or even critical reference to a single person....Her story has other — and more militant — highlights that make it one for women to read with satisfaction and with pride in this successful woman office-holder's point of view about the duty of public servants."

Emma Guy Cromwell, whose age was not precisely determined, died July 19, 1952, a year after suffering a stroke which made her an invalid. Her obituary described her as "a political pioneer among Kentucky women." She is buried in the Frankfort Cemetery.

Notes

[1]Kleber, John E., editor-in-chief. *The Kentucky Encyclopedia*. Lexington, KY: The University Press of Kentucky. 1992. p.160.
[2]Personal interview. Lexington, KY. April 26, 1994.
[3]*The Courier-Journal*. Dec. 11, 1939. Section 3, p. 1.
[4]*The Courier-Journal*. Sept. 3, 1937. Section 4, p. 5.
[5]*The Courier-Journal*. March 11, 1943. Section 2, p. 1.

An Additional Comment

Mrs. Cromwell wrote her autobiography in the language of her times. She referred to Kentucky's black citizens as "colored," and, in direct quotations, used the dialect that was commonly attributed to black Americans at the time of the book's publication in 1939. These references have been modified, edited and/or deleted in this edition.

The Original Dedication

To the Masonic Order of Kentucky, a great factor in shaping my destiny, this book is respectfully dedicated.

The Original Preface

Aside from whatever observations may occur here and there on the philosophy of life and the meaning and influence of women in politics, this book is a narration of facts. It is a plain record of some of the main happenings in the life of a woman in politics in the early, formative years of womanhood's struggle upward and onward.

Most of it comes from the memory of the writer, as may be seen. To make it authentic in date and relation to other events, use has been made of the Kentucky Statutes, reports of the various departments, reports of the Library Commission, the Kentucky State Park reports of the years 1932-1935, catalogue of records, documents, and papers of the Kentucky Governors, 1792-1926.

Thanks are due to Mrs. W.T. Fowler of Lexington, Kentucky, and Colonel Bruce Reynolds of New York, author of The Sweeties in Sweden and other widely read books, for reading the manuscript and for valuable constructive criticism.

Emma Guy Cromwell
Frankfort, Kentucky
April, 1939

Introduction

During the past few years many friends have urged me to write this book. They have argued that an outline of the incidents in the life of a woman pioneer in politics would be of interest. In yielding to their insistence I shall be well repaid if I can, in any degree, raise the standard of thinking among the women of my state as they go to the polls year after year. If, in addition, I can point the way to any aspiring young woman who may be considering how to make her way in the world and give courage where she might falter, I shall be more than happy.

My mind goes back to the many who all along the way have given me loyal support and to them my heart goes out. First, looking back I see a long line of ancestors who gave me background, whose achievements as pioneers in Kentucky and in other states gave me courage. None of us can rightly appraise the debt owed to ancestors, especially to fathers, mothers, and grandparents. One can, however, give to them a full measure of appreciation and gratitude.

My own father and mother live for me in the words and recollection of others more than in my own, and to the silent influence of their lives I owe much in the shaping of my own life and thought. My father was Ashley Duncan Guy. He was born in southern Kentucky. His grandparents were born in Warwickshire, England, and very near their birthplace yet stands "Guy's Mill," on the river Avon, said to be the oldest water mill in the world. "Guy's Cliffe" is another romantic spot in this the home county so beloved by Shakespeare, who had his birth there so many years ago. The Duncan in my father's name comes from the family of that name in Scotland which by tradition belongs to the Clan of Robertson.

My mother was Alice Milliken Quisenberry, daughter of Harry Quisenberry and his wife, Frances Hail. Other family names among her connections were Milliken, Wilkins, and Herndon. The latter line is connected with the Wallers, Georges, Digges, and other families of early Virginia.

1

I have spoken elsewhere of the ideal life I led for a few years as the wife of the late William Cromwell, an attorney of Frankfort. When he passed on to a higher life my whole being was centered around the budding life of our son, William Foree Cromwell. To William I gave the full measure of a mother's devotion and watched with growing pride his development into a man of character, scholarship, and integrity. I gloried in his career in the army during the World War, and later in his upward climb in business. When in a sudden accidental tragedy he was taken from me, there seemed nothing for me but an empty heart. Time has softened but has not dimmed this grief, and I have found a panacea in hard work, and filled my life with duty and my heart with thought for others. I can say no more.

To the Masonic Order in Kentucky this book is dedicated as a slight payment on my debt to this noble order, who were guardians of my childhood, who provided teachers and schools and prepared me for the work that awaited me as a woman.

Again, one's birthplace and childhood home is a background that has much to do with making or marring one's future. In this I was fortunate. Allen, Warren, and Simpson counties of my own Kentucky are all home to me, and they evoke the sweetest memories. They are mentioned at greater length elsewhere, with due appreciation for their location, history, and people.

In my private and public life I owe debts of gratitude for friendship, fellowship, and understanding that can never be repaid. Far more names than I can mention here are included among those who have helped me from day to day as the years have rolled by. My heart grows too full for adequate expression as my mind surveys the past and remembers all the loyal, faithful friends and kin who have helped me with kindly criticism and words of encouragement as this book has taken shape, and to them I give heartfelt thanks.

All this is said with a very humble spirit. It is my hope that my work, my ideals, and my modest achievements may be used by a kind Providence to guide precious girls to fuller life; to point the way to ambitious souls; to give faith, hope, and help to other women. True happiness lies in serving others, by sharing with them life's problems, by contributing to the creation of true, pure, and noble conditions.

I

A Woman Enters Politics

I light my candles from their torches.

Several years before women gained the suffrage, they were permitted to hold some elective and appointive offices of importance. About that time it was my good fortune to be elected as State Librarian by the Kentucky Legislature. When Senator Tibbis Carpenter entered me in the contest for this state office there were already three other Democratic women candidates in the field for the nomination, which had to precede the opening of the Legislature. These were Mrs. Mary Brown Day of Frankfort, Mrs. Caswell Bennett of Henderson, and Miss Pauline Hardin of Lexington. Those who remember these three cultured and able women can realize what their opposition meant.

Senator Carpenter, one of the many kind home friends who had my future at heart, told me one day to get ready to go with him to Frankfort. He had consulted a number of State Senators and Representatives who all thought I could easily win. These first political friends of mine were Senators Powell Taylor of Henderson, Robert Brown of Warsaw, Henry Martin of Midway, Thomas Tippett of Morehead, Charlie White of Elizabethtown, Charley Moore of Frankfort, and Jack Wills of Winchester.[1] The position sought was alluring in name. I had loved books all my life and nothing could have suited me better than to have the opportunity to read and further develop my taste along that line. I had no special library training, of course, as this was an almost unheard-of thing at the time, but being ambitious and willing to work it seemed to me then that was sufficient. Experience has added the magic word, "Opportunity," and I yet think these, with patience, honesty, and persistence make up the seven magic symbols that spell "Success."

The first thing necessary was to assemble suitable clothes for the trip. Mrs. Carrie Taylor and my cousin, Mrs. Ben Milliken of Bowling Green, superintended this and saw that everything was of good material and correct in every way. I was very proud of my outfit and even went a little into debt, trusting to the promised position to reimburse my depleted purse. This assembling of a wardrobe was very different from today when one can procure ready-made clothes at many shops. Then patterns, materials, trimmings, and finishings all had to be purchased separately, and one good dress took up several days of a seamstress' time and it was finally on the good taste and skill of the dressmaker that the — as we would say today — ensemble depended.

We left Bowling Green two days before the Legislature met, because they told me that they had to lobby and "put up fences." These were new terms to me but I did have sense enough not to ask too many questions or talk too much. Miss Lizzie Johnson, one of our very charming young women, who had traveled a great deal, went to Frankfort with me, and she proved a fine companion.

Our first night was spent in Louisville, where we met the solons who were to "put me over." While there Senator Carpenter added many more to his list of workers. It looked so good to me that I felt I was already elected. They kept talking about trading, lobbying, and the "caucus," all of which gave a glimpse of a world strange to me. I have never yet met so many people at once and was never so uncomfortable. It was a medley of many different kinds; legislators, state officials, office seekers, and lobbyists from every point of the compass.

I remember being introduced to one distinguished-looking legislator who wore a long black coat and silk hat. He told me I was as "pretty as a speckled pup," and that he thought he would vote for me. I swallowed my discomfort, accepted the intended compliment, and thanked him.

After dinner the men held a conference and we were free to go to a show or to rest. This was a relief as so much conversation tended to be confusing and the admonitions of my friends were rapidly reducing me to a yes-sir and no-sir person, a result which I was determined should not be.

After the conference Senator Carpenter assured us that there was nothing to worry over, that certain workers had agreed to look after their parts of the state and there remained no doubt of my nomination. He may have thought that I needed encouragement, for I found that the real fight had not yet begun. Next morning we were all up early, had breakfast amid much confusion and talk and hurrying to and fro, then boarded the train for Frankfort. On this trip nothing was discussed except the caucus and lobbying, and so much importance was attached to them that I determined to find out exactly what it was all about. I did not recognize the words as old acquaintances of Civil Government in school. As soon as comfortable in my room in the Old Capital Hotel in Frankfort, instead of ordering ice water, I had the porter bring me a Webster's Unabridged Dictionary, for which I gave him a tip, as we used to do in college when we wanted a secret kept.

I found that caucus meant a special meeting of a political party to nominate candidates for office, while lobbyist meant one who solicits support for men or measures. This explained in a very practical way the words I had learned in school without thinking of their application to real life. Thus I entered my first adventure in what was to be for me a career for many years to come.

Miss Johnson and I were told to be ready in a few minutes to meet some newly arrived members of the Legislature, Senator Carpenter wishing me to meet them before the other candidates had a chance. Everyone was so agreeable that I believed everything they told me. Imagine my surprise and disillusionment later when I learned of some votes against me. I could not understand then, but years of experience have taught me that in politics people sometimes do the school-child act of "crossing fingers" when promising. They think that, "All is fair in love and politics." I am happy to believe that these finger-crossers are often the disillusioned ones in the final count. I like to feel that honesty and integrity and straight thinking and talking win out over double dealing.

There were two Populists in the Legislature, Mr. Edrington of Lyon County and Mr. Poore of Pendleton County, Mr. Edrington seeming to hold the key to the situation.[2] Since then the son of Mr. Edrington

5

and his granddaughter have been among my best workers in campaigns in Western Kentucky. The reason for Mr. Edrington seeming to hold the key to the situation was because the two major parties were in closer combat than is usual in Kentucky while this third party held the balance of power. There was trading, as usual in politics, and one of the Senators tried to find me to confirm my position. I was in care of Mrs. Charlie White in her room while the trade was under way. This was not only new to me but rather disturbing. I had heard of swapping and trading horses in my home town on Trading Alley beside the court-house, on County Court Day, but on such days and on election days all such places were forbidden spots to girls. I had no idea then that votes were traded as well as positions for people. I thought that honor and integrity and ability were all that counted. I found there had to be much adjustment and exchange of power in high places before things were on a stable basis.

However, in a long experience, I have learned that in spite of trading and lobbying, the vast majority of the men and women in politics are truly loyal to friends and to principles and do their best for their state and communities according to their ability.

Very soon someone knocked on Mrs. White's door and she said to me, "Get back into that alcove there." I obeyed and sat behind the tall headboard of the antique bed, as innocent as a lamb. Perhaps Mr. White had warned her they would look for me. She met Mr. Poore at the door and in reply to his query said to him, "Did you look in the parlor?" He said, "I have looked everywhere and just must see her before the caucus meets." She told him she would try to find me and out she went and locked the door while there I sat not knowing what move to make next.

In a short time she returned and told me to come out and get ready as they were to take us out to dinner and then go to the caucus. In a few minutes Mr. White came for us and we were met in the parlor by Senator Carpenter and others. I felt like a fugitive from justice for I did not know what had happened. I shall never forget when we marched into the big, crowded dining room of the hotel. Our table was reserved and was the center of attraction. Though feeling rather uncomfortable, the beautiful dinner my friends were giving me added to the excite-

6

ment and thrills.

There are not many places in the world of today where there is packed so much of interest and glamour as in a pre-legislative session in the Capital City of Kentucky, and it was true then.[3] It was all rather overwhelming and inevitably sent my mind back to Byron as these words raced through my memory:

> "All Belgium's capital had gathered then
> Her beauty and her chivalry
> And bright the lamps shone o'er
> Fair women and brave men."

Time sped on to the caucus at the Old Capitol, as eight o'clock was the hour. When we arrived we found several other candidates (for other offices) and my opponents all waiting to go on trial before the tribunal of legislators from all points in the state. The house was so crowded there wasn't even standing room in the balcony. With a heavy stroke of the gavel the meeting was called to order and the roll call proceeded to determine if there was a quorum before the balloting started. This was thrilling to me then and continues to be so every time I hear it when the representatives of the people gather to make the laws and guide the destiny of the state.

One candidate after another was put in nomination until finally the office of Librarian was reached. When Charlie White, Representative from Hardin County, arose and put me in nomination, such eloquence had never fallen from the lips of man. The cheers were great, and I wondered if it were really I who was being lauded. Then, immediately, Senator Carpenter rose and in his dignified manner pleaded with the members of the General Assembly to stand by his home candidate for Librarian. In his mellow, benign voice he reminded the crowd that the "Pennyrile" never asked for much and he hoped that every section of the state would remember to cast its vote for his candidate from that faithful district.

Kentuckians do not need to be told the location of "The Pennyrile." Others may not know that it lies between Louisville and the Jackson Purchase. The name comes from the fragrant pennyroyal that grows there so luxuriantly — and this in common parlance is called "pennyrile."

The balloting soon started and to my surprise I won the nomination easily and I felt like shouting "Glory Hallelujah" right there in that great audience. This was a wonderful victory and many of our friends leaped over their seats to congratulate me as the Democratic nominee for State Librarian.

The election was to follow in a few days when I must defeat my Republican opponent, Mrs. Georgia Shelton, of Columbia, Kentucky. Here the battle really started, as the General Assembly was very close as to party affiliation, the balance of power being held by Mr. Edrington and Mr. Poore. During the twenty-eight days I was tied up with my opponent these two stayed with me. Finally, on the twenty-eighth day, when the ballot was taken, and was again a tie, a Republican Senator, Honorable Hays Petrie of Elkton, arose and said, "I cast my vote for Emma Guy, the little woman from the Pennyrile." He had told me he would do this if his vote was necessary to elect me. He kept faith with me and saved the day.. There was great rejoicing through the state among my friends, and many nice things were said about me in the press.

I felt as if the beam of Aladdin's lamp had been turned on me, and a new world had opened to my vision. I little thought then that this line of work was to be my career and that my fate had led me to my life work as one of the pioneers in office-holding by women. This one vote was the turning point.

I had read and studied government in school, passed my examinations and received my diploma at Howard College, Gallatin, Tennessee, but had never seen a Governor or other state official. These, with legislators, were all to be classed along with Socrates, Demosthenes, and Plato. I was timid and shrinking and liked it only too well when my advisers warned me not to talk too much. I can hear the echoes today of the shouts that went up from the legislative hall of the Old Capitol when my first election ended in triumph. "Hurray for our little Pennyrile girl. You can't beat her." Judge Virgil Baird of Glasgow, Judge of the Court of Appeals, Bob Morningstar of Bowling Green, Charlie Lewis, and Elliott Beard of Shelbyville, and others of my supporters were highly elated.

After receiving many congratulations and the good wishes of friends from over the state, I was very glad to start homeward to plan and dream and attend to the practical problems of taking up my residence in Frankfort. Miss Lizzie Johnson and Mr. Morningstar accompanied me as far as Bowling Green. In Louisville that night he took us to the theater. It was my first time to see a real play. The theater was large and beautiful and the surroundings so spectacular that I was dazed until the curtain rose and the characters appeared in Shakespeare's A Midsummer Night's Dream. Then I felt at home for our class in college had worked very hard as amateurs to stage this comedy.

Just in front of us we heard a couple talking during intermission — of my race and the victory won. One of them said, "Wouldn't you like to see that little woman who was elected State Librarian?" And went on to remark, "They say she is attractive, a college graduate, of fine family, but an orphan without means." "Yes," was the reply, "she worked her way through school by coaching rich girls from the South and carried off more honors than any of them, but she is so timid her friends are worried for fear she cannot hold the place." It is hard to realize now the stir caused by the entrance of women into public life in that day.

Mr. Morningstar could hardly be restrained from introducing me then and there, but I forbade it. This conversation put fire into my soul and renewed my determination to hold the job and to be a credit to my friends and to the Masonic Fraternity to whom I owe a debt of gratitude that can never be paid except by making good in all I undertake. This order has been my prop and stay in the past years. My father, who passed into the Great Beyond before my earliest recollection, was an ardent Mason. He would honor and appreciate more than ever the knighthood and chivalry of the Masonic Order if he could look down and see their loyalty and protection to one of his children.

The next morning how bright the sun shone, and oh, how beautiful the world looked and the people all so good! I seemed to be the center of attraction for the first time in my life which had been so different from that of the average girl. From early childhood I had just plodded along in school, under the care of the Masonic Fraternity, then through high school and college, passing along from one class to another always with the present problem of knowing the next lesson and wondering where the money was coming from to buy the books needed.

9

On one occasion while at college I sold a beautiful pair of skates with silver mountings to my roommate for ten dollars. These had been given me by my first sweetheart. Oh, how I hated to give them up! It almost broke my heart. I knew he would not find out about it as he lived in the East. It so happened that our paths never crossed again. A girlish heart soon mends, and the ten dollars was vital. With the money I bought second-hand copies of Byron, Burns, Longfellow, Milton, Whittier, Pope, Shelley, Keats, Scott, and a History of the World. A wonderful bargain then and still prized possessions in my library. Every now and then I go there, take out one of these volumes and spend a delightful evening reading page after page, following the rich thoughts of these masters of expression. Memory lingers here where I learned to love the classics which were well worth the great sacrifice made in parting with my skates.

It was not long until I was again in Scottsville, my home town, where I had lived during my mother's life. But mother and home were gone, only a few relatives and scores of good friends left, who all came to rejoice with me over my promising start in life. For several days it was the talk of the town and everyone wanted to know all about the election, the legislators, officials, and the splendid library of which I was to take charge on the first of June. The more I repeated all that had happened, the more it seemed like a dream.

Even my good black friends were all interested, especially Uncle Isie, who bossed the young folks of the town and made us all step around by threatening to tell on us, always reminding us that we belonged to "quality folks." I can see him today in memory as he used to strut around, up and down the streets, with his head tied up with a clean white rag, telling us what to do and what not to do, saying, "I'm not going to have my white folks' children running the streets tomboying around like they don't have good sense." I wonder if he could come back today what he would say if he could see the changes — in thought, word, and deed.[4]

All my Allen County friends had heard of my good position and were greatly interested in helping me to get ready for the new responsibilities. They helped me in every way, from selecting my wardrobe to advising me as to my work and play under new circumstances and surroundings, which from their own experience they knew would be so different from my former life. They knew that until this time I had been as secluded from public life as if brought up in a convent. I can never be grateful enough for all the nice things that were done for me then and my love for my county and section of the state grows brighter and brighter as time goes on.

Dear old Allen County! How her people have stood by me through thick and thin! And connected with it always by geography, history, and tradition is Warren and also Simpson, the latter being my birthplace. The very rivers and the creeks which were familiar to me in childhood are beloved names now. Its beautiful river is the Big Barren. Its creeks water fertile and productive valleys. Some of these creeks are Puncheon Camp, Big and Little Difficult, Bay's Fork, Drake's, John's, Trammel, Long, and Rough. Each name tells a legend of early pioneer days and later agriculture and industry. The wheat, corn, oats, and tobacco of this region are famous even in Kentucky, that prides itself on these products. In these later days the oil of that section has a story all its own, too long to tell here. The limestone and red clay soil has sustained a hardy and progressive people.

The very names of these counties breathe patriotism of the old order. Colonel John Allen and Captain John Simpson went together to the "gallant but disastrous event on the River Raisin" and both made the supreme sacrifice. They were both Virginians of that early day when patriots were bred to live for their country and to die for it if need be. These two studied law together and practiced in Shelbyville, Kentucky, before they marched away to their final fate in the War of 1812. Captain Simpson first saw service at the Battle of Fallen Timbers under General Wayne in 1794.[5]

It was the usual thing for Kentucky counties to be named for Revolutionary patriots, or for those of "(The War of) 1812," and the martial and loyal spirit of these brave men lives yet in the counties that bear their names. There are no truer Kentuckians than those who make their homes in these counties. Warren County was named for Dr. Joseph Warren who fell at Bunker Hill, June 17, 1775; Scottsville was named for General Charles Scott.[6] How these grand old names ring!

It was all Indian country and in our childhood there were many tales told to us of Indian mounts and forts. White travelers passed through Allen County as early as 1770, and its first settlement was in 1797. The deer, the elk, and the buffalo with numberless smaller animals of the wild have passed away, first succeeded by the hardy pioneers, then by a progressive modern citizenship that has fostered homes, churches, schools, culture, and education that equal any other section. Allen County is still known for its fishing and hunting, its horses and hounds. Shy quail seek cover in its fields and woods, and red and gray foxes tempt the finest hounds to many a chase. Listening to a fox chase, or going on "possum hunts" were among the pleasures of youth at that time.

Allen County boasts of many public men who in the Legislature held their own with any other statesmen. Among many of literary bent who could be named, one stands out as the subject of stories told us over and over by Uncle Tom Brown, who used to relate how Opie Read, noted writer and kinsman of many in the county, was editor of the Scottsville Argus in the early 1870s, how he would walk to Bowling Green, twenty-five miles away, to get his newsprint, relating that he would carry his shoes and sit down to put them on when near the city.[7]

If I wondered sometimes how to meet the situation at Frankfort in circumstances so new to me, my trust was in Providence to bring everything around and to direct my destiny. In this my faith was rewarded then and ever since. One of the finest gifts of our Heavenly Father has been this direction of my life and the many loved friends who have helped me always. My heart ached at the thought of saying good-bye to those who had been my stay and whose friendship, love, and kindness I needed more and more.[8]

At last the day arrived to say farewell to my friends and start on my journey. I knew I was going to the Capital City to take charge of the State Library; further than that I had no vision of my future. A feeling of sadness and regret crept into my heart at the thought of leaving friends and dear old Allen County, which was a world within itself to me. No matter where I may roam, Simpson, Allen, and Warren will always be home. It must be remembered that the distances then were immeasurably greater than now. Travel was difficult in many ways;

12

roads were poor; trains were slow and very coal-sooty indeed as compared with the streamlined air-conditioned cars that glide along the tracks today, not to mention the automobiles that make travel on our good roads a pleasure deluxe.

I shall never forget the morning I left Scottsville in the town hack to catch a train at Bowling Green for Louisville where I would have to change trains for Frankfort. Many friends came to say "Good-bye and God Bless you."

I have always felt that a mantle of blessing fell on me with the prayers of the good people back home, a covering of courage that gave me endurance to carry on in my work as well as in my manner of living. They come back to me today, the sweet prayers of my aunts Bettie Brown and Sudie Atwood, Mrs. Laura Spillman, Mrs. Frank Pitchford and Mrs. Sylvester Welch.

I was soon comfortable in a seat behind the big bay horses that were to draw the hack, but the waving good-byes and cheers that went up choked me, and I wept tears of mingled sorrow and joy. Into my life had come a complete change, and things could never be the same. I must go into a new world and adapt myself to conditions and circumstances, but what fine conditions and miraculous circumstances to come to one who had known only the sheltered life of the small town and the school! What opportunities, too! In the morning of life, it is well we cannot look beyond the veil to see all the sweetness and the sorrow, but must take whatever comes day by day, a bit at a time.

As the bays went prancing over the hill, I heard the school bell ringing. It seemed to me that it was ringing down a curtain on the past, as it gradually faded away as the bays pranced on. It was sweeter to me with the memories it evoked than the "Chimes of Normandy," which I was privileged to hear in later years. As the wheels of the old town hack rolled on, they seemed to keep time to vagrant fancies from my loved poets, such lines as:

"All are architects of fate,
    Working in these walls of time,
    Some with massive deeds and great,
    Some with ornaments of rhyme."

13

And then Scott's "Lay of the Last Minstrel," as it repeated over and over:

> "Breathes there a man with soul so dead
> Who never to himself hath said,
> 'This is my own, my native land'?"

And, again, Tennyson, the Poet Laureate, came to mind in words that linger in his most beloved song, "Crossing the Bar." At this last thought so sweet and gentle, I drew up the reins of my mind, for the association was too solemn for one who had life before her. Soon the many sounds and sights of the way engrossed my attention as I watched passing people and wagons and buggies.

In Bowling Green I had just time to buy a ticket, check my trunk, and board the train. This time the journey to Louisville and then to Frankfort did not seem so long. I was soon in a comfortable room at the Old Capital Hotel and had met many charming people. It was not long until I was fortunate enough to be located in the hospitable home of Miss Lutie Ware, where there were many more who became true friends. Among these were two dear ladies who became my trusted advisers, Mrs. John Milam and Mrs. William Hudson. As an evidence of their loving interest, Mrs. Milam's best remembered admonition to me was to read the Ninety-first Psalm every day; Mrs. Hudson's mind turned to my social fitness and she told me to read everything on etiquette and to keep up with the trend of the times. Both had in mind always my best interests.[9] I lived at Miss Ware's until my marriage to William Cromwell of Frankfort, one year later.

On a morning that is unforgettable, I began my new work. Ed Hines, formerly of Bowling Green, was my chief adviser. He escorted me to the State Library, where I met Charlie Willis, who was to be my assistant. Mr. Hines had my bond ready, and he went with me to the office of Governor William O. Bradley to have him approve it, as was provided by law. I had heard of bearding the lion in his den, and that seemed to be my fate. Governor Bradley was the newly elected Republican Governor, while I, as a Democrat, had been through such a grueling experience in attaining my office that I feared the worst. My newness in politics made me take everything too seriously, and I was painfully aware of my inexperience. So when I signed my bond my hand shook so I could scarcely hold the pen. No doubt this was more than amusing to such a seasoned campaigner as the Governor, but he was very polite and formal and kind.[10]

After the bond was signed he said to me, "Miss Guy, did you think I was 'Auld Nick' with horns?" I replied, perhaps with little tact, "Oh, Governor, I did not know." From that time we were the best of friends. He was always very considerate and thoughtful whenever we had any business to transact, and he must have often smiled to himself at the scared little woman in the beginning. I can only hope that he noted some improvement as I gained in experience and knowledge of the work. He was very broad-minded and tolerant, and I shall always cherish his memory with admiration.

Others remembered at this time for their many kindnesses and courtesies are Captain W.J. Stone, State Auditor and Southern gentleman of the old school; Frank Johnson, Treasurer, a rugged individualist of great integrity and high sense of duty and honor; and Charles Finley, Secretary of State, a conscientious public official. These and others gave me good advice, and what meant more to me then, treated me as an equal in the high duties of serving the state.

On that first morning my office was made beautiful by a profusion of flowers sent by friends, while many telegrams and letters attested to the interest felt by those who knew me or my parents and forebears. All this was exciting and thrilling but my heart still sank when I contemplated the legal tomes that were strange in their very appearance and yet more strange in their contents to one who was a mere schoolgirl. I surely knew this was not a "position" but a job and a working job at that.

The black porter was a wonder at knowing the books and their locations.[11] He could neither read nor write, but yet had a marvelous fund of "book knowledge." He had also a fine philosophy of life that never failed him and a great deal of information gained from experience and contact with the legal minds of the men who from time to time ruled the state and used the library. He helped me over many embarrassing places. We had not the system we have now in force in all good libraries and the work largely depended on memory. I used to go to the office at a quarter to eight and study the locations of the books, their titles, and to some extent, their contents.

The porter had a philosophy expressed something like this: "Don't worry, little miss, it will come out all right." This was comforting but not always adequate. For instance, one morning a note was sent in which I simply could not read. After pondering a moment, I remembered that Chief Justice Pryor had told me always to come to him when in doubt. So I took the note at once to the dear judge and told him that someone wanted a book, but I could not see what book or even read the name of the sender. He took it, looked at it awhile rather quizzically, and said, "Child, I wrote this. I don't blame you. I can't read my own writing after it gets cold." I said, "Judge, please do not tell this on me." He said, "Don't worry, the joke is on me and not you. Very few people can read my writing."

Many interesting things happened during this term as State Librarian. One that made a great impression was a very satisfactory interview I had with Lieutenant Governor (W.J.) Worthington, when he was acting as Governor. Some lawyers from Louisville came to the library and asked me to present some papers to him requesting a pardon for a young man who was serving a sentence in the penitentiary for killing a man. The trouble had arisen over a game of cards, and whiskey had been the cause of it all. The young man belonged to a prominent family, and the feeling had run high, and many believed his conviction had been largely for spite. They told me all this and enlisted my sympathy.

I did as they requested, took the papers to Governor Worthington with an explanation and the request that he read and consider the matter. The next day he sent for me and said, "Little girl, I am going to pardon this man. I believe he has been punished enough." Today, that young man is one of the leading businessmen in a large Eastern city, has a happy home and family, and no one there knows of his wild-oat days. This was a good deed done by Governor Worthington who passed into the Great Beyond without knowing the splendid results of the pardon he gave then. I have often thought that if it were possible for the public to know the many who go straight after a prison experience and pardon, much good might be done. Where one goes wrong, many do make good after a pardon, but from the nature of the cases, the one bad result is always well known while the good results are buried in the consciousness of the men and their families.

Judge Joseph H. Lewis, a member of the Court of Appeals, was another interesting character. We were so close to the pioneer ideals then that if a man were strong intellectually, his constituents did not care about his personal habits. Judge Lewis was very fond of chewing tobacco and was a great whittler. So good soft sticks were always kept for him to whittle on. He would sit for hours chewing and whittling and making sage observations. We could not induce him to use a cuspidor. He would call the sergeant of the court, and tell him to take that darn thing out of his way as he wanted to spit in the grate.[12] Oftener, instead, the beautiful new rug suffered, but none dared to chirp.

The sergeant was a great help in getting out the catalogue of the library. He knew the library thoroughly, was very competent and a typical Southern gentleman, loved by everyone. Charlie Willis, my splendid assistant, was invaluable. He was the right one for the place; everyone liked him, and it was a real pleasure to work with him. We were very proud of our catalogue which, by law, had to be renewed every six years. In this time the books grew in number until the task was not merely a revision, but amounted to a new cataloguing in toto.

Judge George DuRelle was one of the most polished judges of that day. He was always faultlessly dressed, had a Chesterfieldian manner, and was a brilliant lawyer besides. He was another who had volunteered to smooth out the rough places in my pathway. So when a group of interesting people from the East came to my office and wanted to be presented to the Governor, I had no hesitation in calling on Judge DuRelle to tell him of my difficulty and to ask him to tell me all the little formalities of such an occasion. He coached me a little, and I went back and soon got an audience with the Governor and made the proper presentations without a slip. This reminds me that in addition to learning the business of being a State Librarian, I was kept busy all the time waiting on the crowds that came in, and in this I had the constant assistance of Mr. Willis and the porter.

I shall never forget the first Legislature that met after I became State Librarian. It was one of my duties to seat the members of the General Assembly, and the porter, with old-time courtesy, would show them the seats which were assigned to them on a chart we kept. On the opening morning, he came to me greatly disturbed. One member of the Lower House had not taken his seat upstairs with the other members. He had found him on the first floor and told him the House met upstairs. The dear old man had told the porter that he had been elected to the Lower House and was not going into the Upper House. I took the chart and showed the member about the seating capacity and told him that both Houses met on the same floor upstairs. After much persuasion, we succeeded in getting the legislator into his right seat. He did not make any the less valuable member for this confusion, for we often find that common sense means more than sophistication in running the affairs of state.

In the Legislature there were many interesting events and outstanding characters. It was a day of oratory, and argument and great changes were in the air. Among the best remembered were the many women who were lobbying for suffrage. The leaders were Miss Laura Clay, Mrs. Desha Breckinridge, Mrs. Ida W. Harrison of Lexington, and Mrs. Edmund Post of Paducah. They were women of master minds, and often while listening to their arguments I wished I might equal them in speech and logic. It seemed that the men were afraid of them because they could hold their own against any odds. These women were the shining lights that illuminated the path for the freedom of womanhood in Kentucky. They were among the leading pioneers in paving the way for woman suffrage. We, who have enjoyed the fruits of their hard work, should appreciate their labors and honor their names, and remember what they did for all women everywhere.

During this session a United States Senator was elected amid great confusion, and the trading and swapping for votes beat any County Court Day where horses and mules are swapped and traded. And they were all so jocular and unconcerned about it all. In giving a reason for unseating one member, they said it was because he was bald-headed, and that another was unfit because he parted his hair in the middle. This recalls the fact that there was truly a great prejudice against a man parting his hair thus. He was condemned as a "dude" and there could be no greater slap than that in the circles that chose our lawmakers.

Now United States Senators are chosen by popular vote, and the stormy scenes in the Assembly Halls are no longer enacted. The battleground has been shifted to the primary and general elections, and all the voters can participate in the battle of ballots.

I went into office the first of June, and one year later was married to Mr. Cromwell. My work went on just the same until the close of my term when I was very glad to turn over the duties to Miss Pauline Hardin, who was elected by the Legislature to succeed me. After our marriage we moved into our home in South Frankfort. I had been happy in the companionship of the good friends at Miss Lutie Ware's but was supremely satisfied in my home, where the visits of our many friends were always welcomed. Mr. Cromwell was a man imbued with the genuine Kentucky hospitality, and my comparatively brief married life held the only true contentment I have ever known. My childhood home had been broken up by the deaths of both parents, and my career had been one of struggle and stress far more than that of the average girl. I welcomed the calm and quiet of home life and had it continued would never have chosen a public career.

Our Heavenly Father had led me through struggles and privation and had encouraged my ambition and determination and at the same time opened a way into home life so that I could for once know what it was to be in a safe haven, sheltered and protected. I had enjoyed and appreciated the opportunity of holding one of the best positions open to women in that day. The years spent at home with my husband and boy are a blessed and priceless memory. You who are so blessed should be completely contented, for around the family fireside is the most sacred spot on earth. It is here that true happiness and contentment are found.

In my own case the sweet recollections of that time are as pictures that hang on memory's wall, and it is on them that I gaze on evenings when tired and worn with office work. It is to that time I look back for inspiration to keep on in the field of political success where it has been my privilege to labor. The uncounted friends who have loyally supported me in my every ambition will not think the less of me if I say that I would have preferred to remain in a peaceful and happy home. But when death steps in and takes the best loved ones away, then it is that we doubly appreciate the new fields that have been opened for women. It is then that a career can compensate in some measure for all that has been lost in what was once woman's only sphere. This reminds me of an old poem:

> "They talk about a woman's sphere
> As though it had a limit...
> There's not a place in heaven or earth,
> There's not a life, nor death nor birth,
> That has a feather's weight of worth
> Without a woman in it."

And may I say to home women, keep such happiness while it is in your possession. Treasure it as a pearl without price. Hold on to it as to your hope of Heaven. But if home happiness is snatched away and duty calls you to business or politics, remember that one can be as clean and honorable in these fields as in home and church. Indeed, one can hold on to all that is best in home and church and still climb to the top of the ladder of success. This is the heritage of the noble women who were leaders in the fight for woman suffrage. It is our glory today that as women we can still to "our own selves be true," and we can know beyond a shadow of doubt, we will "not then be false to any man."

> "But God gives patience; love learns strength,
> And faith remembers promise,
> And hope itself can smile at length
> On other hopes gone from us."

Chapter I Notes

1. Although described by the author as "Senators," some of these men served in the House of Representatives. The Kentucky Senate Journal of February 6, 1896, lists C. W. White and J.D. Wills as representatives voting for Mrs. Cromwell, and she refers to "Representative" White later in the first chapter; there is no vote recorded for Thomas Tippett or, somewhat surprisingly in view of the author's comments, for Senator Carpenter. The others included in the list were recorded as Senators voting for Mrs. Cromwell. It should be noted that the House and Senate met in joint session for the

purpose of electing the librarian.

2. The Senate Journal notes that Representatives W.J. Edrington and H.J. Poor (note the spelling difference) both voted for Mrs. Cromwell for state librarian.

3. Pre-legislative conferences were common in the days preceding the modern emergence of the legislature as a strongly independent branch of government; some were held in the state's resort areas, providing an opportunity for socializing as well as the election of legislative leaders. The last such pre-legislative conference, according to the Legislative Research Commission Library, was held in November, 1981 at Kentucky Dam Village State Resort Park.

4. The author did not provide a full identification for "Uncle Isie." Also, the dialect used by the author in this and other passages was that which was commonly attributed to black Americans at the time of the book's publication in 1939. It has been modified or deleted by the editor in this edition.

5. Col. John Allen was a Kentucky legislator from 1801 until his 1838 death at the Battle of River Raisin. Capt. John Simpson was speaker of the Kentucky House of Representatives in 1811. He was elected to the U.S. Congress in 1812 but never served.

6. General Charles Scott was Kentucky's fourth Governor during 1808-1812.

7. The author continued:

"The annals of the county bear the names of such worthies as William T. Anthony, Barton W. Stone, John J. Gatewood, Frank Pitchford, J. Wilson Foster, Joseph W. Hester, William J. McElroy, Thomas J. Morehead, Tobias W. Burton. Of the old families some best remembered are Huntsman, Bryant, Wilson, Calvert, Brown, Guy, Walker, Hughes, Spillman, Read, Hood, Pitchford, Kreekmore, Hams, Crow, Payne, Lovelace, and Johnson; while Joe and Jim Kirby, noted fox chasers and possum hunters, lived across the line in Warren County.

"Andrew Jackson was a great hero of the old days to citizens of this county, so near to Tennessee. My mother's great-aunt, Mary Anne Wickwire, used to tell of the comic and tragic happenings of old times when my great-great-grandfather, John Hail, one of the founders of Franklin, Simpson County, and a close friend of Jackson's, was active among the pioneers and in furthering Jackson's plans. Old Hickory had spent nights at the Hail home, and I have today the plain white sugar bowl from which they sweetened their toddies, while a cousin, Mrs. Roscoe Huntsman, has the demijohn in which peach brandy was always kept."

8. The author continued:

"One of the last to call on me was Ellen Fishback, the black woman who used to run down to Howard College to see Myrt Shive, Bessie Welch (who were my roommates), and me. She brought us large baskets of good things to eat and notes from the boys who would fix her up to come and pay her expenses. It was always a great trip for Ellen. When she left me this time she said, 'Child, I'm coming to see you when you get to Frankfort because I know you have too much raising to take the big head and forget your black folks who helped to raise you and love you. You belong to the quality folks.' And sure enough she did come for a visit later, and there was great rejoicing on both sides. My butler, Spence Blanton, who was a senior in the black normal school (and who is now principal of the City Colored School in Frankfort, doing a wonderful work for his race) was very nice to Ellen and drove her all around to see the places of interest."

9. The author added:

"Hugh Hudson of the Farmer-Hudson store is the highly esteemed son of Mrs. Hudson."

10. Governor William O'Connell Bradley was the state's first Republican governor, serving from 1895-1899.

11. The porter was identified only as "Uncle Mose."

12. The sergeant was identified only as "Captain Hill."

II

A Woman Blazes the Trail

The world is a wheel, and it will all come round right.

With full suffrage for women a reality, by 1923 everyone was asking very seriously what women would do with it, what it would mean in nation and state, and what changes were on the horizon as the sun of a new freedom rose above the clouds of the past. Individual women were asking seriously, "What does it mean to me?" "Will it be best for women to run for office?" "How will they measure up to new duties and responsibilities?" and perhaps the most vital of all such questions, "What price power?" "What price office?"

They all thought, in one way or another, "Now, it is up to us!" They remembered a well-phrased thought, "Honor is a harder master than the law." They were on their own, as the trite saying goes. No one of them realized this so poignantly as those to whom came the first opportunities to run for office, to approach the public with a new appeal, to ask for work and responsibility in a new field.

About this time there were several business propositions and changes of location offered to me, and while I was wondering just what to do, I took counsel with John Noel, one of our leading financiers, well known for his keen and logical thinking.

He listened to some of these propositions, and when asked if he thought some other location might offer better opportunities, he looked at me steadily and said very firmly:

"Mrs. Cromwell, had you ever thought of 'letting well enough alone'?"

Many times I have been glad of his wise advice so briefly and pointedly given, for the way was even then opening for real service to my community and my state.

23

In the spring of 1923, there was much discussion of placing a woman on the state Democratic ticket, and rumors began to reach me that I might be asked to take this place. Some said they did not want any petticoat officials as yet. Others replied that it would strengthen the ticket since women would surely demand recognition. Naturally, the first questions were: What office? and What woman?

The very first to formally approach me on the subject was Dr. Louie Harmon, president of the Business College of Bowling Green, who came to see me to tell me that he had heard my name mentioned repeatedly as a probable candidate for Secretary of State. He added that he hoped I would consider this because many of my friends, judging from my previous service as State Librarian, were anxious for me to have the distinction of being the first women to hold an elective state office in Kentucky.

It was certain that many difficulties would beset the pioneer who blazed the trail. One often heard the expressed views of many men (and some women) who held out to the last that women were not able to run an important office competently, although they usually camouflaged this bold statement by talking of the hardships of campaigning and the many difficulties and problems incident to office holding. Others were broader minded and saw with clearer vision that a new day was dawning. So, when a delegation from the western part of the state called with the same request that had been brought to me by Dr. Harmon, I deliberated very seriously and asked for time to consider. Even though it was the opinion of many influential voters that my name would strengthen the ticket, there was much to be thought of before allowing that name to be used. As a great soldier of the Sixties once said, "My name was my most precious possession" and this proposition was not one to be accepted lightly.

So, I talked with Senator Robert Brown of Warsaw, Judge James Cammack of Owenton, Allison Holland and Senator Thomas Combs of Lexington, Governor James D. Black of Barbourville, H.K. Bourne and J. Wirt Turner of New Castle, Senator Charles Moore of Franklin, Judge J.E. Robbins of Mayfield, General James Garnett of Louisville, Judge Charles Marshall of Shelbyville, Charlie White of Louisville, General Hubert Meredith of Greenville, Seldon Glenn of Eddyville, and my cousin, Tom Cromwell of Lexington. I consulted with them as to the wisdom of making the race for Secretary of State at this time. We went over the situation thoroughly. Rather to my surprise they all said they believed I could win and counseled me to go ahead. More than this, they offered freely to do all they could to aid my campaign. The unanimous support of such men as these decided the question, and I determined to enter and to do my best.

I looked upon this coterie as Paul looked upon Gamaliel, and they taught me valuable lessons in campaign management. Their experienced viewpoint gave me an insight into political life, and I found that underneath the management and the struggle for votes they all looked upon public offices as a public trust. I felt that with such leaders the women could go far: and it is largely due to the broad views taken by such men all over the state that women have been encouraged to study the science of government and to take their part intelligently in elections up to this time. We must admit that the political views of women were rather vague at first. We often trusted our hearts rather than our heads. We were inclined to be a trifle sentimental and sometimes a bit prejudiced. It is a fine commentary on the adaptability of women that they have studied public questions, made important decisions, and built up interest in problems of government both in the state and nation. It is not strange if we are found not yet to be perfect. It is an imperfect and puzzling world, and women have had so little experience in public affairs. Just give them time.

My formal announcement was made in the early spring, and I may be pardoned if the thoughts of this adventure added beauty to the springtime, always my favorite season.[1] That year the birds sang sweeter, the flowers seemed brighter and the little lambs more playful than ever. My own interest did not lag, and there were many opportunities to enjoy the freshness and brightness of the newborn day, as we often left home just as the sun was peeping over the lovely Frankfort hills, in order to cover the many miles necessary if most of the voters in the state were to be seen. This was my intention, and I did not lack much of accomplishing my purpose.

My first objective was to have a close organization; next to give my personal attention to this and all other points that were presented. It is my firm belief that one seeking office, or any other end, should seldom delegate any important task to others. There is just not one thing to be said in favor of anyone sitting in an office at headquarters and sending out others to do the work. If mistakes are to be made, it is better for the one most interested to make them. If promises are called for, it is best for the one who has to fulfill them to make them in the first place. One can keep one's own path straighter than can any other. In addition, in seeking office, nothing takes the place of the kindly word and the cordial handclasp. It is the personal touch that tells.

The advice of my friends who knew the long road ahead of me and the best way of covering the ground was to buy a car. This was my first, a Reo, and in its use I had the valuable assistance of Herbert Dodson, my faithful black chauffeur, who knew the roads all over the state and whose sobriety and loyalty could be depended upon absolutely. I always took companions with me, for what is life without friends who add to happiness and fellowship. It has been unkindly said that women make indifferent comrades, but I have not found it so at any time. In this particular campaign, two of these good friends were Misses Hattie and Emmie Scott, two charming Frankfort girls, who accommodated their time to mine and added greatly to my pleasure and to the effectiveness of my campaign. Miss Hattie spent most of her time at the courthouses doing genealogical work, which is her avocation, while Miss Emmie accompanied me and enhanced the social pleasure of any meeting. It was said that, together, we made a team that could not be surpassed for travel and vote-getting.

Another practical point in campaigning was the economy of time and place. Instead of renting expensive headquarters, which I could not afford, I opened a room in my home and from there came and went and directed the whole campaign. Another point here that may seem strange now was the peculiar feeling that one of my generation felt at seeing her own face staring at her from every telephone post and tree along the way, for it seemed to be necessary to have a great number of posters with my picture and even more cards with my name and that of the office sought. In this my good friend, the late James Newman of the Frankfort State Journal, was my adviser in selecting material necessary for distributing the publicity. I depended on his good taste and common sense to a great degree, and he never failed me.

There were enough posters and cards printed for every voter in the state it seemed, and after my first doubtful start at distributing them, I saw that, as far as possible, everyone did have a card, while my adherents saw to it that the telephone poles were similarly decorated. I did not need a mirror in those days for I saw myself coming and going, and soon did not give it a thought any more than if the pictures were of someone else.

There was quite a bit of comment on this poster and picture card campaign of course, some favorable, some unfavorable. However, the voters soon grew accustomed to a woman's face so shown and the comment died down. I did not need then to quote Burns for some power to be "gi'en" me to see myself as "ithers" saw me, but was certainly more conspicuous than ever I had been or had hoped to be.

It was not unusual for some unknown friend to speak to me on the train or other public place and say, "Lady, I beg your pardon, but aren't you our woman candidate for Secretary of State? I see your picture everywhere, in every bank and business house and certainly on every telephone pole. You are surely well advertised." This always took me aback just a little, but such friends usually added some request as, "Me and my folks are going to vote for you, and I would like for you to sign one of these cards for my little girl." Then I would realize that this publicity was both useful and effective.

With headquarters established and publicity provided for, the next question was where and when to open the campaign. This was decided by the invitation of Mr. and Mrs. Robert Crowe of La Grange, who felt that an appearance at the Oldham County Fair would launch the woman candidate properly. Those who know the flavor of the whole-some, widespread interest of a county fair in Old Kentucky will realize this was a master stroke. Saturday was the "Big Day" when town and country people from several counties abandoned work and gave up the time to play as well as to gain information as to what other farmers were doing. They all mingled with fine good fellowship, ready to accept with good humor introductions to candidates, to hear speeches, and in general to realize that they were part of the wider community of a county and a section of the state.

The late Mr. Crowe had been speaker of the House of Repre-sentatives, and few could equal him in judging the psychology of people, whether individually or in crowds. He and Mrs. Crowe met me at the station, and my stay at their home included delightful drives, long con-sultations as to means and method of campaigning, and hours spent in pleasant conversation before a cheerful log fire, as the evenings were crisp. They told me in a delightful way of some of the pitfalls that awaited an unwary candidate, also relating many amusing and amaz-ing incidents of politics.

As we sat beside the dying embers, I saw in the flames a forest in which there might be many thorn trees and wondered how I would walk among them without becoming entangled. These conferences made me realize that a woman's campaign must be somewhat differ-ent from that of a man running for the same office. The people expect a woman to retain all her feminine charm and at the same time to be able to meet the world with a brave face. A woman is apt to take things too seriously, to be almost too conscientious, and to believe that others are as serious and as conscientious as she in all the statements and promises they make. One soon learns, however, to take most things "with a grain of salt," and in time it appears that, after all, campaigning is really a science based on tact, diplomacy, and common sense, that above all one must be in earnest. It may sound trite but it is true that, "Life is real, life is earnest," and politics is certainly so.

One matter discussed with them was campaign stories, and I told them I hoped there would be no room for any of these to be told about me personally. They did not believe there would be, and happily I have found ever since that if one faces issues squarely and honestly, forgets the possibility of underhanded work and drives to a definite goal, a woman need not fear the results of any untrue stories. Women have their contribution to make to government, and the men are beginning to translate the chivalry and gallantry of old into justice, as they recognize the right of women to stand side by side with them in the halls of the state and nation. This innate gallantry of the men and intense loyalty of the women which I have found to be well nigh universal gave me great happiness when new in the field and just starting out on this first campaign for support for a political office.

I shall never forget my awakening on this fateful day. The sun shone brightly, happy people passed going to work or play, and all the world seemed glad. The word "politics" rang in my ears, and I recalled a verse of Pope: "Old politicians chew on wisdom past, and totter on in business to the last." I devoutly hoped that the entrance of women into politics would brighten the lives of many and would finally remove any slur that had attached to the word which should be one of the finest in the language, dealing as it does with the science of government, which is so vital to every one of us.

That day Mrs. Crowe saw that I met the women while Mr. Crowe and other friends introduced me to the men. Among these friends was Ballard Clark, a prominent lawyer; W.L. Dawson, editor of Oldham Era, and several officials of the county and town who all showed the finest cordiality. At the fair the delightful hospitality of Oldham County appeared to wonderful advantage, nowhere better than in the delicious lunch served which included fried chicken, country ham, beaten biscuits, pickles, cakes, and pies in endless profusion.

This was not a political meeting, but arrangements had been made to present me for a short talk. It has been said that, "Politics is the Kentuckian's meat and drink," and it was not at all unusual to have politics mixed as a sauce with all the other good things spread before such crowds whenever they gathered.

Mrs. Crowe and I sat on the platform where other speakers were also to appear. Mr. Crowe introduced me as the first woman in Kentucky to announce as a candidate for a state office and said that I was honoring Oldham County by making the first appearance in my campaign there. The applause was encouraging, and I said in substance, "Mr. Chairman and Friends: I am delighted to be here today and have enjoyed all the varied interests of this wonderful fair. I appreciate more than I can say the privilege of saying a few words.

"We are not here to discuss politics today but for pleasure, information, and fellowship. However, permit me to say to you good people that I am a candidate for the nomination for Secretary of State in the August primary on the Democratic ticket and will appreciate your vote and influence in helping me to win this nomination.

"I believe the women of the state will help me in blazing the trail as a pioneer for a political office and that, combined with the support, experience, and chivalry of the men, we can win. We are close enough to the days when our forefathers blazed the trails into the wilderness with the ax that we can go forward with the same spirit to blaze the trail for a new day for women when they can stand side by side with men in governing our great country, as well as in sharing in the building of its homes.

"I have enjoyed meeting every one of you. You have been so very kind and pleasant that I do not believe that campaigning is going to be as hard as I have been warned it would be. I believe you will all vote for me and help me to attain my ambition. I promise you to give you good service....Thank you."

The people seemed pleased, and in the primary that summer Oldham County gave me a rousing good vote, so that it seemed that the hundreds with whom I shook hands that opening day did as they promised and voted for me.

It was hoped that I would have no opposition and we thought how ideal it would be if this race could be made without a fight; but I found that a candidate may as well as prepare for any eventuality and that after beginning a campaign it is, "Theirs not to reason why, theirs but to do or die," though the verse must be changed to include, "theirs to make reply." So, one morning when I picked up the Lexington Herald, to my great surprise there was the announcement that Mrs. Mary Elliott Flannery of Catlettsburg would run for Secretary of State.

May I say now that here was a real opponent, a charming and intellectual woman who would be in earnest in her efforts to be nominated. However, to advance a little on my story, I will say that she and I kept on being good friends. We often met and had lunch together. Each kept her own secrets, if she had any, and we closed the heated campaign with no mudslinging and none of the inevitable regrets that follow such a course.

Mrs. Flannery was afterwards the first woman to be elected to the Kentucky Legislature and in that capacity and in the party councils we ever remained good friends and co-workers.[2]

It was decided that my campaigning was to be done by Congressional Districts and the choice of leaders was first to be made, then of helpers who would aid in organization. There was already much interest because of this race between two women, but it takes more than interest to win in politics. Organization is the magic word, the open sesame to the door of office. Choice of leaders is all important.

In northern Kentucky, Ray Smith, a former pupil of mine in a class in Parliamentary Law at Eastern State Teachers College, was an enthusiastic adherent and took his Ford car, loaded it with posters and literature and literally placarded the three counties of Grant, Boone, and Pendleton. He stopped everywhere, telling the people that we had a woman running for Secretary of State, a friend of his, and that he wanted them to vote for her. Friendship is another magic word in politics. His campaigning paved the way there in counties that have always been loyal to me since. Pendleton County is the home of Doctor and Mrs. Crecelius who also worked hard for me and often entertained me in their hospitable home.

Another pupil, C.S. Acre, of Florence, Boone County, also worked hard for my success. I spent a week at the home of his mother, and we worked early and late, meeting with great encouragement, especially from the women, who began to feel that this was their very own campaign.

Mrs. Frank Rothier of Covington and Mrs. Mary Cain of Newport were both leaders in Democratic circles and agreed to be my chairmen. They had been among the pioneer suffragists in that section, had attended all conventions, and worked hard for the Nineteenth Amendment which had been finally adopted under President Wilson's administration. They were anxious now to see the new plan work out and were indefatigable. In Covington along with Mrs. Rothier, Miss Ada Conklin of Latonia proved a stalwart leader with many followers, always ready, tireless, and alert. In that section, too, were Mrs. John Read, Miss Linnie Brady, and a host of others who were yeoman workers in Kentucky and Campbell counties.

Among the men workers were Judge Samuel Adams, Judge Frank Tracy, Honorable Polk Laffoon, Congressman Brent Spence, Ora Ware, Ulie Howard, Shelley Rouse, Arthur Rouse, the late Mr. Hines, and others. They all worked hard with splendid results, and some of them told me they remembered so many occasions when they had enjoyed the hospitality of my home and the Southern cooking of faithful Aunt Winnie Thomas. So I found two other magic words were "home" and "hospitality," as such remembrances helped me when I essayed public life. One of the many charms of Frankfort, our Capital City, is the ready hospitality — the warm welcome to its homes that has meant so much to the men in public life who have come here through the century and a half when the business of the state called them. They have been well received and have appreciated the kindness shown them, and now it is found that my small part in this city-wide generosity to visitors in our midst was to repay me with support when needed.

Mr. Acre had a host of business friends who became interested in my race and who helped greatly. In Covington and Newport I remember the Driskels, George Goode, Charles Brooke, the Neffs, Swartzes, Millikens, Jake Roe, and many others who took a vital interest in this new departure of having a woman Secretary of State. The women looked on me as a true pioneer, and the men seemed to appreciate my promises for an efficient and business-like administration, which I had determined to give them.

Everything was moving along smoothly. Mrs. Flannery and I were working hard, each doing her best, sometimes meeting, joking with each other, taking tea together, leaving with a laugh as we went on to corral more votes. Then came another surprise. One morning The Courier-Journal announced that Judge J.D. Rucker of Ashland was to run for the nomination for Secretary of State. This put a new face on matters, and while I felt that he would draw more from Mrs. Flannery than from me, it made a three-cornered race of which no one could see the outcome. Ashland and Catlettsburg were twin towns, and certainly his candidacy would hurt her most. I did not, however, want any unfair advantage.

The new candidate was a distinguished jurist and also an astute political leader, so it was up to me to go into the eastern part of the state immediately. I always tried to keep ahead of him in my appointments, as I did not want to be challenged for a debate on "The Propriety of Women in Politics." It was best not to inject that question into this campaign, for we were on new and untried ground and must have the opportunity to make good and to prove our worth by performance.

There was a challenge for a debate on this subject by a lawyer who was honestly opposed to women in public affairs, but I sidestepped this by pleading lack of time. I did not want the kind of publicity in the press that any such debate might bring. It was best to keep the issues clear, to win in order to show that a woman could fill an office in a competent way and serve the public efficiently and intelligently. The entrance of a man into the race against two women already was bringing to a head any opposition to women and making it harder for either of us to win.

Once on a train going to Danville to speak, a young man with an ingratiating smile sat beside me in the crowded coach. We spotted each other as fellow Kentuckians and entered into conversation. I learned that he was making his way through Transylvania College at Lexington and was greatly interested in athletics. Indeed, our conversation started on this vein, it was so evident to me that a young man of his build and appearance was an athlete, and it has been a lifelong habit to begin where the evident interest of my companion lies.

I told him, in turn, that I was a candidate for Secretary of State and was going to win beyond the shadow of a doubt. This emboldened him to tell me of his ambitions. Among other things he said, "I'm going to vote for you. Women should be represented in any administration." He added, "I am going to be Governor of Kentucky some day, and it is my ambition to reorganize the state and put it on a paying financial basis. Ever since I can remember they have been talking about state debt. I'd like to see it paid off, and I do not see why the state cannot pay its debt if a businessman can do so."

Need it be said that this young man, A.B. Chandler, is now Chief Executive of Kentucky and is well on the way to seeing his young ambition fulfilled in paying the state debt, besides having to his credit many other constructive and progressive policies.

This is told to illustrate the fact that Opportunity in America is still spelled with a capital "O." The log cabin candidates of the past have their counterparts today in the boys and girls who can enter school with a smile, a few clothes, a few dollars, and a great reserve of dogged determination, and win out in the struggle for recognition in the great world of affairs.

Up to this time, the magic carpet and Aladdin's lamp of the old world stories have become a reality in this country of ours. Without calling on luck, without depending on charity, without recourse to any other aid than a stout heart and a will to work, the opportunities in this country are as great as ever. The serious question for us to ponder as citizens, amid the changes that are taking place everywhere, is this very one of change in our system, of a break with a past that has built our institutions for some uncertain will-o'-the-wisp in the future. We surely do not want any change except a steady, natural progress from a system that has given such opportunities to young men and women who work their way through school and on up to share life's highest honors in business, politics, the professions, and the world of productive labor.

On this same trip I met Mrs. Mae Wells, then Superintendent of the Montgomery County Schools, who was much interested in having a woman on the ticket. She was very popular in that section and rendered me great service.

Mrs. Flannery had already preceded me to the mountains, and I felt that must be my next stop. I rushed to that front in my battle and landed in Powell County, where I was to find out much about the sincerity of the highland people and their unbounded hospitality which cannot be exceeded anywhere. My pictures had preceded me and adorned (?) every post.[3] It was evident that someone had been at work there.

The leader of thought in that section was Uncle Luther Stevens, who had been enlisted in my cause and to whose industry was due the spread of my literature and posters. I had not met him personally before and was greatly impressed with his appearance. With his white hair and saintly face, he looked more like an apostle than a politician. He invited me to "light" from my car and "have a snack" and made me welcome in his home.

The mornings were chilly, so the log fire and the big hickory homemade rocking chair gave me the feeling of rest and refreshment that I needed. I had not realized the hardship of this early rising and rushing from one place to another, talking to so many people each day and perhaps not resting enough. Here in Powell County I gained inspiration and courage that lasted me to the end of the campaign. As the Psalmist says, "I will look up to the hills whence cometh my strength." I thought then that this was meant for me and adopted it for my own.

In addition to the comfort of that home and the peace of the

33

sublime mountains, Uncle Luther delighted me by telling me that he had visited every home in the county and that practically all had promised to vote for me. He had also been to Campton and interviewed some whose names he gave me as leaders, and he felt it would be wise for me to go on into Wolfe County and see the people there myself. Uncle Luther has gone to his reward, but his kindly influence lingers yet in the mountains and will linger with me to my last day. It was at Hazel Green, that noted watering resort, that I met Mrs. Rose Coldiron Conlee who took charge of the women's organization in that section. She rode daily through the mountains pleading with the women to stand by one of their own. Her work and influence were felt far and near and she remains one of my truest friends.

I found at Campton all was as Uncle Luther had said, while at Jackson in Breathitt County, and Hazard in Perry County, Judge O.H. Pollard and D.Y. Combs had my literature distributed and several speeches had already been made in my interest. The women were wide awake and interested. My organization was very complete, and I learned again the great lesson that a candidate must never allow a thought of defeat to enter his mind. Defeatism never wins. That is a helpful point in living that came to full fruition in my mind while on this trip to the mountains. So to these people I owe a debt of gratitude which can only be repaid with loyal service. The mountain people have never failed me and many times have come to my aid without waiting for a call.

My good friend, O.H. Pollard, warned me to go back to Frankfort and make preparations for a whirlwind campaign in Western Kentucky. I have often wondered if he did not have insight into what was going to happen to square out the race with a fourth candidate. I had no thought of this, and on my way stopped at Versailles to tell my leader there, Mr. Sullivan, and the workers that this was the last day for filing papers and the race had shaped up with two women and one man. So, imagine my surprise when, about twelve o'clock that night, I was called on the telephone and told that Ben Marshall of Frankfort had filed his papers to run for Secretary of State in the primary.

I felt heartbroken for awhile, but pulled myself together and began to think and plan. Right here was learned another valuable lesson which has stood me in good stead ever since. In my confusion at having told the Versailles people that the race was all set, I rushed off the next morning to tell them that I had not intentionally misrepresented anything.

At the courthouse while standing in the hall explaining all this,

Mr. Sullivan came to me and said, "Mrs. Cromwell, if I am to manage your campaign here, I am not going to have you electioneering for Mr. Marshall. Don't you know that every time you mention his name you advertise an opponent? Just go on as if you did not have anyone running against you. Build yourself up, not the other fellow." This psychology was sound, and I realized it immediately, but the fact remained that Mr. Marshall was well known and able, with plenty of experience both in work and campaigning.

This situation aroused the women all over the state, and all felt that it would bring out a record vote, which proved to be true. It also resulted in a very hotly fought campaign which attracted attention far beyond the confines of the state. Miss Jeannette Rankin had been Congresswoman before this time, and Mrs. Nellie Tayloe Ross and Mrs. James Ferguson were in public life in western states, but this was the first real campaigning done by women in a state primary for one of the offices of the gubernatorial staff. It was news and was so treated, which was probably as much help as anything outside could be, for in the comments from outside of the state there were a number of editorials that were distinctly favorable to women, and certainly many that aroused the women to know and realize that they were voters and that much was expected of them in that capacity.

My friends warned me of every kind of combine that might be made, and some of my best supporters were doubtful. I told them I would change the old saying to, "faint heart never yet won office," and would do even more than had been planned in pushing my campaign to a successful close. It all developed into one of the hardest fought political races ever waged in Kentucky, or perhaps anywhere else. It was a battle for individual votes rather than blocs, as is so often the case now. Both men opponents were good "mixers," as the saying is, knew the state, and were not afraid of work, and I had already found that Mrs. Flannery was a "foe worthy of my steel." It was one of the cleanest races I have ever seen. There was no mudslinging and no underhanded work, so far as we ever knew. It was a case calling for close organization and personal appeal, of making each one feel that his or her vote was an absolute necessity.

So, in leaving Frankfort, I spent a little time in Louisville consulting with friends and seeing as many voters as possible. From there I went to Paducah in McCracken County. Here I met ex-Senator Eaton, my manager, who had arranged for a conference with leaders, both men and women. Among the latter were Mrs. Roy McKinney, Mrs.

John Lawrence, and Mrs. Edmund Post. These were veteran suffragists and greatly interested in having a woman in the office of Secretary of State. They were friends of mine, who could be depended upon. Not only then, but since, I have trusted to their friendship and good judgment when needing help. This county was thoroughly organized and was won by a large majority.

From there I had to go yet farther on into the Purchase, down to the very banks of the Mississippi River. This trip is memorable for many reasons. One was that I was far away from my home base and had no woman companion with me, something that seldom happened, for we all felt then the need of a certain chaperonage, to say nothing of the fine feeling of comradeship. One incident that occurred stamped this indelibly on my mind.

Near a certain small town in the western part of the state my train encountered a terrible rain and thunderstorm which blew down trees and impeded the way until we had to stop on the edge of town in the middle of the night. Here the station master met us with a flashlight. We had to walk down the track with only this light and the steady flashes of lightning to guide us while the rolling thunder added to the fury of the storm. The worst of the rain had passed but the train men felt we had best get shelter in the town before another storm struck. It was a hard task to walk the railroad ties, and I felt more than a little lonely as my only companions were five men besides the station man.

I kept as quiet as possible, although I felt more like screaming as the continual lightning flashed. One of the men took my bag and they were all most knightly in their care of me. We came to a very steep bank and the guide said, "I don't know if that woman can make this steep place." I said, "I can, if you can." Little they knew that this was a symbol of the long walk I had undertaken in blazing a trail for women in office.

To make a seemingly long story short, the hotel had burned and the only place was a boarding house which they told me was kept by a very fine woman. As it was so late the proprietor did not show up, but one of the gentlemen guided me to my room, which was very nice indeed. I will admit that for once discretion seemed the better part of valor, and I tied the sheets together so as to escape by the window if molested, while I locked the door and barricaded it. Thus fortified, I slept until morning, being terribly exhausted by the events of the night before.

I was awakened by the sun shining brightly in my face and on looking out saw the whole world green and beautiful after the storm. The town by daylight was a very pretty one, and the brightness of the morning was a good omen. The landlady was a prominent club woman and civic leader who became one of my best workers, and always thereafter a friend. This was a lesson on the futility of losing faith. I was glad that I had untied the sheets, unbarred the door, and hidden the evidence of my cowardice. The gallant knights of the road had already taken their departure and we never met again, but I have ever treasured the remembrance of their united efforts to make me feel at ease in a difficult situation. This county was mine in the primary by a good majority, and it was largely due to my hostess of the stormy night.

The Purchase is known as the land where Democrats grow. I toured it thoroughly and my friends organized it in the same way for, once nominated, the election would more or less take care of itself. The Purchase stood by me manfully in this first trail blazing. All through Western Kentucky I met encouragement, for it was well known that I had come from the Pennyrile, and that gave me open sesame to the hearts and homes of all the section west of Louisville. Friends here saved my time and my finances by royal entertainment in their homes.

In my home counties of Allen, Warren, and Simpson especially, my friends and kindred told me that they would attend to my interests and that they wanted me to canvass in those counties where I was not so well known. In all my experience I have never met with greater proofs of friendship than in this my first statewide campaign. Everywhere in that section, and especially in Simpson County, where my great-aunt had lived, I was constantly reminded of the past and of the part played by my ancestors in settling that county.[4]

It was found that many men differed from me and thought that women should not leave the shelter and protection of the home and venture out into public life. I always met with the greatest courtesy and kindness. None of these differences of opinion ever shook any friendship. Indeed, many friends were made by my firm conviction that I was in the right and was traveling along the right path and by my defense of my position. Times change and methods also, but it is still the same old world with the age-old problems and people of common sense and good judgment change with the times and employ new and better methods in getting on in the world and solving its problems. Women and men can work side by side with increased respect for the ability and purposes that animate all when we consider the need of our country and the many policies and plans that must be put into action to meet the necessities of modern life. In all these things women have proved that they can measure up to the full stature of womanhood, even as the best men have measured up. But in that early day it took tact, patience, and persistence for the trail blazers. It was a true test of temper and temperament many times, and perhaps some of the things said and done were for the purpose of testing the mettle of the women who were going out into these new fields. It must have been a temptation to say and do things calculated to stir up feeling just to see how women would meet any given situation.

During the time I stayed in my home counties, a strong organization was quickly perfected, and a number of conferences held. Mrs. Laura Sloss, a favorite cousin of mine, and Clarence Evans, who was a prominent young lawyer, were among my staunch supporters. Sam Maxie, a newspaperman, was another. Ex-Senator Charlie Moore was one who had championed my cause when I was elected State Librarian, and often came to my rescue later when his aid was needed.[5]

In Simpson County my friends were busy working for me.[6] Just before leaving for other fields, Miss Alice Adams, County Superintendent of Schools, drove me to Barnes's School, about nine miles from town. It was here in the rural schools of Simpson County that my education began. Here stood the schoolhouse by the road, like the one made poetic by Whittier:

"The warping floor, the battered seats,
The jackknife's carved initial,
The charcoal frescoes on the wall,
The door's worn sill betraying
The feet that creeping slow to school
Went storming out to playing."

Here a crowd had gathered, most of them former schoolmates, all of them friends. They were greatly interested in my race and happy to see one of their own running for office in the state administration. It made them feel close to their state government and they all seemed to be personally determined to contribute all they could to my success. The school had been replaced and had modern equipment, very different from that of my childhood, but the old two-room building still stood, and it aroused all the sweet and precious memories of childhood. There, too, was the old spring with its rock wall and nearby the very grapevine on which we took turns swinging around to land over on the other side of the big spring, taking care not to let loose and fall into its depths. Such recollections made me forget my ambition for office for the time. It was with real regret that I left the old school-house and the memories of other days, to hasten on to Allen County, where my girlhood, during my mother's life, was spent. I was there for two days; my people formed a strong organization in Holland, Half-way, Gainesville, New Roe, Trammel, and every other section of the county. All the dear old family names! How little I had thought as a child that these names would each and every one be component parts in plans to place me in high position where I could serve these commu-nities in public office, along with all the other communities in the state.

Mrs. Roscoe Huntsman and Mrs. Ed Welch, cousins again, headed my organization in Scottsville. It seemed that every citizen, regardless of party, was interested and attended the meetings held in my behalf. I recall that Uncle Tom Brown went into the Long Creek Section and made a house-to-house canvass, while my cousin and many others worked hard for me, giving up valuable time of their own to further my cause.[7]

It is worth such as this and loyal friends that finally bring suc-cess, and one can never be too appreciative of all such friendships. How the names and faces gather around in memory whenever I try to set down the recollections of those days! Harry Collins Spillman of New York and Dr. Harry Read of Louisville, two of Allen County's favorite sons, never lost an opportunity to put in a good word for me as they went about the state. From Allen County I went to Bowling Green, where the faculty and student body of Western Normal, headed by its princely president, H.H. Cherry, were all my loyal supporters. The Business College, with Dr. Louie Harmon and Murray Hill, had been active from the start. Mrs. Carrie Mitchell, one of our leading suffrag-ists, a splendid club woman and good church worker, went into that county as well as those adjoining and spoke in my interest. To her I owe much in training as she was a splendid speaker, poised, self-pos-sessed, and always ready. She and Miss Laura Clay of Lexington have both been an inspiration to me. I look upon them as mentors who guided and directed my thinking and inspired my ambition. Other Warren County friends and relatives were not lacking in loyalty nor in work.[8]

From this intensive campaigning I returned to Frankfort to find that Mrs. Flannery had toured my own district and had undoubtedly made inroads. The gentlemen who were running were seemingly not nearly so active as we two women. It was my intention to put in more effective licks than any of them. Here on home ground I had an advan-tage, for the roads were good and the car bought at the insistence of my advisers aided me in covering the ground in that section. My faithful chauffeur could always be depended upon, and again I enlisted the Misses Scott, who enlivened the hurried journeys hither and thither as we skimmed the district.

Sometimes I also took my cook, Aunt Winnie Thomas, who greatly enjoyed the trips and who did some yeoman work among her own race. She seemed to feel as if she herself were running. Her ready wit and happy humor took the day whenever she chose to "turn on her personality." She was one who lived her religion daily and had a philosophy that sustained her through every trial. General Tandy Ellis, widely known for his "Tang of the South," has quoted her and said she was one of the greatest philosophers he had ever known.

At any rate, she was true as steel and did everything she could in my interest. At Salvisa one day, I went into a store to confer with some friends. When I came out, there was Aunt Winnie standing by the car with a crowd of listeners gathered about while she was making a speech. She told them in no uncertain terms that I was not afraid of work, could do anything in the world but cook, was just not born to be a cook, but was every inch a lady. This was a compliment that was liable to cut two ways, so that while I thought she made me some votes, she was cautioned not to tell again that I was "no cook." When August came and the votes were in, there was no happier soul than Aunt Winnie, and she firmly believed that her speeches when with me had swayed untold numbers. They did have an effect, for "Not every man," it has been said, "is a hero to his valet," and surely not every woman is a heroine to her cook.

On one occasion a bold knight, speaking in my favor, said in an eloquent address that he did not know whether women should enter the political field just yet. Some folks were not reconciled to women wearing the breeches. He added that he was of the opinion that they could wear them better than the men, and that he was going to give them a trial and vote for the woman candidate for Secretary of State. This was another two-edged compliment, and I took this problem to my good friend, Governor William Thorne, an interesting character, always full of kindly wit and humor, one who would know how to turn this doubtful compliment rightly without offending the gallant gentleman who made it.

Governor Thorne said: "Don't let that humiliate you, daughter. Just say to the next one who repeats that expression, 'Mercy, don't you know that women in this modern age do not wear breeches, they wear step-ins and step-outs. Today we are stepping out, and on the day of the election we will step in.'" This, in turn, was a little hard for me to say, but was valiantly repeated whenever the breeches slogan came up, and soon it was mentioned no more.

One of the hardest points to meet was that women were trying to get jobs that rightly belonged to men. There was some point to this, and it had to be met with tact, for we certainly were doing just that — running for office that had always been considered man's perquisite. This is one of the deepest problems raised by the entrance of women into modern business and political life. It can be answered only by a very broad and deep study of economics in general and the swift changes in modern conditions in particular. In a campaign there was no time to enter into discussions of the changes in business and the rapid absorption of all of women's former home tasks into machine-made jobs. In fact, the women were only following their own jobs out of the home into business and public service.

In addition, there was the democratic doctrine of a chance for all and equality of opportunity for all. There were men who just did not grasp this at first, and they proceeded to throw cold water on the attempts of any woman who had ambition and initiative. As one of the pioneers, I caught my full share of this criticism, and it required tact and thought to get around some of the ingenuous arguments of the stand-patters. This attitude was not confined to the men. Some women took the same stand. All of us are prone to measure by our own yardstick, and some of these women who felt themselves safe in comfortable homes could not see why any woman wanted to leave such a shelter for the hurly-burly of the outside world.

Several instances occurred where the minds of these conservatives were changed, and I shall always be proud that it was my lot to have a part in freeing the minds of some who were bound by all the old traditions to the chivalric attitude of the past. Some failed to realize that chivalry and gallantry are of the heart and soul and are not destroyed by changing conditions. One man in particular who really liked me personally said, "I am so sorry to see you trying to get some man's job, to rob him of a living. Home with the sewing machine and cook stove is the place for women anyway," and so on. It was strange, but such discussions nearly always verged on rudeness which had to be met before it fully developed. The reply to this was that there were many women whose homes had been broken up by death, and I countered with questions as to what such women were to do. This would be followed by statistics showing how many women were really the bread-winners and had as many dependents as men.

This, with other arguments, patiently presented, bore fruit and I was glad to have this very man come to me and tell me he was mistaken in his attitude. So often one can win out by starting a train of thought and leaving the result to the opposite party. When he first talked to me, he included women's clubs in his sweeping arraignment, but when I next saw him, he was all aglow with the honor that had come to his wife who had been elected president of her club. He had changed his mind about that as well as about voting for me. So does the personal tinge all our thoughts. So little does a balanced sense of justice rule us. This is a point for all of us to remember. Put ourselves in the place of another and then decide what is just and right.

I recall one dear woman who told me that her husband had practically forbidden her to vote for a woman, saying that if she had that in her head, he wanted her to stay at home, that one of the men would win anyway and the voters would show women their proper place when the election day came around. He had used just the wrong psychology, and the little woman had determined to show him. I gave her some of my best arguments and warned her not to make a fighting point of the matter, to be very firm, yet not to lose her temper over it. At the same time she was given some literature on suffrage and told that the battle for women's rights had been won and we could afford to be very calm about it and was warned that it never paid to be belligerent. I do not know what tactics she used, but the husband came to me before the primary and made a sort of apology, saying that his wife had been right and he wrong. I did not allow him to think that he was apologizing, and talked to him as if he had always had just the thought in the back of his mind. I said, "Do not take this too seriously. I am sure that you were the first to think that you and your wife would both vote for a woman. You were just trying out her temper. Isn't that so?" He replied, "Yes, I guess it was. At any rate, we are both for you and will work for you at the polls."

To this day we meet with the argument that women have not done much to clean up politics. This is not true, of course. They have already done much. One has only to remember the election days of old and contrast them with the orderly elections of today to know that there is a vast difference. And in public office, while there is yet much improvement to be made, there is a far better spirit and wider vision than of old. Most officials do want to do the right thing. Government is still a trial-and-error proposition, but we are nearer the solution of our problems than ever before if we keep our heads and are not led off by some of the isms of the loose thinkers.

In this race, as it drew nearer to a close, there were very few voters whom I had not seen. There was not one voter in the state who had not been approached by some of my loyal friends. My organization everywhere was close and effective. Organization and energy mean much more than money, promises, and trading. Dependence on the latter results in misuse of money, broken promises, and poor bargains.

The memories of this whole campaign are fraught with kindliness and courtesy. It was wonderful how cordial everyone was. There were many friends of my own and those of my late husband who outdid themselves in showing me around, giving me valuable assistance and, what was more appreciated, inviting me to their homes. Such true friends mean much, and in a heated campaign they are pearls without price.

In campaigning, one must follow a certain course. I would say to go into business houses, courthouses, hotels, and homes, to visit briefly and tell one's errand concisely. One finds that workmen, organizations, railroad people, all busy persons, while they like to be sought out, do not have time to give and are thankful for brief calls and talk that is right to the point. I would say to touch every village. Many of the very best people are in the rural districts. It pays to contact all precinct workers, for after all that is where the battle is waged. There are about five thousand of these precincts in Kentucky and it is there that the hardest fighting takes place.[9] The precinct workers are the soldiers who win the battles for their chosen candidates.

In touring the Bluegrass and in other counties, I found that some women pitied me, a few censured, but most women took great interest in my race. Our own Miss Laura Clay, mother of suffrage for Kentucky women, was my main tutor and adviser, and many a time her wise counsel was sought. We all owe to her a debt of gratitude, and there are other pictures of that pioneer band that hang on memory's wall, including the late Mrs. Desha Breckinridge, Mrs. Ida W. Harrison, and many more.

In an intensive campaign, it was necessary to touch five or more counties in one day. One such tour is typical. At various times, those who accompanied me were Miss Harriet Scott, Mrs. Albert Kaltenbrun, Mrs. Bowman Gaines, Mrs. Robert Noel, and Miss Elizabeth Johnson. With one of them beside me and Herbert Dodson, my chauffeur, and Aunt Winnie Thomas on the front seat, we would start out. One day we left Frankfort at early dawn, the sun peeping up, the dew fresh, the air crisp, and the highway beckoning to speed and promising far greater mileage and comfort than was ever possible in horse-and-buggy days.

That day we went to Lancaster, Garrard County, reaching there in time for high school chapel exercises where the principal had me give a short talk on education. Afterward, I made my usual rounds, met Joseph Robinson and Clay Kaufman, two prominent lawyers; Homer Jennings, County Clerk and a former pupil of mine in Parliamentary Law at Eastern Normal; Miss Sue Shelby Mason and many of our club women who were all interested in my race and who made me feel that I had many friends in Garrard.

From Garrard we drove on to Stanford in Lincoln County, and there met Ed Walton, editor of the Stanford Interior Journal; also Mrs. Harvey Helm, Miss Esther Birch, and other club leaders, who were very much concerned in the advancement of women.

From Stanford we proceeded to Danville, where at the courthouse we met one of my firm friends, a leader of power, Miss Sara Mahan, then Circuit Court Clerk of Boyle County, who afterwards was elected and served as the third woman Secretary of State.

Here I met the two editors, Vernon Richardson and J. Curtis Alcock, who rendered me great service through the Danville Advocate and The Messenger, as well as by personal support, leaving me under obligation to both. We reached Harrodsburg early in the afternoon, called on court officials, business people, and newspaper people, among these Mack D. Hutton, the late James Isenberg, Dr. C.V. Van Arsdall, Hal Grimes, Bacon Moore, and Judge Charlie Hardin, who were among my supporters and advisers in this early pioneering. Mrs. Dan Moore, a charming woman, was a warm friend and loyal supporter whose memory I shall always honor and whose friendship lives on for me in her two daughters, Mrs. Minnie Ball Goddard and Mrs. Owen Van Arsdall, who now reside in the beautiful old home near Harrodsburg.

We reached Lawrenceburg in time to visit the courthouse, to see the editor of the local paper, Kenneth Garrison, who was one of our Scottsville boys. Mrs. Stanley Johnson, Mrs. Mary Dowling Bond, Mrs. J.B. Carpenter, and many other women had organized the whole county. The men in Anderson stood by my cause manfully.

This was the home of Bob Johnson, who had been the college chum of my boy at the University of Illinois and a fraternity brother in the S.A.E. Many times I had been chaperone for their parties during their school days when visiting my son, William Cromwell, in Urbana. Bob left no stone unturned in my interest in Anderson County, or elsewhere, strengthening the ties of bygone days.

These experiences were typical of the day-by-day work. Next after this, we went to Owenton, where Judge Cammach had arranged a conference with some of the leading businessmen of the town and county who wanted to know how I stood on certain issues. I was somewhat embarrassed for fear I might say the wrong thing, so just spoke according to my conscience. The Pari-Mutuel, "The Monkey Bill," and the Prohibition question were the subjects of this questionnaire, all themes on which many appeared to be afraid to speak out.

One man said, "Mrs. Cromwell, down in Owen County most of us want to know how our candidates stand on certain issues we think affect our welfare in county and state. How do you stand on the Pari-Mutuel question?"

My reply was, "I do not stand at all, do not know anything about it, and do not want to know. I never went to the Derby in my life nor to the races, am a member of the Methodist church, and do not approve of betting in any form."

He said, "Good for you."

Another asked me how I stood on "The Monkey Bill," to which I replied, "I believe the Bible from cover to cover. While I am not wise enough to comprehend it all, I simply take it for granted, have faith and believe in the Book of Books."

(On January 23, 1922, William Jennings Bryan spoke to the Kentucky Legislature in support of a bill prohibiting teaching of evolution in state-supported schools. On March 9 this bill was defeated in the House by only one vote. This had started the ball rolling and raised questions which should not be injected into politics. After the Scopes trial at Dayton, Tennessee, in 1925, the furor passed over. There the Great Commoner (Bryan), who had been the head and front of the anti-evolution forces, had laid down and died at the dramatic moment, and thereafter the echoes died away — but to the candidates to 1923 in Kentucky, it was a vital issue that had to be met.)

Next came the Prohibition issue. I told them I was a "white ribbon woman," did not partake of any intoxicants whatever, might be styled old-fashioned by some, but this had been my policy in life both in thought and action and that I had no cause to regret it.

At the close of this conference they pronounced me safe and

sound and again brought sunshine into my campaign. To be favorably received in "Sweet Owen," one of the banner Democratic counties in the state, where Jacksonian principles ruled, was an omen of coming success. It was the home of many outstanding citizens: Even Settle, June Gayle, Robert Ford, Judge J.H. Vallandingham, Judge James Cammack, and many of like caliber. The women did not lag behind the men in interest or in work.

I went from Owen to Warsaw, Gallatin County, where I was entertained by Senator and Mrs. Robert Brown in their lovely home overlooking the beautiful Ohio River. He was one of the leaders of the section, his advice always sought, and a proved friend to his fellow man. They introduced me to nearly everyone in Warsaw and the county. Their daughter, Mrs. Frank Connely, who was my chairman, organized the women. The popularity of these good friends won the victory in Gallatin, a splendid little county the name of which evokes dear memories.[10]

My next stop was Carrollton, home of my husband's good friend, Senator Jas. A. Donaldson. His son, Lyter Donaldson, later was largely instrumental when on the Highway Commission in giving to that section the fine roads that lead in all directions, notably that from Louisville to Cincinnati. Thus he has followed in the footsteps of his father in service to his community.

General Tandy Ellis and Mrs. Ellis, of Ghent, had lived in my home in Frankfort and now proved themselves kindred spirits in hard work for me, as did Miss Ann Gullion and Jenn Howe. All honor to the good people of Owen, Gallatin, and Carroll counties for their loyal support in all my undertakings. It is a pleasure to serve them. From Carrollton I landed in Eminence, home of the late Governor Thorne, beloved of all Kentuckians. When I wrote him asking for advice about entering this race he had answered, "Daughter, get into this race. The night will never be too black, the cold never too severe, nor the rain too hard that I will not heed your call when I am needed in your interest. You must win and you will." His daughter, Mrs. Pearl Crabbe, worked hard at the polls for me and is today a loyal supporter and friend of mine. She is typical of the devoted women all over the state who went early to the polls and stayed late, with perhaps only a sandwich throughout the day, all to work for a pioneer because she was a woman and needed their aid. One cannot fail to believe the women are loyal to their own. And all this in a new and untried field!

As a pioneer, such as these were the friends needed. At New

Castle, among my early advisers had been H.K. Bourne and J. Wirt Turner, prominent attorneys. They had distributed my literature and provided for everything necessary. It was felt that not much time need be spent by me either here or in Carroll County, as I had an army working for me. Mrs. Bourne, Mrs. Mary Carroll, Mrs. Effie Smith, and others were with me and later worked with the Woman's Democratic organization with force and effect — Mrs. Bourne, especially, as she was the pioneer first president of that organization in the state. Mr. Turner told me that Henry County Democrats did not want me to spend a cent for expenses in that county, that they would take care of all that. I said on leaving, "God bless Henry County people for such interest in my race." Again, in Trimble County, the good people greatly encouraged me, telling me that I would carry the county as the organization had been attended to already.

Shelby County was the next stop, where I found the Beards, Marshalls, Lawrences, Jesses, Baines, Smiths, Willises, and other Daughters of the American Revolution and club women all interested and working, and anxious to hear how things were going in other places. Mrs. Mary Adams Baine, a distinguished Kentucky writer of that county, also campaigned with me in other counties. From there I went back to Frankfort to look after my mail, pick up the loose ends, and plan for further trips. As Mrs. Breckinridge said of the suffrage campaign, "It was hard on everything from clothes to courage," and so I needed refurbishing from time to time.

I started then another trip to Western Kentucky, going down the Ohio River. The first stop was at Brandenburg to confer with my workers, Allen Stith, Senator James H. Bondurant, and others, who felt they had Meade County well organized and in good shape. In Breckinridge and Hancock I found that my cousin, Geneva Duncan, and others of that family, who were numerous there, had been at work very effectively. They are all very clannish, our ancestors having come from Scotland to Virginia before coming into Kentucky. The Duncans the world over are clannish and love kith and kin and the native heath of their forebears.

I arrived in Owensboro one early afternoon and found that a host of friends had arranged a meeting for after dinner, at which time I met with Ben Ringo, Levega Clements, Mrs. W.L. Mills, Mrs. Mamie W. Watkins, the Hagers, Gateses, Youngs, Mrs. Bright Harwes, and many club women and representatives from patriotic societies. The dean of friends there was Urey Woodson, editor of The Messenger, well remembered as a great publicist and one often solicited to run for Governor, an honor he would never entertain. With such workers as these to take care of Daviess County, I rushed on to Henderson.

Here, my good friend Mrs. Powell Taylor was waiting for me. She had been educated in music, was a lovely singer, and being from California originally, was unacquainted with politics, particularly the Kentucky brand celebrated in poetry by Judge James Mulligan of Lexington. She was popular in club and music circles and a friend of everyone, so it was rare good luck that she consented to be my campaign chairman. She proved to be as good a politician as musician, and the results justified her fine efforts. There was not a voter in town or county who was not approached by her or her lieutenants, and Henderson was perhaps more closely organized in my favor than any other county, men as well as women, with Powell Taylor, Ben Niles, Leigh Harris, Clarence Givens, Strother Banks, and Judge Ward in the lead.

The whirlwind campaign put on by Mrs. Taylor and her helpers made the race a dominant subject of conversation in the town and county. Mrs. A.O. Stanley and Miss Minnie Mahler arrived from Washington, D.C., in time to join the Henderson women in effective work before the primary, and this added to the interest.[11]

On the day of the primary they showed their mettle. They assembled at the polls by seven in the morning and in every precinct in town and county stayed on the job, calling in lads and lasses to aid them and to swell their ranks as workers, to hand out cards until the polls closed on a busy day's voting. This was a maiden experience for these women, and they got a real joy out of it and have always been unusually active in all elections since. Mrs. Taylor's watchwords were system and thoroughness. It was her determination to get out every vote in the county. She visited, or had someone to visit, every precinct several times through the day to see that all had a way to get to the polls and showed the men that this could be done. The result was a record-breaking vote. There had been some "doubting Thomases" among them, but they were then fully convinced of the value of women's work at the polls. This was expressed by Leigh Harris, editor of the two newspapers, in an editorial when he said, "Gentlemen of Henderson County, we will have to take off our hats to the women, for they have proved themselves better political workers than the men. While we fought right with them, they showed us new ideas in pluck, energy, and endurance. It is they who deserve the credit of putting over their pioneer woman candidate here today, with a larger vote than that given to the Governor."

It was during this campaign with the good people of Henderson that a vision came to me that gave me very great happiness in its later fulfillment after I became Park Director. Others had the same vision and helped, but it is a matter of pride that the thought came to me thus early, to have at Henderson a park that would be a memorial to the great Audubon, so closely connected with the early history of the town.

Time was closing in and my presence at Frankfort being needed, I hastened home, where there was serious opposition. It is needless to say that I did not expect to carry this county, for my opponent was a man born and reared here, one who had a host of friends and relatives, who could call every man in the county, and thousands in the state, by name, and who had an enviable record as an able public official. At the same time, I could not afford to quit, but tried to make the very best showing possible, relying on my own home counties of Warren, Allen, and Simpson to overcome the majority that must be his in Franklin County.

My next trip was to Louisville and several days were spent in organization and meeting people. While in Louisville, Misses Nell, Rose, and Nora Cummings, nieces of my good friend, the late Charles P. Mooney, of the Memphis Commercial Appeal, who used his Kentucky Edition in my interest in the Purchase Section, took me everywhere and visited with me stores, railroad stations, business houses, banks, schools, and convents. The latter, of course, of the Catholic religion. I may say here that members of this great Church have ever been my ardent supporters. This is as it should be. Religious freedom is our most precious heritage. There is no room in a democracy for intolerance. People of all creeds should stand together against all tyranny. Despotism begins with the destruction of religious faith.

From Louisville I went to Bardstown, Nelson County, one of the then-hotbeds of Democracy, yet a place where the women were more conservative in their attitude. However, there were many wide awake and faithful. Mrs. James Rouse and others were on the firing line espousing the cause of a woman on the ticket. It is interesting to note that today these women have blossomed like the rose and now always take the lead as one of the very best organized groups in the state.

Those were yet, more or less, horse-and-buggy days, and at Bloomfield, my good friend, Mrs. Thomas Wickham, would hitch up her old gray mare to the buggy and she and other women would start out early in the morning with stacks of posters and cards, stopping all along the highways to tack up posters or to deliver cards. Taking their lunch, they would drive all day, stopping at farm homes and talking to both men and women, telling them it was advisable to have a woman on the ticket. They went on into Spencer, Taylor, and Anderson counties with this missionary endeavor. It was in Spencer that Mrs. W.W. Bowlers and Miss Katie Beauchamp of Taylorsville joined the chain of workers; and in Taylor, Mrs. W.J. Wade of Campbellsville and others were added. This coterie has remained in service and they have made splendid workers in every primary and election since, getting their start in this eventful race of 1923, when a woman needed help to blaze a pioneer trail.

Only ten days until the primary! That meant much work to be done and fast moving to do it. Central Kentucky was pivotal. On a flying trip through the Bluegrass country I was accompanied by Mrs. Albert Kaltenbrun and Mrs. Bowman Gaines, of Frankfort, who were both my loyal supporters and good workers, always ready and willing to lend a helping hand. Into Scott County we went, where we found an Amazonian army of women who had already done so much work that it seemed unnecessary for us to linger there. Among other items was a house-to-house canvass of Georgetown, which had been made by Mrs. Amos Hamon, now Mrs. Dogged, aided by Mrs. John Shuff, Miss Mary Herndon, and others, who used all their time and energy to fine effect.

From there I went to Paris, in Bourbon County, where I met a host of loyal supporters. I had previously given my course in Parliamentary Law in the high school, with Dr. Lee Kirkpatrick in charge, and it seemed that every boy and girl in the school was on the firing line doing his bit. They were ably led by the school head and faculty. Judge Fanniebelle Sutherland, public-spirited and alert as always, was my champion with the Daughters of the American Revolution, the Federation of Women's Clubs, Professional and Business Women's Clubs, and other organizations. One of my captains was J.W. Prichard, who organized the younger set. He is now at Yale, where he is making his mark. Who knows but I shall sometime in the coming years have the pleasure of voting for him as a member of Congress, as he is in my district.

From Paris I went to Harrison County, accompanied by Mrs. Mary Adams Baine of Shelbyville, who was a native of this county. My cousins, Miss Bettie Cromwell and John Cromwell, led the fight there for me. They had great influence. Everyone loved Cousin Bettie, while her brother, John, is now mayor of Cynthiana. I profited by their popularity, also by that of Mrs. Baine, who had a host of relatives. My good friend Mrs. Jesse Basket of Cynthiana spoke in several counties in my interest.

Next into Fayette County, where there was much opposition, owing to the unavoidable fact that it was a sort of second home to Mr. Marshall, and the loyalty of boyhood friends to him was hard to combat. Here I had a bunch of stalwart friends who never failed me. Among them were Miss Laura Clay, Mr. and Mrs. Allison Holland, Mrs. W.H. Forshee, my cousins Mrs. Luella Cromwell Minter and Tom Cromwell, Thomas Combs, and others who were for me one hundred per cent in Lexington. Another who was always my friend and helper was the late Honorable Desha Breckinridge, whose advice was invaluable. He was a man of broad sympathies, an understanding heart, and the ability to make his influence felt, a friend to be sought, and an enemy to be feared.

This left but two days to Frankfort, and I put them in to the very best of my knowledge. This was my adopted home, and many friends rallied to my support, for this four-way race had created quite a furor. It was a question of whether one of the two women would win or whether one of the men would be victorious. I felt that I would win. My faith never faltered and this gave courage to my supporters. There was no thought of defeat, but the question was, "By how much majority?"

Then August fourth, the fateful day, arrived and there was a record-breaking vote for the nomination cast in the primary. It was a question of whether Kentucky women had upheld a woman candidate, and whether men had carried their traditional Kentucky gallantry and chivalry to the polls to do justice to womanhood. At four o'clock the polls closed, ballots were counted, the boxes were hurried to the courthouses, and reports began coming over the wires. Many hurried to Louisville to headquarters to hear the results there. I waited in my home to hear the final reports, for to me home was the center of my life, and it was important to me to be there to hear the results of what we women felt to be a crucial test.

These questions were settled when the vote was counted. The two women had won over the two men. Mrs. Flannery defeated Judge Rucker of her home county, with over 33,000 votes in the state. He had over 25,000 in the state. I received over 42,000 votes and carried 51 of the 120 counties. My majority over my closest opponent, Mr. Marshall, was about 5,000; over Mr. Rucker, more than 16,000.

51

The press had played a noble part in this victory for the woman pioneer who had blazed a new trail to the statehouse. Friends had stood by and, better than that, had run the race with me, many of them feeling it to be a personal triumph. This was especially true of the women who had aided my cause.

Since full suffrage has been granted to women, they are eligible to hold any office in our country and are equally responsible for the kind of government under which we live. It is our duty to help keep the wheels of government well oiled and running smoothly. Woman's progress has been gradual, becoming more marked as both men and women learned that one could not advance without the other. Most uncivilized races hold women inferior to men, but as civilization advances, it is recognized by thinking people that all citizens must be fitted to share in the nation's support and betterment. And "Who shall shut out fate?"

Today we have many millions of eligible women in the United States, and all should be interested in the party of their choice. It is through the ballot that government is built up or torn down; therefore, it is our duty to study and understand public questions, so that we can vote intelligently on the issues of the day.

Women's place in the political field is becoming more effective every year. They have had the ballot long enough to learn that their power is felt throughout the nation.

The privilege of the ballot has made the home circle more interesting than it was in days when only the men discussed public questions, and women were supposed to be just listeners.

Following the motto of our state, "United we stand, divided we fall," we can make our nation the greatest in the world.

We should be interested in the ballot, for it is the one way in which public opinion may be expressed. In the Democratic Party of Kentucky today we have more Democratic women voters, so statistics show, than we have Democratic men voters. But at first our women were slow about voting. They are now realizing that it is a duty as well as a privilege and are voting almost as well as the men. If a woman once sees her duty, she seldom fails to respond.

The primary was over, and not only was it a victory for the women in Kentucky, but it helped the womanhood of the nation. It was a great victory, and, as all elections should be, was conducted on a high plane and won without any mudslinging.

My opponents were among the first to send telegrams of hearty congratulations, and Mrs. Flannery came to see me to talk over the coming campaign and the part the women must take in the election. Many telegrams, letters, and long distance calls congratulating the pioneer came not only from within the state, but from many other states. One telegram from a prominent Democratic leader in Oregon said, "I am proud of Kentucky and of the gallantry and chivalry of our men in opening the official door to the womanhood of my native state. If you need me I will come down and campaign for you." Many other interesting telegrams were received and all were appreciated not only by me, but by the women who had joined the men so bravely in this great victory for women.

> "We strive until the goal is gained,
> Then look for one still unattained,
> Our records point the course we take,
> To greater records we can make,
> For hope springs not from what we've done,
> But from the work we've just begun."

Chapter II Notes

1. Spring of 1923.
2. The author continued:

"This friendship has extended to her daughter, Mrs. David Howerton of Ashland, Kentucky, who has worked side by side with me in later campaigns and is today a true friend."

3. This parenthetical question mark apparently reflected Mrs. Cromwell's modesty about the use of the word "adorned" to describe the effect of her photograph.
4. The author continued:

"She (the great-aunt) had told me that my great-grandfather, John Hail, was one of the founders of Franklin and that he and Andrew Jackson were bosom friends. Among her stories were those relating to visits that General Jackson made to her father's home and to the fact that she and all the other children loved him. They found him one who could be loved and trusted. She said that he was always unfailing in courtesy and kindness to women and children and that no one who ever saw his fine patrician face and heard his inspiring voice ever forgot him. She was one of the old school who put great stress on ancestors and on blood. Some of the past generation might be greatly disturbed to see one of their posterity campaigning and holding public office. But these older people were not lacking in sense or in adaptability, and I believe they would have kept up with the times. They would have moved with progress and would have been ready to pioneer in the modern causes as they were in the wilderness and along the trails where they followed the Indian paths and hewed out their fortunes even as the men hewed the logs for the fine stout houses they built for shelter and comfort."

5. The author continued:

"I shall always love and respect his memory, and his son, Honorable Lee Moore, has a warm place in my heart because of the generous spirit of his father, who was ever ready to give me fatherly advice and to further my interest in any way he could, especially in politics."

6. The author continued:

"These included the Neeleys, Hills, Goodnights, Duncans, Millikens, Slosses, Robeys, McClanahans, Adamses, Maxeys, Bryants, Pebbles, Evanses, Mitchells, Harrises, Granters, Richardses, Wrights, and practically every family in the county."

7. Those mentioned by the author were: Cal Guy, Sam Read, the Hugheses, Johnsons, Bradleys, Mulligans, Paynes, Lovelaces, Frank Pitchford, Dr. Calvert, Dr. Meredith, Bob Welch, and Frank Brown.

8. Those mentioned by the author were: the Potters, Dents, Thomases, Simses, Rhodeses, Merediths, Guys, Isbells, Dickersons, Smiths, Skileses, Millikens, McElroys, Wrights, Kirbys, Cherrys, Harmons, Sledges, and Thompsons.

9. There are currently approximately 3,250 voting precincts in Kentucky.

10. The author continued:

"There is no spot I enjoy more now than Warsaw, in the hospitable home of the Connelys (one of my adopted homes), where I meet again the good people who stood by me in bygone days. When there it is like a pleasant dream to waken in the morning and look out on the placid Ohio while the cheerful Sabbath bells are ringing. This is a church-going town and her people cling to the old customs. It is refreshing to answer the call of the bells and join my friends in worship at their church and always enjoy Dr. Herbert Tinsley's able sermons.

"As in the morning, also in the evening, one can repeat the lyric lines of Thomas Moore,

> 'Those evening bells, those evening bells,
> How many a tale their music tells.'"

11. The author added:

"Among the women working were Mesdames Dixon, Baskett, Thixton, Henson, Ward, Harris, Mahler, Misses Towles, and the clubs of the town, whose individual members were for me almost solidly."

III

The Sweet Fruits of Victory

There's a divinity that shapes our ends,
Rough hew them how we will.

The bells of victory for the nomination which rang out on August fourth throughout all Kentucky delighted the women, who rejoiced that for the first time in history a woman had been nominated in a primary for one of the important state offices. The strenuous campaign had acquainted them fully with the issues, had aroused the dormant ideals for public service, and had made them fully realize the meaning of the right of suffrage.

Mrs. Flannery and I were two pioneers, and fortune favored me. Neither of us left a stone unturned that would win votes or serve to uphold the dignity of womanhood in this new hour of the dawning of a full citizenship. This had been a comfortable victory for me, although not a landslide. The latter could not be expected when four well-known candidates were in the field, each seeking to win.

It was about midnight when news of the nomination flashed over the wires, and before noon of the fifth the result was certain. Telegrams from far and near poured in. One cablegram came from the Lamberts of Chicago, who were touring Europe, and many messages from the western states where women were fully imbued with public spirit. It was gratifying to see from the tone of all these that this pioneer trail-blazing of mine was regarded not only as a personal victory, but also as a harbinger of a better day for women everywhere, when their opportunities would be greater, their privileges more numerous, and their standing as citizens taken for granted.

Illinois had been the first state to ratify the Nineteenth Amendment to the Constitution. This, as now enacted, reads: "The rights of citizens of the United States shall not be denied or abridged by the United States nor by any state on account of sex." The first territorial legislature of Wyoming in 1869 gave women the vote. The Territory of Utah did the same thing the next year. Both came into the Union as states in 1890 and 1896, respectively, with clauses in their constitutions that granted suffrage to women.

Colorado granted women suffrage in 1893. Idaho enfranchised women in 1896. One by one, other states fell into line, until by the end of 1919 the women of thirty states had the right to vote for presidential electors. The Great War, which we remember with sadness for many reasons, had also its progressive side. It certainly did advance the cause of women as they worked side by side with men in the United States and in France and England. The superior ability and sublime endurance they showed then had a large share in changing the attitude of men when woman suffrage came up for final and serious consideration.

It had been a little more than 300 since the London Company of England had said in granting 100 acres of land to each man and woman who would "make the adventure" of settling in Virginia, that, "It is not known which is of the greater service to a new state, men or women." This had been said, and they had acted upon it before the first House of Burgesses met in 1619 at Jamestown. Had this first fine belief in the value of women citizens been made the basis of citizenship through all these years, I cannot help but believe that the United States would have been better for the experience.

The first woman elected to the United States Congress, Miss Jeannette Rankin, took her seat as representative at large from the suffrage state of Montana in 1917, three years before suffrage was extended to all women citizens of the whole country. Miss Rankin's all-too-short public career made many friends for suffrage, and many said that if women of her dignity and character could be elected to office, there should be many of them enter such service. They felt especially drawn to her for her vote, given with tears, against the Declaration of War. God bless the women of our country and speed them to victory in their firm stand for peace.

On November 21, 1922, Mrs. Rebecca L. Felton of Georgia, appointed to fill the vacancy caused by the death of Senator Watson, was sworn in as the first woman Senator of the United States, holding the office for a few hours.

In the national and state elections of 1924, more than one hundred and twenty-five women were elected to important offices. Chief of these were the first two women governors: Mrs. Nellie Tayloe Ross of Wyoming and Mrs. Miriam A. Ferguson of Texas.

In my election as Secretary of State in both a primary and general election, Kentucky became one of the pioneer states for the women of the nation.

This was true although the grand old Commonwealth had been the next to the last state to ratify the Nineteenth Amendment. Her sister state of Tennessee was the last. Kentucky had, however, not been unmindful of the abiding interest of women in affairs that affected the home, as she had granted school suffrage to women before this. And it may not be known so well, for many years even before that, widows with children had in Kentucky the right to vote in local school elections.

This briefly is the beginning of women in elective service generally.

There remains little to tell of the campaign after my nomination, for changes had been in the air and the old comfortable majority of the Democratic Party was threatened by a militant Republican Party newly aroused to its own responsibilities.

The result of the August primary gave as leader of the ticket the Honorable Campbell Cantrill of Georgetown, a popular member of Congress for many years. His lamented death at the close of the campaign brought forward as substitute the Honorable William J. Fields of Olive Hill, also a Congressman of ability, who led the ticket to victory.

The result of the August primary gave as a ticket: for Lieutenant Governor, General Henry Denhardt of Bowling Green, a military figure of importance; for Secretary of State, Mrs. Emma Guy Cromwell of Frankfort; for Attorney General, Judge Frank Daugherty of Bardstown, a leading factor of Nelson County in civic life; for Auditor, William Shanks of Stanford, a leading banker; for Treasurer, Ed Dishman of Barbourville, an outstanding citizen; for Superintendent of Public Instruction, Dr. McHenry Rhoads of Lexington, an educator of note; for Commissioner of Agriculture, Newton Bright of Eminence, a leading farmer; for Clerk of the Court of Appeals, Charles O'Connell, Sr., a popular citizen of Louisville. For the first time in history a woman, Mrs. Elizabeth Lyon, was made Assistant Commissioner of Agriculture under Honorable Newton Bright and rendered splendid service to the people, proving herself most competent.

Another woman who has rendered valuable service in this department is Mrs. Christie Park, who was Secretary to the Commissioner of Agriculture through four administrations, a compliment to her efficiency, ability, and tact.

The Republican ticket was headed by former Attorney General, Charles I. Dawson of Pineville and Louisville; Lieutenant Governor, Ellerbe W. Carter of Louisville; Secretary of State, Miss Eleanor Wickliffe of Bardstown; Attorney General, R. Monroe Fields of Whitesburg; Auditor, James A. Wallace of Irvine; Treasurer, F.M. McCain, Mayfield; Superintendent of Public Instruction, W.L. Jayne of Morehead; Commissioner of Agriculture, Lewis Martin LeBus of Cynthiana; Clerk of the Court of Appeals, John H. Asher of Pineville.

It was said that the two women opponents kept pace with the men, played their part satisfactorily, indulged in no mudslinging, and in general won the plaudits of their respective supporters. They both realized the truism that honey catches more flies than vinegar and were both considered good organizers. So, as in the primary, there were no regrets over poor sportsmanship or hard words.

The strenuous part of the campaign covered more than six weeks, and most of us throve on the hurry-up, stop-and-go program we had to carry out. A few were fagged, but the excitement kept us going. Added to this and the realization of the importance of each move was the joy of meeting friends and of receiving so much genuine Kentucky hospitality.

What to talk about and how to divide the subjects was often a moot question. I remembered the popularity of the speaker who said he always "talked about ten minutes" and worked hard to formulate my thoughts and to express them in such a way as always to be brief, speak to the point, and never outtalk my welcome. As to a place on the program, I preferred not to be either first or last, and my wishes were usually regarded in this matter.

Next came the question of saying something that was of interest to the people in their homes and useful in daily life. In this the candidate had a golden opportunity. On one occasion I was accompanied by a young lawyer who was full of his college, obsessed with his reading, and withal extremely sentimental. He was taking along a copy of Moore's poems, and when he was asked his subject he told me he was going to read and comment on, "The Vale of Kashmir."

I replied, "If you are, please let me speak first, for I want to talk to these people about their problems in raising and marketing their tobacco and other crops and how to educate their children in a practical way. I will let you follow with the poetry, but let them hear me first, please." I knew they were far more interested in the crops of their own hills and valleys than in the adventures of Lalla Rookh. Fanciful and romantic as that story is, everything has its place.

Frankness along with diplomacy is a proved method. Friendliness wins and bookish speeches fail. The oratory was left to the men, as my whole thought centered on the women and what they wanted. I knew that, as they had begun this battle with me, they wanted me to talk to them of their problems, that they expected some real results in the betterment of their own condition by the entrance of women into the political arena.

I had somewhat the advantage of the men there. They had been in the political game so long they played it according to their old rules and their own ideas. I was timidly venturing on new and untried ground and did not hesitate to confer often with my women lieutenants, trying very hard to keep abreast of the times as to just what they wanted me to say. We took it all more seriously than the men did. Old custom and usage had dulled their interest. It was all new and strange to us, and we tried our wings slowly but with increasing power as the campaign progressed. I truly believe that the major part of the women felt that my interest was theirs and went into the fight wholeheartedly, feeling that much depended upon it.

I was told that this was true of the Republican women also. Miss Wickliffe was on their ticket. She proved to be a candidate who felt that this was her opportunity to mean something worthwhile to her sister women.

If ever I feel downcast because the women seem to be neglectful or heedless of their civic duties, I hark back to those pioneering days and remember well the women who stood by me on this untried battlefield, how they stood together, worked together, and exemplified Kentucky's famous motto, "United we stand, divided we fall!" And again, if I need heartening amid many discouragements and much seeming indifference, I look with pardonable pride to the organization of our Democratic women and the inspiring history of their achievements.

Our pioneer president of the Woman's Democratic Organization was Mrs. H.K. Bourne of New Castle, who started the movement off in a progressive and constructive way, seeing the need that developed through this first campaign for a woman official. She was followed by Mrs. Davis Howerton of Ashland, who continued the same policies and pushed forward along the same lines. Then Mrs. Thomas

Underwood of Hopkinsville had an extremely successful regime. She had many advantages to bring to the work, as her late husband had been a nationally known publicist and her son, Thomas R. Underwood, is the able editor of the Lexington Herald and always alert to the developments of the day. Mrs. Underwood left the organization in the capable hands of Mrs. Eleanor Hume Offutt of Frankfort, who had gathered together a fine corps of officers and district directors who are competent and interested in aiding her in carrying on the work with zeal. She has inherited her interest in civic affairs from her late father and mother, Dr. and Mrs. Edgar Hume, of Frankfort, leaders in the cultural and community life of the city.[1]

It is presumed that the other political parties recognize the value of women's organizations as do the Democrats. This is as it should be, for there is no stronger force in elections than the women, and it is their province to help mold public opinion. In doing this, women should never allow themselves to be swept away into the strong current of world events which is now flowing like an angry gulf stream through the hitherto calm ocean of world affairs.

The plans we put in action at that time have been continued to this day. The captains of each precinct stayed at the polls throughout the day from 6:30 a.m. to 4:00 p.m., checking the voters as they came and voted. Then we had generals who had cars and could drive them, and these we used to bring voters from a distance or those who had such household duties they could not spare much time to vote.

Early in my life I was deeply impressed with the immense value of one vote. It happened this way. I have before referred to Uncle Isie, who was such a unique character in my home town. He was a mighty Democrat and would not have missed the election for anything, but always held out for some fine clothes to wear on the great occasion of casting his vote. That was one of the election expenses that always had to be attended to, and on time.

That year his heart was set on a high silk hat, white shirt, and red tie, and a certain sweet-smelling oil for his hair. The busy men appealed to the school girls to help them out, and several of us during the noon hour got busy and collected the items for this outfit and sent them to his cabin. With a little time to primp, and these gala additions to his attire, he came out looking as dignified as an African chief on dress parade. It was a sight to see him strut up to the courthouse, where he voted the straight Democratic ticket, thus voting for Mr. Fallis, who was the candidate for Representative on that ticket.

The sequel is that the seat of Allen County's Representative was contested when the Legislature met, and in the final count Mr. Fallis was seated by a majority of one. We always said that Uncle Isie's vote elected Mr. Fallis, and this made such an impression on me at the time that thereafter, and especially in this, my first real campaign, I had in mind all the time the potential value of any one vote.

This is a good idea for every voter to cultivate. It adds to the worth of the individual when he can feel that he is valued for his own personality and that every act and deed of his stands alone in the final count and is singled out for inspection. We are sometimes apt to minimize our own value and worth, especially as to influence.

The great evangelist Sam Jones had a story that illustrated this. He had an argument with a man of little note in which he insisted that he should amend his ways and live better because of the great influence this would have on others. The man said that no one knew or cared what he did, that he did not have a penny's worth of influence anyway. This gave Jones an idea and he said, "Come along down the street with me, my friend."

He led the way to a cigar store which had in front a wooden Indian gaily painted, with feathers, arrows, etc., such as was then used to adorn all tobacco stores. He called the proprietor out and said to him, "That's a fine Indian you have there. Did you buy him?"

"Why, certainly," the man replied. "Nobody gave him to me."

"Why did you buy him?" was the next question.

The man looked at him as if he thought he had little sense and replied, "For his influence! To show the people where to come to trade."

Next, "What did you pay for him?"

"Fifty dollars," said the storekeeper, with a disgusted look, which turned to admiration when he heard Jones's next remark to the friend with whom he was arguing.

"Now, see," said he, "if a wooden Indian has fifty dollars' worth of influence, don't you think you have at least that much?"

The story goes that the argument was effective. We hope so, for each human being has an infinite value in the sight of his Creator. And in the conduct of his government, each one has a very great stake. So, none of us should limit our patriotism, for none of us knows when or where our single influence will be needed to preserve the institutions, the laws, the customs, the traditions, and the history that are so dear to us all.

The democracies of the world, won at such cost of blood and

treasure, hold the individual to be the center of government which is conducted for his benefit and in which he has a share of control. All despotic forms, on the contrary, emphasize the state and tend to make the individual one of a mass of people who may be handled in blocs by those in power.

There are two things expected of candidates which are sometimes greatly exaggerated and sometimes too much minimized. These are contributions to campaign expenses and participation in social events. In regard to the first, I knew as a pioneer that the men were wary of asking a woman candidate for her contribution, so without solicitation I was ready at our first meeting with a check and planked it down on the table. I realized then and know now that there are many legitimate expenses that must be met, and it is only fair that everyone pay his or her share. This includes rent of headquarters, postage, stationery, clerical workers in the office, and transportation of voters, where this is not donated. Some of these are sometimes met by volunteer workers, but it cannot always be depended upon and a sufficient fund is necessary to carry on any campaign, and this is in addition to the personal expenses of each candidate.

Here was another place where a woman must set a precedent. I did not expect nor allow the men to pay my fare or other expenses, to wait on me, or to be hampered by my presence. Why should I? I was entering a field that had always been theirs, and it seems to me in this modern day women should not wish to be treated as social butterflies, especially when they are taking places beside the men in public life and business.

On the contrary, I tried to be even more thoughtful than if they were guests in my home, I tried to see that they were comfortable, and suited, as far as possible, my time to theirs. Chivalry and gallantry come naturally to Kentuckians, but these are in the heart and should be taken for granted. Women when they are taking places in the wider world should not expected to be shown all the little exaggerated niceties. Men and women, too, can be entirely courteous and kind without making a drawing room exercise out of a journey, or a speaking. Above all, any affectation is out of place. Common sense, here as elsewhere, is the best rule.

In regard to social functions, the simple rules of social usage apply here as elsewhere, and a woman entering public life need not worry over her appearance or manners if she has been accustomed to the best in other places. Simple dress, in accord with the place and time, cordial manners, without effusion, no airs and graces that are not perfectly natural. Indeed, naturalness is the open sesame. Just be yourself, and the effect will take care of itself.

After this election, one dear old lady who was my devoted friend paid me a great compliment according to her lights that came from other days. She said, "I don't believe in women holding office, but since they have elected Emma, I am for her heart and soul. One thing I know well. She will not run around to parties with nothing on her arms like these society women do."

If I have sometimes gone "formal" and worn sleeveless or other modern dress that might have shocked my dear old friend, I hope the spirit of her confidence has been kept and her belief justified that I would keep a level head under changing circumstances and different surroundings.

The Golden Rule of kindness, to be genuinely interested and to place the comfort of others before our own, is the infallible test that applies whether we live in a tent, cottage, or palace, and whether we work in a field, kitchen, or office. There is no barrier nor chasm between the woman in business life or public life and the woman who is manager and leader in her home and church. The same rules apply.

I campaigned with my fellow candidates in practically every county in the state, covering much of the same ground as in the primary fight. The men did not do quite so much. It was not necessary for them. A woman was an oddity in the political field then and it would not do for her ever to be absent when called for. This was not hard for me for I prided myself on punctuality, always arrived a little ahead of time to see the women and organize them. One of my pet slogans was that we could let the men be the orators, we must be the organizers. Yet I never allowed my part of the speaking to fall flat or be found lacking. My comrades complimented me often on that fact.

It was not because of any desire to overlook us as women that sometimes our speaking was not wholly provided for. It was just that the men were not accustomed to women taking part, and some did not yet realize that the vote of the women was a reality to be reckoned with. Only once do I recall that my part was entirely forgotten. This was an important Eastern Kentucky appointment. One of my women friends reached me by phone and told me this, adding that the women would be disappointed. She and I did not dally, but went directly to headquarters with our plea, several telegrams burned the wires, and never again was the woman candidate left out.

Our usual course was to have dinner at the hotel or in some private home where we were guests, then proceed to the courthouse. This dinner hour was a gala occasion, for the men do enjoy a good meal.

Following dinner, the march down the aisle of the courthouse was fraught with far more thrill to the women then than it is now. One or more of my friends would always bear me company, and it was a delicate compliment that almost always I was introduced by a woman. One such occasion is well remembered. At Stanton, Mrs. Rose Coldiron Conlee was asked to introduce me. She made a splendid short speech, placed woman on a pedestal and connected her former ways of life and history with her new opportunities.. The applause was deafening, and I felt that perhaps I might not measure up to her eloquence. However, it was an occasion when there was "glory enough to go around," and the audience was most generous to me. She had opened the way for me to say many things that were inspired by the splendid way in which our every word was received.

Often we are surprised to find that women as well as men are good at extemporaneous speaking, as was Mrs. Conlee on this occasion. She is one of those who from that time on has been a most effective worker and leader. We have gained greatly in discovering these hidden capabilities and talents, and this is the direct result of the suffrage and the increased emphasis put on woman as a citizen.

This all seems trite now, when the men have fully realized that it is a good thing for any political party to have one or more than one woman to strengthen the ticket and to appeal to the loyalty of our women voters. It is essential, of course, that such women have high ideals and be willing and able to study the part they are to play in sustaining the principles for which they stand and to live up to the promises they make to fulfill all their many duties in office. They must realize that their conduct is always under scrutiny. They must be on guard that no friendship or comradeship will disrupt other loyalties. Above all, they must take account of the natural jealousies that arise between home women and public servants, and must be doubly sure to always take into account the possibility of disturbing the sacredness of any home ties.

Kentucky has had all too few women who have been willing to subordinate their lives to the strenuous labor of campaigning and holding elective office. However, those who have attained these honors had made up in high quality whatever they may have lacked in numbers. There have been in the Legislature: Mrs. Mary Elliott Flannery, who began her state career in the campaign which we are now discussing; Mrs. H.G. Jorris of Jamestown, Russell County, a Republican, one who was loyal to women and several times did me the honor to befriend me; Mrs. S.B. Blackburn of Greenup County, whose high ideals made her much beloved in her community, and Mrs. Cecil Cantrill of Lexington, an astute political leader, one who is having a notable career in her home town where she is one of the city commissioners and has several times acted as mayor pro tem with dignity and ability.

That Kentucky women could make good in the public arena is amply proved by the fine showing they have made in the literary field. Dorothy Dix, highest paid columnist in this country; Alice Hegan Rice of the "Cabbage Patch;" Mrs. Attwood Martin of "Emmy Lou" fame; Elizabeth Madox Roberts, author of "The Great Meadow;" the late Mrs. Annie Fellows Johnston, who created "The Little Colonel," beloved the world over; Mrs. Mark Ethridge, who has recently entered the literary world; Mrs. Eleanor Mercein Kelly of Saturday Evening Post fame; these and dozens of others who have made names for themselves show conclusively what women could do if they turned their attention to governmental problems as well as literary attainment. The inclusion of political science and kindred subjects in high schools and universities should develop in the coming generation of women the consciousness of their citizenship, pride in their patriotism, and the desire to be a component part of the vast fabric of state and nation.

It is the duty of every man and woman to be willing to take upon themselves the burden as well as the privilege of government and to appreciate fully the inheritance our forefathers left. "They built the foundation in the days of Washington and Jefferson, and as a duty we must safeguard the building."

One item from many concerning the workers will show how indefatigable the women are. One woman in Eastern Kentucky who had a large district worked it down to the last voter. She did this without spending money. She planned ahead and had everything donated. She used four cars and loaded them well with rugs, galoshes, and wraps and, what was even more important, with pies, cakes, and fruit which were greatly relished by the voters. Starting at 6:30 in the morning, going in different directions, each of these women drivers under her direction labored through the whole election day, bringing in one merry party after another, all laughing, talking, and having a jolly good time.

No wonder the election days when this captain was on duty were looked forward to as gala occasions. At the risk of too much moralizing, is this not a commentary on how and when we can attend to the duties that are ours? It is not necessary to pull a long face or to preach. Fun can be found all along the way, and we and the world are better off for this good fellowship.

As the campaign drew toward its close the political lines were held more taut. It was a year when election of our ticket was not a foregone conclusion, and we were told to turn on all the steam. Few things equal in excitement and suspense the closing meetings of campaigns. Headquarters, loyal friends, and busy candidates all feel that a few hours have a magnified importance. It is true in this as in the one vote. One hour lost, one phrase spoken at the wrong time or place when nerves are tense and the result in doubt, do often spell gain or loss. The more experience one has in politics, the more of such slips one can remember.

We were instructed to make a whirlwind campaign for these closing days. Going to Barren, Monroe, Cumberland, and Metcalfe counties, I first made Glasgow, home of Joe Richardson, gifted editor of the Glasgow Times and an ardent worker. Here Congressman Creal, Miss Bess Howard, now County Court Clerk, and I made a speaking campaign. The Congressman was of immense help, being a stump speaker of scarcely less ability and of the same type as Senator Pat Harrison of Mississippi, who has won national fame by oratory and wit. Miss Howard was an organizer par excellence, well known and popular. Senator Frost of Metcalfe County, another man of outstanding ability, aided us here. At Burkesville, I was joined by Mrs. Curtis McGee, one of the most charming women of our state, well known in patriotic society circles and an effective worker wherever found.

In the First District our meeting partook of the nature of a rally and was featured by a mammoth barbecue. Senator Alben W. Barkley was one of the principal speakers, and I was introduced by Senator W.V. Eaton, which gave me quite a send-off. Senator Barkley needs no words of praise here as he is a national figure now and his policies and labors are international in scope. He is the kind of Kentuckian of whom in old times they used to quote, "There were giants in those days." His sledge-hammer debates and his always plausible and strong arguments bring conviction every time.

The Purchase and much of Western Kentucky are so thoroughly Democratic there is not much need of speaking except to rouse and rally the voters and ensure their attendance at the polls. The people want to meet their candidates and to arouse enough enthusiasm to get out the record vote for which that section is famous. A barbecue cannot rightly be described to one who has not seen one or participated in one at some time. Great barrels of burgoo, sides of roast pork and lamb roasted slowly for hours on spits over bedded fires in long trenches, sauce so piquant and hot that the famed East Indian curry is not comparable. Great piles of light bread, big dishes of pickles, cut up tomatoes of giant size, sliced onions for those who wish to add them, long tables spread and overloaded with these viands, while the happy barbecuers and burgoo-makers linger on the outskirts, listening for the praise they know will be theirs when the toothsome barbecue is sampled.

Another memorable meeting of those closing days was in Hopkins County, where young Bob Tapp did yeoman work for the ticket, and especially for me, going into every home in the county, tireless and enthusiastic. When the battle was over his was one of the very first telegrams to tell me of my victory in his county. The next telegram was from Senator Gates Young of Owensboro in Daviess County. Neither of these could wait to let me know how things stood. At our meeting in Owensboro, Senator A.O. Stanley turned loose his silver-tongued oratory and the applause has never been surpassed. He outdid himself as a spellbinder on that occasion, and the people responded with ready, roof-lifting noise, even more than he usually evoked.

Lawrence and Bruce Hager who succeeded the fine old stalwart, Urey Woodson, as editors of the Owensboro Messenger-Inquirer, were indefatigable. Their publicity was profuse and to the point and was responsible for much of the enthusiasm shown that day. The women were in evidence there as elsewhere, and as the campaign progressed it was heart-warming to watch the mounting interest in their participation. The novelty of the situation was forgotten, and from that time there has been no real criticism and little doubt of their efficient work and their ability to campaign and to hold office. In the midst of the campaign we all had to meet the issues of the Pari-Mutuel, the "Monkey Bill," and Prohibition. I had already taken my stand and suffered no further uneasiness. I was glad to be a conservative in living and thinking and to verge on the old-fashioned in my ideals. I found that this stand was pleasing to the people. If it is ever feasible for politicians to be ultra-radical, I believe the people will not expect the women to follow the extremes. It seems me that women should be balance wheels and should not let the pendulum swing either too long or too short. A couplet of Alexander Pope applies here:

"Be not the first by whom the new is tried,
 Nor yet the last to lay the old aside."

When the campaign was ended and victory won I did not find that I was tired. Some few who took part professed to be fagged out. I had kept calm, had my regular hours of sleep, had not allowed worry over the outcome to interfere with my appetite, and thrived on the hustle and bustle.

It has always been my determination that, should defeat be my lot, I would be a good loser, which I fancy is the only way to be also a good winner. However, defeatism was not allowed to creep in. I just put forth my best efforts and left the matter in the hands of Providence. I had never a moment's doubt that victory would be mine. That technique of success is a mainspring deep within each of us, and we should not allow outside influences to either enthuse or depress us to the breaking point of nerve exhaustion.

The next few days after election I was extremely busy answering telegrams and messages of good will. I felt it would be the height of discourtesy to neglect to reply to even one of these thoughtful good wishes. And then the next thing for all the successful candidates was preparation for taking up the duties of office and going through all the social formalities that attend a change of administration in Frankfort. I felt rested and refreshed, yet there was a period of preparation before me not fully known to my friends, who felt that now the campaign was successfully ended there was nothing to do except choose some suitable dresses and accessories and get ready to take part in the inauguration, the receptions, and social functions that would follow. I will admit that it was a problem to know exactly "what to wear" for these notable occasions, and wondered how I would get the time to attend to this.

For in the back of my mind was a plan to gain some training for the new duties that were to devolve upon me. I had been, throughout the years in Frankfort, quite close to the administrations and knew very well that if I entered on the new duties unprepared in knowledge of detail and in the modern systems that were coming into use in various states, I would make but a halting beginning. The work would hang heavy over my head if I did not make myself familiar with the methods being used in other places.

So, while my inner circle of friends were discussing, "What

must Emma wear?", I slipped off to Nashville, Tennessee, where I understood there had been inaugurated some new methods in the work of Secretary of State. Indeed, it was being discussed a lot, and there and in one other state, I spent quite some time, no on knew exactly where, thought I was away for a rest. But I was in the Tennessee capital where Mr. Hastings, Secretary of State, put at my disposal all the training and experience he had, while his assistant was most gracious in showing me every detail of the office system. This was a part of my duty to the women of my state who had stood behind me so valiantly. I determined for their sake to do the very best job I could and to absorb every bit of technique and detail possible. When I came home, my heart was very light, for I felt that I could easily grasp the work to be done. Knowing that my office would be regarded as a model, good or bad, I determined that it should be a laboratory where we would work out the very best methods for Kentucky.

Before leaving for Nashville my very good friend, Mrs. Lelia Leidenger of Louisville, had offered to superintend my wardrobe. I knew that her taste and choice would be in keeping with the position and with my purse and would be exactly what I should have. What an uplift to have such a friend in need! One familiar with shopping, with the materials and modistes. I had no uneasiness there.

It may be of some interest to women to know just what Mrs. Leidenger advised and what was the result. My street dress for the inaugural process or parade was a lovely dark blue cloth with hat, gloves, and accessories to match, and a Hudson seal coat. My reception gown was a handsome black panne velvet with high neck and long sleeves. For the office, of course, my plain and simple light wool dresses for winter and lighter crepes and prints for summer were the same I would have worn at my home.

For some time before any inauguration, the citizens of Frankfort are up and getting ready for the occasion, attending to the thousand and one details that have to be worked out and preparing for record-breaking crowds. There are also other details of precedence, not quite as many as in Washington, D.C., but plenty at that, for it is due the people of the state that everything about the inauguration of their chosen officials should be done in decency and order, as well as in perfect taste.

This work is done through committees and, as I was the only elected official who lived in Frankfort, I naturally attended practically all meetings. When the Committee for the Reception met and the arrangement was announced giving the place of officials in the receiving line, I noticed that they had, without regard to precedence, placed me almost at the end of the line, although the Secretary of State ranks third in line, next to the Lieutenant Governor. It was a little embarrassing, but I knew that, if allowed, many would notice this change in precedence. The honor is to the office and not the individual, so I called attention to this. Colonel Edmund Taylor, widely known and loved as "The Admiral of the Kentucky River," said in his princely manner, "Surely, we must follow the proper order." Pruett Graham, Mason Brown, Mrs. Timmy Hay, and Mrs. Sherman Goodpaster also spoke up immediately and said, "Why, of course, how thoughtless!" This is given as another of the occasions when we had to change our ways of thinking because a woman became a state official in her own right.

This precedence is followed not only in social affairs, but in order of official rank, so that there is no chance of mistake nor change when the officials are absent from the state or incapacitated. According to the following rank, they serve as Governor when it is necessary. First, the Lieutenant Governor; second, the President pro tem of the Senate; and third, the Secretary of State; fourth comes the Attorney General, which closes the legal ranking for this purpose.[2]

All was ready for the inauguration on the eighth of December. Great preparations had been made by the leading citizens of Frankfort, regardless of party affiliation, to keep "open house," as is the custom. It happened at that time I had two vacant apartments. So, I not only filled my residence but every available space in them with beds, and entertained forty guests, friends from out in the state, in a mammoth house party. As they came in they were met at the door by the butler and told to go upstairs and locate themselves. There they found tacked on the doors notes that assigned them to their quarters.

The Inauguration Day dawned with sunshine on the "old Kentucky home" and cheerful weather, a condition always welcome in Frankfort, where sometimes the weatherman is not so generous. The procession was formed near the old statehouse on Broadway and moved up St. Clair Street, across the old bridge to Shelby, thence to Capital Avenue, to the front of the new Capitol, where a large stand had been erected for the ceremonies which were witnessed by as large a crowd as had ever gathered for that purpose. Inauguration of a Governor of Kentucky makes up in sentiment and background for any diminution in size and importance from a national inauguration of a president in Washington. At least it seems so to all true Kentuckians. The stately dome of the new Capitol rises above the scene and behind it and to the sides all around rise the immemorial "Hills of Frankfort," below which glides the Kentucky River in sinuous curves, pausing here between its palisaded cliffs as the stream of life moves across and beside it. Above on the Cemetery Hill is the last resting place of Daniel Boone, some twenty Kentucky Governors, Senators, Admirals of the Navy, and notables of the state.

The busy modern statesmen and citizens carry on the work begun by the pioneers. As they take the oath of office, their eyes rest on the sacred hill above and look downward to the streets whose very names bring back the glories of the new republic and the young state whose business they swear to carry forward, to whose enduring fame they dedicate themselves anew. It is always a thrilling scene and gains new glamour with each passing four years of statehood.

On this occasion all was in readiness and the ceremonies went forward with speed and precision, and withal, with such dignity as befitted this recurring patriotic ceremonial.

After hearing the oaths of the new officials to support the Constitutions of the United States and of Kentucky, the crowd dispersed to late lunch and to make ready for the reception and the ball that followed, to which every Kentuckian is an invited guest. At the reception, as always, a line a block long formed, passing slowly along the corridors of the Capitol, in perfect good humor, although foot-weary and tired. It took something like an hour and a half for any one person to reach the Governor, his lady, and the receiving line, as they moved forward by inches. On either side of this line as many more stand by to watch the slow progress to the desired handshaking in the lovely reception room on the second floor of the Capitol building. These spectators seem to gain as much pleasure from seeing formally dressed citizens as those do who actually join the procession, perhaps more, for they are more free to move about and to take notes on dresses, modes, and fashions as displayed by the participants.

For those in the receiving line, as well as the crowd, this was a tiresome proceeding physically, but there was an uplift to it all; there was compensation in seeing again the happy faces of those who had helped by their votes and hard work to put us in this place of honor and acclaim. For the Governor and Lieutenant Governor, it was the beginning of a hard four years of work. For the rest of us, there was to be a respite of about three weeks during which time we were busy with preparations to take over our offices and begin a new regime with new forces and to show to the state our appreciation of the honors and responsibilities that had been given us. All this was a part of the "sweet fruits of victory," but no more so than the duties of state that awaited us and challenged us all to do our best to carry on the history and tradition of our beloved Commonwealth.

This was in the days of Aunt Winnie Thomas, with chauffeur Herbert Dodson as butler; and three meals a day were served buffet fashion, with good friends to attend to the serving. At lunch on Inauguration Day, there were two hundred friends besides the forty house guests. Everything went smoothly, and fun and jollity prevailed. It was like a gigantic Christmas celebration, an occasion long to be remembered.[3] It was a pleasant interlude between the strenuous campaign and election and the heavy duties that awaited me beyond the massive doors of the Capitol in the office of Secretary of State. Our happy days together closed with the singing of "Auld Lang Syne."

At the inauguration, the Governor and Lieutenant Governor were sworn in and entered upon their official duties for the great Commonwealth. The other officials are sworn in the first Tuesday in January and are then ready to join the Governor in service to the people. This was the first time in the history of Kentucky that a woman was a member of the official family to help plan and build up the state.

These are but indications of a new day for women. The new problems of women in politics are not ones that can be solved by a moment's thought or in a decade of public life. In its full implication it involves the economic problem of machines against the work of human hands.

It involves the discoveries of modern science that have changed not only thought but methods of work. Henry Adams, in his "Education," calls the entire problem of womanhood in this century the most vital of all problems of force. He says that, "All these new women have been created since 1840; all were to show their meaning before 1940."

Henry Adams in setting this date did not give time enough for the problem of women's place in this modern world to be worked out. We have not the time and space in these pages, even if we had the ability, to outline any solution. It is a fact that times have changed. There is yet a long way to travel before we can say that women are doing their best in the places they can fill. We do feel that progress has been made in Democratic countries in the position of women, and we hope that no backward steps may be taken.

One thing is sure, women in public office are on trial and they have an opportunity never before in history given to any one group. It is their great responsibility to live up to the challenge of these modern times, and to prove themselves worthy of the trust that is theirs. The long process of freeing the spirit of womanhood began when the Scriptures declared that, "In Christ Jesus there is neither male or female." Pray God the complete fulfillment of this high calling will come in our time and in a way that will make every woman citizen proud that she is a woman, when her sister women are proving themselves worthy to wear the crown of complete womanhood, when each shall be equipped, as Wordsworth wrote, with:

"The reason firm, the temperate will,
Endurance, foresight, strength, and skill;
A perfect woman, nobly planned
To warn, to comfort, and command."

Chapter III Notes

1. The author continued:

"Her Executive Board includes Mrs. H.K. Bourne of New Castle; Mrs. D.M. Howerton, Ashland; Mrs. Thomas C. Underwood, Hopkinsville; Mrs. Curtis McGee, vice-president, Burkesville; Mrs. J.A. Kaltenbrun, recording secretary, Frankfort; Mrs. J. Campbell Cantrill, corresponding secretary, Frankfort; Mrs. Lawrence Hager, treasurer, Owensboro; Mrs. Samuel M. Wilson, chairman of the legislative committee, Lexington; Mrs. Owen Moreland, chairman, ways and means, Lexington; Mrs. John L. Woodbury of Louisville, and Miss Linnie B. Brady, Covington, board members from the state at large; Mrs. Samuel Connor, Bardstown, Democratic National Committeewoman; Mrs. Emma Guy Cromwell, state organizer and parliamentarian; Miss Ann Gullion, Carrollton, editor of the Democratic Woman's Journal. I pause here to pay tribute to Mrs. V.O. Gilbert, who was for years the efficient and faithful treasurer of the Journal. She has had to resign after such long and loving service, on account of ill health in the family. The difficult and ofttimes thankless job has passed into the capable hands of Mrs. Woodbury, who succeeds Mrs. Gilbert.

"Many prominent women scattered throughout the state are on special committees. The directors in charge of the nine Congressional Districts, who are responsible for the organization and working of their districts, are: Mrs. R.L. Johnson, Clinton; Mrs. Bright Hawes, Maceo; Mrs. Roscoe Huntsman, Scottsville; Mrs. Elliott Riddell, Louisville; Mrs. Tom Wickham, Bloomfield; Mrs. L.F. Crecelius, Falmouth; Mrs. John Read, Covington; Mrs. Mary Cain, Newport; Mrs. Robert Dunn, Richmond; Mrs. Roy Helm, Hazard; Mrs. Espy Goodpaster, Owingsville; Mrs. Edward Garland, Somerset.

"Another effective Democratic worker in Frankfort, with charm and tact, who was for some years connected with various departments, is Mrs. Mable Glenn Barton, now the wife of Captain A.H. Conner of Alexandria, Virginia, and Washington, D.C."

2. Under a constitutional amendment adopted in 1992, the governor now retains his

authority when outside the state; the order of succession in the event a governor dies or is incapacitated remains unchanged.

3. The author continued:

"Some of those helping with service were Mrs. Laura Sloss of Franklin, Mrs. Roscoe Huntsman and Mrs. Ed Welch of Scottsville, Mrs. Lena Chapman of Columbia, Tennessee, Miss Nell Cummings of Louisville, Mrs. Marie Dogged of Georgetown, Mrs. Luella Cromwell Minton of Lexington, Miss Bettie Cromwell of Cynthiana, Mrs. Lelia Dempsey and Miss Sarah Hayes of Madisonville. Among the viands served were old ham, beaten biscuits, chicken salad, coffee, pie, ice cream, and cake. Senator and Mrs. James Rash of Hopkins County, and Mrs. Powell Taylor and Mrs. Laura Stephan of Henderson, and Miss Virginia Welch of Scottsville entertained us with music, old ballads, and songs of long ago. Leigh Harris of Henderson was official announcer for the music and the meals."

IV

Scaling the Wall of State

All that glistens is not gold.

I was sworn in as Secretary of State on January 10, 1924, by Judge Augustus Thomas of Mayfield, Chief Justice of the Court of Appeals, then and now regarded throughout the state as the sage and wit of that august body, as well as one of the wisest of the judges who have held that office.[1] Kentucky's oath of office includes the sworn statement that the applicant has not fought a duel with deadly weapons, neither acted as second, nor carried a challenge for any duel. A smile went over the audience as the Chief Justice intoned this antiquated part of the solemn oath to attend to the duties of office and to uphold the Constitution of Kentucky and that of the United States of America.

In spite of the solemnity of the occasion and its significance for Kentucky womanhood, no auditor could suppress a feeling of amusement. To me the oath was of double import because I was, in effect, doubly representing the women of the state as newly recognized citizens and as women. The thought came to me that in a sense I had fought a triple duel for this honor and responsibility to which I swore my fealty for the coming four years. Had I not taken part in a pitched suffrage battle for the rights of citizenship, as one of the many women who saw further into the future than others? Had I not then entered into a duel of wits and endurance with three other candidates for the nomination in August? Then, thirdly, had I not fought a real duel with another woman as opponent in the final race which had been won in November previous? Although there had been no deadly weapons used, nor any poisoned arrows of the tongue, the fact was that it had been a duel to the death — of ambitions.

The crowd at the opening of an administration is always a large one. This time it surpassed the usual size. Friends of my own and of the other elected candidates were there from every corner of the state, its length and breadth, city, town, and country. Reporters swarmed all over the place. Especially remembered are young Tom Underwood of the Lexington Herald; my cousin, Tom Cromwell of the Cincinnati Enquirer; Vance Armentrout of the Courier-Journal staff; George Willis, Sr., of Shelbyville; and particularly the late Judge Robert Worth Bingham, who honored the occasion by his presence as a public-spirited citizen and owner and manager of the Louisville Courier-Journal. He was a figure then of national interest, and it was no surprise to his friends when he later became Ambassador to the Court of St. James and had many other well-deserved honors heaped upon him as long as he lived to serve Kentucky and the United States.

Those sworn in at that time were Emma Guy Cromwell, General Frank Daugherty, Ed Dishman, W.H. Shanks, Dr. McHenry Rhoads, Newton Bright, and William O'Connell. The Governor and Lieutenant Governor had been sworn in at the statutory date in December. So, at this time my turn came first according to the precedence of the Secretary of State in the official family of the Governor. Never in my life was the overruling of a kind Providence felt more keenly than on that day. In one instant there flashed on memory's screen a picture of my orphaned childhood and my rather lonely girlhood, followed by a great wave of thankfulness for the kind friends of my father's Order of Masons, as well as for many others who had given me aid in the business world. Other thoughts crowded in, too sacred to mention, too poignant to think about when calmness and poise were necessary for these new duties. As Lowell has said so fittingly:

"Behind the dim unknown
Standeth God within the shadow,
Keeping watch above His own."

In my new office my desk was hidden with a mass of flowers that had been sent from generous friends who took this beautiful way of wishing me well in the journey of four years that lay before me. The outgoing Secretary of State, Fred Vaughn, genial and kindly always, received me with the utmost cordiality as he turned over the office that had been his during the preceding administration.

My visit to other states had given me an insight into the duties that awaited me, and I had a system of work planned and immediately proceeded to put it into practice. Having kept my own counsel, even my closest friends did not know of this special preparation, for I had found long since that it is wise to "never tell all you know, nor believe all you hear."

The desks of the staff members were designated, and as they took their places they found typewritten slips with a partial list of the duties assigned to them. This made for an orderly system and there was much comment on the lack of confusion and the amount of work accomplished in a short while.

The Governor had selected as Assistant Secretary of State a young lawyer from Hardinsburg, Sam Monarch, as this official handles the records of the gubernatorial office and is more or less responsible directly to the Chief Executive. The Corporation Desk was handled by Mr. Roberts of Louisville, a competent businessman. My two secretaries were Miss Lennie Lewis of Mayfield and Miss Mary Malloy of Kuttawa. They proved themselves extremely competent, as did the others of my staff. I may be pardoned for emphasizing their efficiency and loyalty as they handled the business of my own desk and were so close to me personally. Others of the staff who did yeoman work for the office were Mrs. Nola Hanberry of Hopkinsville, widow of the distinguished Circuit Judge, Jack Hanberry; Mrs. John Phillips of Frankfort; Miss Josephine Fonville of Bowling Green (now Mrs. Robert Porter of Frankfort). Later as the expanding duties of the office required more help, I added to the staff Miss Frances Hazelrigg of Mt. Sterling, who later married John Carroll, son of the distinguished Chief Justice and compiler of Carroll's Statutes. Then Miss Lela May Stiles became a member of my official family, and no comment on her efficiency is needed when it is remembered that she has since had a distinguished career in Washington, D.C., and is at present one of the personal secretaries of President Franklin D. Roosevelt in the White House. Near the close of my term my assistant, Mr. Monarch, resigned and Colonel Bob Dixon of Louisa was appointed. This did not disrupt the office nor plans in the least, as he had influence and experience and was congenial, as well, all qualities that are indispensable in a public servant, whether elected or appointed.

Many amusing incidents occurred, especially at first. One day a rather pompous gentleman came in, one who had a reputation as a globe trotter and who bragged that he had walked all around the world. He said, somewhat abruptly, "I want to see the Secretary of State." I said, "Very well, how can I serve you?" He replied, "I want to see the man of the office." "If so, you will have to walk into another state, for we have a woman Secretary," I replied. He looked at me hard and long, then said, "I have some important papers to sign. Do you think you can sign them?" My answer was, "Watch me and see." In leaving he said, "Gosh, I believe women can do anything." Somewhat nettled, I replied: "Yes, except walk around the world, and they are too busy doing useful things to attempt that."

Another day a corporation lawyer from New York came into the office, looked around and, the Corporation Clerk being out, saw only women. He asked, "Is this the office of the Secretary of State?" I replied that it was and asked what we could do for him. He said, "I want to file some corporation papers, but don't suppose you know anything about corporations." My reply was, "Just tell me what you want and we will show you that women can transact business. All we want is a chance." We soon had his business attended to, before he had time to make any more remarks. In leaving he said, "Women are really doing things these days. I want to apologize for my abruptness." This was accepted courteously and the card filing system on which we were engaged was explained to him. He then said we had the best and most up-to-date office he had seen anywhere and made up with complimentary comment for his offhand manner of approach.

My office had a great opportunity to serve the public of that day, and the occasion soon arose when we could serve the future by reclaiming priceless records of the past. Just below us in the basement were piles of documents in barrels and boxes with many dumped on the floor in endless confusion. Dirt and dust of years — yes, of a century or more — lay thick upon them. It seemed at first just a gigantic housecleaning job, one which appealed to a woman as being certainly within the scope of her traditional duties.

On examination, however, were found pen-written papers of great value, the records of all the administrations, from Isaac Shelby, 1792, on to 1924. Here were the signatures of all of Kentucky's Governors, not once but many times repeated, also many documents with signatures of those less notable, who had played their part on the stage of Kentucky affairs and passed off leaving their acts and deeds as a basis for the government of today. Here were lessons in patriotism, in service of civilians and soldiers, in devotion to duty under strange difficulties as well as in the ordinary life of the people. Many of these were souvenirs of the day of the goose-quill pen and the unfading oak ball ink.

Year after year, as these documents had accumulated, they had been pushed further and further back, until finally dumped into the basement. Most of them had been written in a time when there were no filing systems, no cabinets of polished wood or steel, no adequate way to preserve them so that they could be available for research, for genealogical data, or just to stand as mute records of laborious work, done in the service of the public.

Standing there and surveying the chaotic heaps, it was noted where the writing lay exposed that infinite care had been taken by the penmen who wrote these documents in beautiful script, that the good ink had scarcely faded and the fine paper had kept its textur,; which all testified eloquently to the splendid workmanship of our forebears and told of the painstaking care in the choice of materials for use of the public officials of Kentucky. Day after day, year after year, these records had accumulated. Now, what should be done with them?

Along with the realization of the historic and sentimental value of all this mass of material there arose in my mind's eye a vision of what should be done to preserve them. A few historians were consulted and they were intensely interested. Two of these were Dr. W.H. Goodrich and Dr. William Koch of Ann Arbor, Michigan, my former instructors in Library Science, and they were enthusiastic in their advice to go ahead, and heartily agreed with me that it was a priceless heritage to hand on to future generations.

Looking at the Herculean task that lay in the dust before me, piled in all sorts of grotesque heaps, and knowing it would take time and strength and endurance to complete it, the determination grew to make the effort.

We could not count on any extra appropriation, and our regular budget would not take care of it. So it was determined to appeal to my office force to take on this extra task. Most of them realized its value and were willing to go into it, using odd times when not too busy with other detail work. All became enthusiastic before we were far into the task, and we spent many of the hours that could have been given to leisure and recreation on this job which we came to see was a truly patriotic piece of work.

Miss Mary Malloy was designated as the secretary to handle this special work which I directed. It took two years, working as we did under difficulties. We were furnished two men from the Reformatory to clean and arrange the papers and they proved very efficient. "It can be done" became our slogan, and we pushed on to completion until every letter, record, requisition, list, and document of every Governor from 1792, the first, to the third year of Governor William J. Fields, was neatly filed and catalogued. They included the Executive Journals which are a complete history of any administration, also pardons and other matters belonging to the prisons and eleemosynary institutions. In fact, the variety is as wide as the varied elements that go to make up the state government, and each has the personal touch of someone who put heart and soul into the work as well as those lives which were touched by all this detail. All was classified, put into jackets, titles typed, numbered, and placed in filing boxes in sectional steel cases, making a record of twenty-five Governors that was practically indestructible, well preserved, and made usable. These steel cases were carried over to the Old Capitol, where many of the records had their origin, and there they were deposited in the archives of the State Historical Society under the watchful care of Mrs. Jouett Taylor Cannon, who is adept in all that pertains to archives and knows well how and where to direct research workers who find these records increasingly valuable as they use them more and more. To get them transferred to the Historical Society, it was necessary for me to have an order from the Sinking Fund Commission, of which I was a member.

Miss Malloy had a keen eye for the unusual and the incidental. She had been trained in business under the care of Dr. Louie Harmon of Bowling Green. She often called attention to items that amused all of us who were working so diligently on the records. One striking letter was from an early Governor to his wife, and he was admonishing her as to the extravagance of a fur coat. But he closed by saying, "Dear, buy anything you want, but don't get the old man too deep in debt, for I won't be Governor always. There come a "lighting" time with all of us. So watch our pocketbook."

Other interesting letters showed sidelights on our history.

As a reminder of the many connections of Kentucky with Tennessee, we found this:

A copy of a letter from the Governor of Kentucky to his Excellency the Governor of Tennessee.

Frankfort, Kentucky
February 25, 1821.

His Excellency Governor McMinn.

Sir:

By a resolution of the Legislature of Kentucky and a copy of which is enclosed it has become my duty to have the line between this state and Tennessee run and marked agreeable to the third article of the convention entered into by commissioners delegated from each state and approved by the Legislature of Kentucky February 11, 1829, from its commencement to where it strikes the Cumberland River near the mouth of Obeys River.

Your excellency will see, by a reference to the article of the convention above mentioned, that this work is to be done, by a Surveyor from each state, and at the joint expense of both — Permit me Sir to call your attention to this subject, as the Season of the year is approaching, most proper for performing the labour — please transmit me your views on the subject — I will be ready at all times to make the appointment of a Surveyor on the part of this state.

Accept my good wishes for your health and happiness and believe me to be your most obt. Servt.
John Adair.

Surveyor — Kentucky
Colonel Wm. Steel — Woodford County
Colonel Lovney — Tennessee
William H. Harrison — referee for Kentucky
and W. McHenry — referee for Tennessee

As an echo of the War with Mexico, we append this facsimile of a letter found among these old documents:

Executive Office
Frankfort, Kentucky
September 8, 1845

Sir:

Your communication of the 28th ult., advising me that General Taylor in Texas, is authorised, in case he should need them, to call on the Governor of Kentucky auxilliary troops, has been received.

In reply, I have the honor to assure you that the citizens of my state have lost none of the patriotic ardor which has ever heretofore distinguished them, and which has led them to be among the first to defend our common Country from foreign aggression. I will hold myself in constant readiness to comply with any requisition of the Government at Washington; and I beg leave to assure the Government that any call upon the militia of Kentucky will be promptly and gallantly responded to.

Wm. Owsley,
Governor of Kentucky.

To: Hon. W.L. Marcy,
    Secretary of War.

During this long tedious work it was much discussed in the Capitol building, and no doubt some commiserated with the staff on the amount of extra work they were encouraged to do. The usual criticism was that it was foolishness to keep those dirty old papers, that they had all best be burned up to get rid of them.

One head of a department said once, "Mrs. Cromwell, why don't you burn up all that old trash in the basement? You will work yourself and your staff to death, and no one will appreciate it. You are just foolish to do it." My reply was, "It may be foolish to do so much work, but I believe when we complete it and show you what we have done, you will see that it is a fine heritage to hand down to you and yours all these records of the work of our ancestors." "Maybe so," he replied, "but you will have to show me." When he was told that it was all being done under the Dewey system, he thought that Dewey, hero of Manila, was meant, but I let that pass and I was surprised when after the work was finished and in good shape that he came to me voluntarily and said it was as fine a piece of work as he ever saw and added that it would be priceless to others who would come after. So it is often, the eye must see for one to be convinced. It is not everyone who can visualize a completed perfect file of material when they look on the matter in a chaotic state.

One day the porter of the department came to me and said, "Miss Emma, you know what some of these white folks is calling you?" I said, "No, John, what is it?" He said, "It is 'Lady Antique.' I told them you was a lady, but, Miss Emma, what do 'antique' mean?" I tried to explain to him and told him that we knew what we were doing and for him to help out and that he and others would be proud. Also, that it was best not to listen to outside talk.

Among the interesting papers and records we found much that

pertained to the building of the statehouses of the Commonwealth, their sites, cost, and details of construction. Also much regarding the four Constitutions under which the government has operated since its beginning. This will be discussed in another chapter.

We had not been first on the ground, for stamp hunters had been there before us, and the amount in valuable stamps that had been stolen from these old documents is impossible to compute. Many of them are now priceless, and this vandalism was responsible for some of the great disorder in which we found the papers.

One visitor came to me early in the work and asked that we give him all the stamps left as he wanted to use them for a laudable missionary enterprise. He was told that all these stamps belonged to Kentucky and that the Secretary of State had no authority to give them away or to divert their use.

One discovery found tucked in among the aged papers, well hidden for many years, was a quart of fine old Bourbon whiskey. This was during the days of prohibition, when many who might have liked to sample this were more or less afraid. Yet there were several who called at the office and asked to try out this ruby red troublemaker. They were told it had been there so long that there might be poison in it. It was emptied into the lavatory and drained away through the plumbing pipes. There was poison in it from its very beginning and it was a principle with me not to countenance the distribution of such at any time.

It was somewhat of a surprise that when we had completed the filing and cataloguing of these records, we had not located the original of any one of the four Constitutions of Kentucky. I inquired of many, and no one had any idea where they were or how and when they had been removed from among the old state papers. Among those consulted were Mrs. Cannon of the Historical Society; Ballard Thruston, Otto Rothert, and Miss Kinkead of the Filson Club. All were greatly interested, but all our inquiries availed nothing.

John Doolan, a prominent attorney of Louisville, gave valuable suggestions in this search and informed me that, according to law, if we could find these original papers they could be recovered at no expense to the state, for there was no power that could sequester them from their rightful owner, the people of the Commonwealth.

To Kentuckians, this search was comparable to that for the Holy Grail, and every step suggested was taken. A cousin of mine in Chicago, J.K. Lambert, before the close of my term as Secretary of

State, told me he thought the original of the first Constitution could be located probably in the University of Chicago. I went there at once, visited him and his wife, and we turned up several clues and thought we were on the eve of a great discovery. My term of service ended soon after this, and nothing came of it at the time. In another chapter will be related how and when we did locate the first Constitution of Kentucky. Search is yet being made for the other three, and no doubt the time will come when they will be brought to light. They belong to all Kentucky and the historians of the state will never be satisfied until they repose in the rooms of the Historical Society, which is housed in the Old Capitol building, one of the architectural treasures of the United States, the work of the great designer Gideon Shryock. Every year architects and artists come to Frankfort simply to see this splendid classic building.

One of the pleasures that came from this exacting work was an invitation to address the Filson Club of Louisville on preservation of old documents. The officers and my fellow members of this club all appreciated the valuable work done, and I will never cease to be grateful to Mr. Thruston, Mr. Rothert, Lucien Beckner, Miss Kinkead, and others, who encouraged me in this classification and preservation of our old records. There are others of our state who will go down in history as deeply interested in the preservation of records and the proper housing of archives.[2]

Among other hurdles that an official has to take is that of interviews for the newspapers. No one has a higher regard for the press than I have, for it has stood by me always and my nomination and election at this particular time were largely due to editors throughout the state. The newsmen know of my gratitude to them and my great respect for them. It is to the press that we all look for the continuation of that freedom of speech that is essential if we are to survive as a nation and a free people.

At the same time, there are always reporters on the lookout for news that will add "color" to their publications, and some of these thought a woman official was fair game. Then it must be admitted there are some who do snoop and who seek by fair or foul means to pin something on public servants, or who serve some party or faction and seek unfair advantage by beginning with an interview and by cross-examination methods eliciting some admission that might act as a boomerang to the official who may at first feel flattered by the attention.

One such occasion is remembered when a wise-looking young

reporter came to me for an interview early in my service as Secretary of State. Something in his attitude put me on guard and warned me that he wanted my reaction to some controversial issue. He began by asking his first question on the moot racing issue of the Pari-Mutuel machines. He said, "Mrs. Cromwell, my paper wants to know how you stand on the Pari-Mutuels." My reply was, "I know about as much about Pari-Mutuels as a jellyfish knows about politics. I read something in the papers occasionally. I do not gamble. I never played a game of cards in my life. I merely know that in cards there is a Jack and a Jill. I never attended a horse race. Let me suggest that you go to some of the men who may be interested in telling you what they think. There is nothing to be gained by betting and betting devices. I suppose one is about the same as another, all devised to work the suckers."

This was an occasion

"Where ignorance is bliss,

'Tis folly to be wise."

This promising young reporter was told that if he wished to see our new filing systems or to hear of the project we were beginning to preserve the old and valuable records of the former Governors, it would be a pleasure to give him the time and to tell him of the work which we hoped to make constructive and effective in conducting the business of the state. Thus was he diverted. Whatever had been his motive in coming, it was gratifying to see his real interest in the work and his response to the businesslike methods we were putting into effect. It is certain that if each elected and appointed official had in mind the orderly conduct of business and would not dabble in all sorts of isms and factions, we would all be better off.

This brings to mind the fact that by virtue of my office, I was a member of seven important boards. Being the only woman, the reporters seemed to think it would be "easy pickings" to find out just what was going on. The age-old idea that women cannot keep secrets and that they eternally talk too much caused me to be besieged on every hand for "tips." Now I do not believe in "star chamber" sessions, and think that the people's business should be conducted in the open. Yet we know well that if everyone knew everything that was proposed and knew all the beginnings of worthwhile projects in the making, the way would be open for checkmating on the part of factions or real enemies of good government. The servants of the people should be open and above board, yet they should have some sort of privacy as to their plans until they are well on their way, just as businessmen or

85

those who invent and patent new things. They should have a measure of secrecy until their work is well started, and then it can stand or fall on its own merits, without undue propaganda on the one part or undue pressure on the other, from those who would overthrow it before it has a fair chance to succeed or fail.

So when approached by reporters and interrogated as to what had occurred in any meeting, they were always referred to the Minutes. Then, it was up to the secretary and chairman of the meeting as to whether these could be made public property at that time. It was my firm rule never to give out information from any board or committee meeting. This was part of my settled policy as guardian of the interests of the women as well as of all citizens. I knew that if any slip occurred through me, the slur would be on the incompetence of women generally and determined never to let my sister women down in this way or any other.

During my regime, the National Association of Secretaries of State was very active, and I attended every meeting of that body and was honored by being made recording secretary and parliamentarian. Being at first the only woman secretary who attended the meetings, the courtesy and consideration that was accorded me is one of the most pleasant memories of my life. Gallantry is not confined to Kentuckians, and I met kindness always.

One of the conventions attended was in Miami, Florida, and was as brilliant as that great city could make it, with all the surroundings of the tropics and the glamour of the great winter resort. Here was my first service as an officer of the organization and the opportunity to be useful. The secretaries who attended took their work very seriously. Altogether much good was accomplished in the matter of systematizing records and insisting on higher standards in office work.

There were some very pleasant social events connected with all the meetings, one at Providence, Rhode Island, being especially remembered.

"Little Rhody" may be small in size, but her citizens are large of heart and generous to a degree. That year there were added two more women to the secretarial group, one elected and another appointed as assistant. United States Senator Metcalfe, the great leader of the textiles interests, had his home there, and he took particular pains to be kind to Kentucky's representative. One reason for this was the fact that he was a descendant of one of Kentucky's noted Governors of the same name.

He personally entertained with a clambake. The clams were baked on the sand at Marragansett Pier and the banquet held in one of the magnificent hotels that line the beach in that region. Not only clams, but all kinds of seafoods in many varied forms were served, and the setting and decorations were beautiful. One always finds that Kentucky has a unique standing everywhere and soon grows accustomed to honors given because of nativity in the Bluegrass State, but seldom has a Kentuckian been so embarrassed by being named as guest of honor when not expected to be more than one of the crowd. The Senator was influenced perhaps by his Kentucky ancestry and wanted to emphasize this, but the feeling of one of our present day "Major Bowes' amateurs" came over me when he came to me and said, "May I have the pleasure of escorting Little Kentucky to the dining room?" Here, though being very prominently seated at his right, the fun and jollity of the occasion soon prevailed to conquer any embarrassment. How different was the serving of the lowly baked clam here amid the luxury to its origin where "along the ebbing edges of saline coves you find the precious wedges."

The clams were served steaming hot in their shells, covered with a white napkin and accompanied by a small bowl of drawn butter. Those accustomed to the dainty seemed to have no difficulty in breaking open each shell gracefully and by making a long tongue quickly engulfing the tender morsel with a fillip and downing it in a wink of time. Looking around, it was seen that many of the visitors were no more adept than I was, and there was great fun as the hosts enjoyed our momentary discomfiture and proceeded to teach us the proper way to eat a clam.

In the midst of this lesson the bargain was made that, in return for the instruction in clam eating, we would teach our hosts when they came to the various states how to eat some of the dishes native to other parts. In Kentucky, we promised this would be the famous burgoo and barbecue. And so on to the ways of cooking and serving, all very interesting and strange to inlanders, as most of us were. All this was interspersed with the stirring music of the Marine Band. When time came for toasts, again we had to meet the high good humor of our hosts. Several things occurred to make me proud of Kentucky, and as the wit went around it seemed easier to respond for my native state. Senator Aldrich, for one, mentioned with compliments Tom Wallace of the Louisville Times, as a convincing speaker, eloquent, and a fine example of what one editor could do for a hobby like the conservation of natural resources.

This gave a cue for Kentucky's toast when the time came at the last of the evening. It seemed a good time to speak of Kentucky's great natural resources and beauty and to proceed to her orators, of whom were mentioned many of the leaders of that day, including Senators A.O. Stanley and A.W. Barkley, M.M. Logan, Mrs. John South, also Governor Edwin P. Morrow, along with many others. It seemed an inspiration that all the delving into old records had brought to light a number of facts concerning Governor Thomas Metcalfe, and it was fitting that here, when his descendant was host, these might be briefly recounted. All fitted in, and the group were very kind in receiving with applause the effort of "Little Kentucky" which, as always, was given in the name and for the good fame of Kentucky womanhood.

Naturally the South came in for a share in the general good will toward Kentucky. Many nice things were said of Dixie Land, and it seemed as if "bygones were bygones." It was amusing, however, to hear next day, when a number of club women called socially at our hotel, that some expressed surprise that the South had recognized women. Indeed, in a not very tactful way it was intimated that when the South did anything worthwhile, it behooved the world to look and stand agape as at some strange thing, a seven days' wonder. This is merely by the way. The hospitality and usual tact of New England followed us all in memory as we left for home with a good taste, not only of clams, but of splendid people, fellow Americans all.

Another pleasant recollection is of the many acquaintances from other states who became my friends. One of these was Mike Holm of St. Paul, Minnesota, a vice-president of the association. Still another was Louie Emmerson, afterwards Governor of Illinois, who became also, with his good wife, my close friend. He always invited me to the functions at the Mansion at Springfield, pleasures I had to forego because of the press of duties.

One of the happy occasions of this kind I did attend. When he was nominated he called a convention of the secretaries of the northern states, and I was invited from the southern division. This was a courtesy and carried with it all expenses, with the privilege of bringing a friend. Mrs. Kinnaird, wife of the Senator from Barren and Edmonson counties, was with me at my desk when this urgent invitation came and she read it with me. As she was one of my close friends, I immediately asked her if she would go with me, should I decide to go.

She, like myself, hardly knew what to say, but when the Senator came in he was enthusiastic and said that we must go. So I wired acceptance and the next morning tickets came, Pullman reservations, hotel accommodations and all. The time was rather short and our journey to Chicago was like a dream, such a fine trip out of a clear sky, with not much time for consideration. Mrs. Kinnaird and I were met at the train by Dr. Wm. Ramsey and J.C. Newman, who had been assigned to escort us to our quarters at the hotel, where we had choice of meals in either American, Italian, French, or German dining rooms. A private secretary was assigned to me and, as there was at the time much urgent business, she proved very useful in taking dictation for a number of letters. So there was no lapse in carrying on the business of the office at home.

The ladies in the party of the Governor-elect gave a very beautiful luncheon at which we were guests of honor. Such a profusion of flowers could only have been shown in a large city like Chicago, while all the table appointments were on the most lavish scale. In the interval before the banquet of the evening, we visited the sights of the city, rested, dictated letters, and made ready for the evening's entertainment. Dr. and Mrs. Ramsey escorted us to the banquet, where we met Governor and Mrs. Emmerson and at once felt at home, as we had worked together as officers in our secretarial conventions. The crowd was congenial and the conversation and toasts were such as might have been expected with such a brilliant throng.

At the banquet the table was laden with flowers. A substantial and beautiful meal was served, the menu cards being splendid souvenirs of the occasion. The places of the various invited representatives of state were marked with black satin banners lettered in gold. My few remarks when called upon were confined to the fact that Kentucky had been a pioneer in honoring womanhood with elective office, not forgetting, however, to remind them that Illinois had been first to ratify the Nineteenth Amendment to the Constitution, which gave suffrage to women, and that that state had been among the first to send a telegram of congratulation to the Kentucky woman who was elected the first female Secretary of that State. It would be ingratitude to the women of my state were not all such honors received in their name and for their sake. The toast which Mrs. Kinnaird gave to the women of the great state of Illinois filled me with pride as it gave another proof that our Kentucky women always measure up to the full stature of womanhood when called upon in any capacity.

A reception followed and the good fellowship lasted until the morning papers were on the streets, a late (or early) hour for the Kentuckians, and I fancy for the others as well, for all were busy people engaged in the important work of their own state governments and private business. The next day was spent in drives, with a visit to the theater, and then return on the following night train back to the routine of the office, which made the luxurious trip seem more like a dream than ever.

Not only in other states but right at home, there occurred many happy interludes when one could forget work for a brief season and give up the time to play. Such an occasion was a banquet given in Frankfort by the Women's Club to the members of the State Federation Board and friends, when Mrs. Allie S. Dickson of Paris was state president. The new Capital Hotel was very new then and the brilliant affair with lights, flowers, and fine food could hardly have been surpassed in any gay capital of the world.

The Frankfort women, accustomed as they are to social functions, shone like stars that evening. Short speeches were the order of the occasion and many toasts were given. The one assigned to me was, "What Would Grandma Say If She Could Be Here Today?" Below are included some excerpts from my response that are neither poetry nor wisdom, but given here merely to show that women in congenial company can relax and enjoy life.

"What would Grandma say of women out eating alone while hubbies are heating their suppers at home? What would she say of women who run for office like men, have lots of fun, and get elected, then, too. What she'd say? 'Boo hoo, my world has surely come to an end.' And there are others who are aping their brothers, are trying to smoke, to gossip and joke, some women who bet, some who are 'wet,' some women who swear, some who bob their hair, who powder their noses and faces at all public places. She would say of these, 'They are setting some paces.' She would say, 'I see that old fashions are out, why none of these modern mothers are stout, what has become of the fat — and whence comes this waved hair worn with never a hat. And the blushes I see,' says Grandma, 'Ah, me, they are fixed as a stare, how do they keep them there? They look like they're painted! And horrors! Not one of these speakers fainted. Why fainting and tears in my maiden years were our mainstay when we wanted attention from our men.' But Grandma was in her day a lady wise and soon would show no surprise, but realize that the modern woman although she goes out and runs all about, when given a task that is hard to do just buckles down and puts it through. That she has found it pays to know

90

more than one thing well, and that it doesn't pay all you know to tell. We think that our times are just about right when these many fine friends have met here tonight, and Grandma would be quite hard to please if she did not admire such grand women as these."

It was during this term of office that the Democratic convention was held in New York City — the one which lasted three weeks and almost bankrupted us all in sleep, pocketbooks, and clothes, to say nothing of precious time spent. Being the only woman holding office, I was interviewed many times and many snapshots were taken of our party, which Urey Woodson, with his old-fashioned gallantry, called one of the highlights of the convention. Others of the party were Mrs. A.O. Stanley, Henderson; Mrs. Edmund Post, Paducah; Mrs. John L. Woodbury, Louisville; Miss Bess Howard, Glasgow; Mrs. Mary Elliott Flannery, Catlettsburg; Mrs. H.K. Bourne, New Castle; Mrs. Dan Moore, Harrodsburg; and Mrs. Campbell Cantrill of Frankfort, who was then national committeewoman.

This convention was the first to be broadcast over radio and thousands over the country gathered at receiving sets, reporting they heard more static than anything else. All agreed, however, that it was wonderful to hear the roll calls as the various states responded, as vote after vote was taken without result. On the ninth of July it was ended by the nomination of John W. Davis of West Virginia and Charles W. Bryan of Nebraska for president and vice president. The deadlock had been between McAdoo and Al Smith. The opposing candidates on the Republican ticket were Calvin Coolidge and Charles G. Dawes, and we immediately plunged into the midst of a heated national campaign which resulted in a nine-year interlude out of office for the Democratic Party.

It was shortly after this New York convention that the Secretary of State served as Governor for a short time. Governor William J. Fields, and also the Lieutenant Governor and the President pro tem of the Senate were all out of the state at the same time, which caused the duties of the Governor's office to devolve upon the Secretary of State. The same thing happened when Miss Sara Mahan was Secretary of State. This brought to us the honor of being the first women to serve as Governors of Kentucky, even though the time was short. Who may be next, only time can tell. There was no publicity given to this because some of the politicians thought it best not to have any stir made about it, as everything was moving along so well and there might be some comment in the press or by the public that would hurt "the party." The women who knew of this episode agreed with us then that it might be better to pass up any mention of this as we had so recently rained a victory in electing a woman Secretary of State. The women, as always, did not wish to push their cause too fast, but asked only to be allowed to show their worth. We were not so well versed in politics as we are now, else we might have used this incident to promote the advanced sphere of womanhood in the state.

During these short times, we two women did not do anything spectacular, issued no pardons and appointed no Colonels. Along this line of woman's duties and how to perform them a quotation is apropos from Miss Lena Madeson Phillips, formerly of Nicholasville, now a successful attorney in New York City. In addressing a national convention of Business and Professional Women, she stated, "It is up to the women in business, professional, or political life to perform their tasks better than the men, to keep on the job and do it well. These tactics will do more than anything else to put us to the front in every walk of life."

I recall once while visiting in Washington, D.C., Senator Sackett asked to have the privilege of presenting the Secretary of State from Kentucky. He escorted me to the offices of President Coolidge, where I heard more of the conversation of that silent man than was usually granted to visitors, judging from all reports. The Senator said, "Mister President, this is one of the women Democrats with whom we have to reckon in Kentucky."

The President responded, "Mrs. Cromwell, there are worse things than being a Democrat south of the Ohio River."

My reply was, "Mr. President, I quite agree with you," and the laconic interview ended.

***

A constructive work undertaken was compiling a booklet for prospective candidates which gave the laws, rulings, and regulations for filing papers and other information. Three weeks of hard work were expended in collecting every helpful suggestion possible. Then the manuscript was submitted to a Frankfort attorney and finally to Gardner Byers, Assistant Attorney General of the state. When he had gone over it carefully, he pronounced it legal and proper in form, and several hundred were printed for distribution to those interested. It was greatly appreciated, as it was a handy handbook of all the needful information that had hitherto been scattered here and there in various statutes and rulings.

Near the close of the term, while on a trip to southern Kentucky on business, a wire came to me stating that the reliability of the booklet had been called in question, which meant that this honest effort to aid any and all candidates with accurate information was about to become a boomerang in my own race for State Treasurer, which was then impending. Starting back to Frankfort immediately, it was necessary to stay overnight in Louisville, where for once worry did crop in to banish sleep. I had called Miss Malloy, who was more or less familiar with the pamphlet, and she, on the instant, called in Frank Johnson, my attorney; Miss Ora Hazelip, always a dependable standby; Carl King, attorney of Lexington, and Raymond Connell, an attorney of Paris. These staunch friends worked all night in the State Library gathering proof to sustain the statements in question and by morning when the nine o'clock train bore me to Frankfort, the attack had fallen down and my purpose and correctness in putting out the pamphlet were fully vindicated.

If one is not extremely careful, the best intentions may be turned against one in politics. Watchfulness is required always, sometimes watchful waiting, more often watchful working that includes oneself and loyal friends. Never at any one time have I had such a quick attack and such quick response. Those five friends merited my unbounded appreciation. Such loyalty is never to be forgotten. Mr. Johnson has passed on to his reward, but the other four remain my firm friends to whom I owe an obligation that can never be repaid. This was a crucial time when my work was weighed in the balance and not found wanting. My whole career hung that night on the intelligence and loyalty of these self-sacrificing friends. The sage of Ecclesiasticus says, "A faithful friend is a strong defense; and he that hath found such an one hath found a treasure."

The issuing of this booklet was criticized with intent to discredit my work. It created quite a stir. Several prospective candidates had ridden all night in order to be sure to file notice of their candidacy at the proper time, for they had been told tall tales of the mistakes in my booklet, with a great hullabaloo concerning its inaccuracies. The whole condition thus created was chaotic and only the all-night vigil of my good and true friends kept it from being a statewide issue. When it was over and it had been fully proved that all my statements were correct and the pamphlet just what it was meant to be, a help to candidates, then the tide turned and every bit of the clamor redounded to my benefit. This is another time when my debt to the press can never be adequately paid, for its representatives were very tolerant, kept watch over developments and waited until it was all settled before printing anything and then, as the sequel showed, they had very little to print, for all had ended well.

Among other constructive things put over during this term were a catalogue of all the office records; card catalogue of all matters pertaining to the 72,000 corporations, both domestic and foreign; a pamphlet on corporations; and the historical work already mentioned. The double-checking system of handling election records, which passed through this office, was put into service, a great improvement on the old hit-or-miss methods. These innovations added greatly to the efficiency of the office, and in the long run lightened the labor of all the staff. Besides this it stood us in good stead on several occasions when matters pertaining to our office were called into question.

There was one notable case when this double-check system saved the day. Had we not had it in force, doubt might have been cast on this woman's office, as a glaring irregularity appeared on the books handled elsewhere which might have made us innocent victims of circumstances. Thanks again are due to woman's intuition that took no chances when dealing with the public. No matter how much work is involved, it always pays to be on the safe side. One naturally felt she was on trial all during this term and must be on the alert and make good every promise to the people with whom an elected officer must never break faith.

This incident occurred in the race of 1928 and involved a dispute between two candidates on the Republican ticket as to the number of votes claimed by each. The general public was not conversant with our double-checking system, nor with the fact that either I or Miss Malloy always stayed with anyone who examined any records in the office. Every step was properly and legally attested and then there needed to be no fear of any investigation that might be instituted.

In the course of events, the Secretary of State was called upon to testify before the Grand Jury. She felt that the big record sheet was a sheet anchor, and how she did hold on to it as she appeared in that room, feeling as if on trial personally before twelve distinguished citizens, with the subconscious feeling, "Someone is trying to drop the mantle of blame on my office." In the last analysis, the system and care we had used, of which this record sheet was the visible proof, had to be saver of reputation, almost of life.

When questioned by the Commonwealth Attorney as to our

methods, I told him it had been my policy not only to safeguard the public but to protect my office by a double check on all our work, and offered the sheet which would prove and explain that any irregularity had not taken place there, that neither the Secretary of State nor the office force were in the least responsible. One grand juror said afterwards, "They cannot get back of that, Mrs. Cromwell." The way in which he said it amounted to an epithet, but as it carried conviction of the fact, that could be forgiven.

The prosecutor asked some very tangling questions, which were answered as best might be, with the full realization that there was nothing to hide, yet with some reservations of personal dignity which sometimes such questions would seem to annihilate. One was, "Mrs. Cromwell, how many feet from your desk to your vault?" The answer was, "Never having stepped it, I do not know." Then he asked, "Well, about how many?" to which the reply was, "That would depend on who stepped it. Some people's steps are short and some long." Then he said, "Your Honor, I wish you would have Mrs. Cromwell answer my question direct." To this the Judge replied, "I think the witness is replying very directly." Suffice it to say that the accuracy of our records was fully vindicated and the burden of proof in this instance was shifted elsewhere.

With the office duties well in hand and the details running smoothly, the end of my term as Secretary of State was approaching. Friends who had seen and known the labor expended in this office came to me in encouraging numbers and asked me to run for Treasurer of the state, as in Kentucky officials cannot succeed themselves in the same office.[3] The duties of the office I held, in running for this nomination, were not neglected. This was a matter of conscience and, had it not been possible to keep the office running efficiently, I would never have entered this next race.

It may truly be said that there was no such struggle as in the first trail blazing. Many knew me better, knew my work and my ideals, and then the general public had become accustomed to a woman running for office and there was not that peculiar kind of opposition to be met. The race was not without its opposition, of course, about the same as in any race, but nothing comparable with all the questions that confronted me earlier. My record of service could be used with some pardonable pride to further ambitions. Arguments as to the propriety of a woman in office did not have to be presented this time. There was one objection brought forward which had to be met with full force. This was that the office of Secretary of State had been more suitable for a woman, that the office of Treasurer entailed handling vast amounts of money and that "naturally" a woman could not handle money in such quantities. It had to be admitted that women were not accustomed to handling millions, but we must not forget that they are the buyers, the budgeteers of the homes, and that they have been splendidly trained in thrift and the safe handling of nine-tenths of the earned money in our country in smaller amounts. So, instead of not being capable of handling large sums, women have had precisely the right kind of training necessary for handling the money that belongs to others, to the citizens of the state.

As John C. Calhoun said, "The very essence of a free government consists in considering public offices as public trusts, bestowed for the good of the country, and not for the benefit of an individual or a party."

One of the most interesting happenings of the summer of 1928 was the visit of Queen Marie of Rumania to the United States and to Kentucky. It was the first time we as a nation had entertained a queen, and there was much questioning as to proper methods of procedure among officials as well as society hostesses. The Americans had cast off kings and queens and proclaimed themselves free and independent. Indeed, it had been the direct ancestor of Queen Marie against whom our forefathers had rebelled.

But all such wounds heal with time, and "blood is thicker than water." While Queen Marie was ruler of a central European country, she was of English blood and birth, a granddaughter of Queen Victoria, who is revered by all Americans for her common sense and goodness. There was much adulation of Queen Marie, and those who read of her were told that she was beautiful, charming, and gracious, that she was very democratic in manner and life and withal very friendly.

Those of us who met her found this to be true, although she was very tired from her many and long journeys when she came finally to Louisville. Later when we read more of her life from her own story in the Saturday Evening Post and heard of the trials and tragedies of her later life in the news, we felt a kinship with her as a woman who had suffered the common lot of women and who had courage and endurance along with her other queenly qualities.

The Brown Hotel in Louisville was to be her stopping place and several suites were decorated and furnished in her honor; gorgeous linens, dishes, everything fine was provided to serve her Majesty the

Queen. Due to my position it was an honor to be a specially invited guest during this time, and it was a privilege to see the rooms prepared for her before she occupied them. In the Assembly Room her people unrolled a red velvet carpet from the door to her chair. The Queen entered on the arm of Kentucky's Governor, Honorable William Jason Fields. All stood as they entered. She was beautifully gowned, her principal ornament being a long string of pearls. Her poise was perfect, and she met all with a gracious greeting.

To each she gave the impression of being especially interested in him or her. She seemed to be greatly pleased at meeting a woman who had been elected to state office and was kind enough to say she would love to have a chat later in regard to women in public life here in the states. She said in concluding, "I am very happy to meet a woman official and would love to speak with you later," but the crowd was too great for more conversation then and, although I was seated at a table very near the one she occupied with Honorable Robert Bingham and Mrs. Bingham at dinner, there was no further opportunity for conversation.

If one could have met her with time to spare, it is certain that she would have been genuinely interested in our way of doing things. But in the press and hurry of that time when all was in a fever heat at the idea of entertaining a queen and her young son and daughter, little time could be taken for any conversation that would have been satisfactory. One does not doubt her interest in democratic institutions nor her longing for the simpler ways of living, for the state in which she moved and lived did not make her happy, as we know from her history. The life of a queen is one long struggle to keep the love of her people and to help keep her whole family in power and place.

Prince Nicholas and Princess Illeana were with their mother, and all three seemed to be happy in each other's society. The daughter of a friend of mine came rushing to her mother to tell her she had danced with the Prince and that he was not as good a dancer as her Louisville beaux. We did not hear how well the Princess danced, but to everyone present the occasion gave a great thrill and was something to be remembered as long as memory lasts.

The dinner and ball were over, and all went home tired, no doubt Queen Marie and her royal children more tired than most, for they had a difficult part to perform. It was said that the principal object of her visit to this country was to enlist the moneyed interests in lending money to her country. If that were so she had a triple burden — as a woman, as a social guest, and as a diplomat. "Uneasy rests the head that wears a crown" was always true, and Queen Marie found it so more and more until she lay down to her last long sleep, not so long ago, not yet an old woman, doubtless living a shorter life than if she had been placed by fate in a lowlier position.

She will always live in my memory as having the gracious bearing and kindly, generous spirit that would make her kin to true hospitable Kentuckians who delighted to entertain her on her short visit to our state.

Early next morning after all this festivity, my office claimed me, as we were then deep in the salvaging of the papers of the former Governors. Here, I could not help thinking the Queen might have seen much to interest her had it been possible for her to have joined us in perusing these important documents from a bygone day.

It seemed fitting that among the very papers we handled next day after meeting Queen Marie and her royal children were some relating directly to the visit of Lafayette, who was invited to Kentucky in 1825, accepted, and was highly entertained. Many papers have been written about this journey by historians. The dates of this visit were about a hundred years before that of Queen Marie, and the great Lafayette had seen kings and queens come and go in his time and was a true patriot who delighted to be called an American. Indeed, he had citizenship in two countries, for Congress conferred American citizenship on him in addition to his natural French citizenship.

On November 17, 1824, Lafayette was invited to visit the state. On May 8, 1825, he arrived in Louisville; May 14th arrived in Frankfort, visited Versailles, Lexington, then Cincinnati on his way back to the East. Everywhere he received the greatest ovations. The old Revolutionary War soldiers were especially delighted to welcome him, and he in turn was overcome with emotion in meeting them. His son, George Washington Lafayette, and his secretary, Levasseur, were with him, and many fascinating true incidents have been narrated concerning their visit to Kentucky.

Perhaps the exact wording of his invitation as copied from the original records in the high-flown language of that day may be of interest.

Frankfort, Kentucky, November 22, 1824.
To General Lafayette
General Lafayette
     Sir:
     The Legislature of Kentucky acting in accordance with the feelings and wishes of the people of this state, authorize me in their name to write you to come and partake of their hospitality. I have the honor to enclose certain Resolutions on this subject, concurred in unanimously, expressing the deep sense entertained of your worth, of your valuable service to our infant Republic and of your constant devotion to Liberty.
     The part you took in the American Revolution in the glorious struggle for independence, your gallant and generous conduct throughout its trying scenes, are recollected with gratitude, and indelibly impressed on the hearts of all. In the retrospect we admire your brilliant achievements, and delight in contemplating the pure and sublime motive which enlisted you in the cause of freedom; we see the efforts of a noble mind, rising above prejudice and looking forward with enlightened forecast to the success, in a distant and obscure colony, of that moral power which was destined to give a new direction and character to political institutions, and to improve and enlarge the sphere of human happiness. Penetrated with these views and filled with gratitude at the recollections they awaken; we rejoice in common with our fellow citizens at your arrival in the United States, and are anxious to see and welcome to our homes the companion of Washington. It is fondly hoped and confidently anticipated that you will visit this country, and look upon the new world that has risen like enchantment from the wilderness since you fought on the Atlantic border. You will see in the rapid growth and improvement of our state, new evidence of the success of those principles you so nobly contended for, and the countless blessings we enjoy under that Republican form of government you so eminently contributed to establish.
     Permit me to assure you on behalf of my fellow citizens that no event of the kind could give them greater pleasure than your arrival in this state. They are anxious to greet you in person, and testify their affection by offering the tribute due from grateful hearts to the nation's benefactor.
     With sentiments of profound respect, and affectionate regard, I am, Sir,
Your obt. Servt.
(Signed) Joseph Desha.
Gen. Lafayette
City of Washington.

     From royal visits and polite social functions, we turn to the arduous duties of office. The close of my term as Secretary of State was a satisfying although strenuous time. The work of the office went steadily along, and my campaign for State Treasurer kept pace with it to a successful ending. One felt that the vote in this Treasurer's race would be a silent approval of the record made as Secretary of State.

     On looking back as we closed one file after another, we could see tangible evidence of the work of four years, in which the high points were the cataloguing of all the Governors' administrations, introduction of a business-like filing system for the current work, card index for corporations, double-check system for compiling election returns, printing the pamphlet of rules and laws governing candidates for election, and a host of lesser duties, all together making up intensive labor with lasting results for good.

The detail of office work had been well attended to and the wide aspects of the duties and responsibilities of the Secretary of State opened into a vision of a better day for state officials when all would be actuated by the motive of duty, do their work in a spirit of patriotism, feel the kinship of all citizens who long and look and pray for the good of our country. Public office calls for single-mindedness in service, and only through such an approach can America become truly great. We only multiply our duty to Kentucky and our love of its broad acres by forty-eight to become citizens at large of our glorious country. May it ever be the refuge of the oppressed while all of our citizens work unceasingly for "the greatest good to the greatest number!" It seems to me that the office of Secretary of State is a little more closely linked with the National Government than other offices, since it deals directly with the perpetuation of our duties as citizens in relation to other citizens, to other states, and to the government at Washington.

It was an added happiness to realize that, in spite of the great amount of extra work accomplished, we had lived strictly within our budget and each year turned back some money to the state. It was a pleasure to turn over this office to another woman, Miss Ella Lewis of Leitchfield, who was capable of carrying on the work with the same progressive ideals we have tried to attain. It was in a sense a justification of womanhood that the voters of the state, men and women, had elected a second woman to fill the important office of Secretary of State.

Chapter IV Notes

1. The Court of Appeals was the state's highest court when Mrs. Cromwell wrote her autobiography in 1939. Constitutional reforms enacted in 1975 restructured the state's judicial system, designating the Kentucky Supreme Court as the highest court.
2. Those cited by the author were Mrs. W.T. Lafferty, Henry Cleveland Woods, Mrs. W.T. Fowler, Dr. Edgar Human, Dr. W.R. Jillson, Mrs. John Price, Providence, Mrs. Lelia Dempsey, Madisonville, and Dr. Jonathan T. Dorris of Richmond.
3. Under a constitutional amendment enacted in 1992, Kentucky's constitutional officers now are permitted to serve two consecutive four-year terms.

V

Again — Victory!

Everything hath a wherefore.

When friends that one knows to be tried and true constantly urge a certain course of action, it is generally safe to follow their advice. When they add that they will put all their force and influence behind that course in unfaltering support, one can go ahead with little doubt of success. Thus, during the fourth year of my administration as Secretary of State of Kentucky, when the office was running smoothly and many efficient methods were in use with good results that were apparent to everyone, my friends began to question, "What next?"

Those who had my best interests at heart would have liked to see this office continue in my hands, but the Constitution of Kentucky forbade, and I was strongly advised to try for another office within the gift of the people, and that was the responsible position of State Treasurer. The first thing to be considered in deciding this momentous question was that here again was an innovation for a woman. Up to this time no woman had been elected Treasurer of any state, and it was one of the offices for which many thought a woman unfitted, however capable she might be in other lines.[1]

Incident after incident occurred where some of my doubting friends questioned the wisdom of what other more courageous ones counseled. One will suffice here. One good friend said to me, "Better not trust your luck too far. Better rest on your successful administration as Secretary of State. Do you really think you can handle forty-five million dollars of the taxpayers' money each year for four years?"

My reply was, "Providence has been kind to me, but really (emphasizing the really), do you think that 'luck' had much to do with the running of my office during the term that is closing?"

It is well to counter with a question sometimes. It provokes thought and shifts the burden of proof. Most people do not like to be "told." They like to state issues and give you the benefit of their conclusions.

To this "doubting Thomas" I put several questions which gave him food for thought, at least. First, "Why cannot a woman handle finances?" And again, "I ask you as a friend who wishes me well, why should I not make use now of the splendid organization of my friends and supporters who have stood by me during this term of office and who stand ready to go with me to further honors and even greater responsibilities?"

He had no answer to this because he knew, of course, that such an organization had been built up, first on friendship and good wishes, then supported by earnest endeavor and real achievement. He could not help but realize that unless used, all this good will would be scattered among other candidates, and after a time it would be impossible to build it up again.

As a parting shot, he was given this, "You will not be able to get a man for the office of Treasurer who has served in that capacity. Any man you support will have to be taken on his record. So why not give a woman the same chance?"

It has been found always that an appeal to justice and fairness has more effect than a statement of abstract rights.

In beginning this campaign for Treasurer a double duty devolved upon me, for each time I left the office it had to be in smooth running order so that my mind could be free to concentrate on hewing out a new path to an office where a woman was an untried quantity, an unknown equation. It proved not to be necessary to do as much trail blazing as in the campaign of four years before. The people were used to seeing a woman out for office, and it was no surprise that Miss Ella Lewis of Leitchfield entered the primary as a candidate for Secretary of State. By this time it seemed quite natural for a woman to seek that office and there was little comment against it. The trail blazing was over in that respect, although new problems did present themselves as one campaign is never quite cut on the pattern of another. Eternal vigilance is the price of success as it is of peace or anything else worth having.

Several short trips were made to western and southern Kentucky, where it was found that Democrats were lining up for two women on their ticket without any protest except the natural one in any race, the protest of each candidate against his opponent and his strong recommendation of himself. In my own case I met with much encouragement. Those who had supported me as Secretary of State seemed quite willing to try me in another important position, and all seemed fair sailing out in the state.

It was somewhat disturbing, when on my return to my adopted county of Franklin, to find on a visit to two of the banks in my home town that the picture of my opponent, Albert Phillips, was prominently displayed. Mr. Phillips was not only influential, but was then Bank Examiner, and in this had a very great advantage. Guy Ramey of Ohio County was also in the race, but did not figure as largely in the running nor in the final results as did Mr. Phillips. The latter was in a strong position with the banks and other financial agencies as they knew him to be efficient and he was well liked by everyone.

On my part there were no hard feelings because some banks felt as they did. Experience has taught that it never pays to presume on any particular support from any group because there are many reasons why a person or an institution thinks or votes in a certain way. The opponent of today may be the friend of tomorrow. It pays in public service to cultivate the respect of opponents and the love of friends, and to root out the weeds of spite, envy, and jealousy, while tending carefully the flowers of friendship and good will that always respond to loving thought and tender care. It is a telling metaphor that likens friendship to a garden; though often used, it is always true.

To be opposed by one who was a Bank Examiner and had made good in that line brought to a head the only real reason that anyone offered against my nomination.

Here is a sample conversation on this point.

"You know, the State Treasurer should keep up with the financial status of the country as well as handle millions of dollars of public money. Then many bonds must be signed and sureties be passed upon for approval. There are a lot of things a woman just can't do."

"Why not?" was an effective answer which brought an apologetic, "I'm afraid you are making a mistake and jeopardizing the fine reputation you have won as Secretary of State. This requires a wide knowledge of stocks and bonds and a deep insight into the finances of the state, the United States, yes, of the whole world."

It was funny to see his arguments flounder between the modern viewpoint and old-time conceptions of woman's limitations, as he went on to praise the ability of women in art, literature, and clerical work, and the skill they exhibit in household management, and so on. All this gave the opportunity for a reply, "Have you ever given a woman the chance to handle public finance before? You know, we can read and write and cipher to the rule of three, and some of us have gone through college. Now, come, my friend, you want to be just and fair. If women have so many fine achievements to their credit in other fields, why not in this? They have been faithful in a few things, you admit. Why not trust them with the many."

He said, "Your arguments are sound. I do believe you can win."

"Don't worry, I will win. It may not be so easy, but everything worthwhile costs effort, labor, and struggle."

May it be said here that the greatest courtesy was extended by my opponents, who never at any time overstepped the bounds of perfect gentlemen as we went about the state or directed our campaigns by correspondence from our respective places of business. Then, and later, both Mr. Ramey and Mr. Phillips assisted me in many ways. After the primary was all over, Mr. Phillips thanked me for defeating him as he realized that another strenuous campaign lay ahead, and he said, "I never want to make another race, especially against a woman. You were always on the job and glided over more territory than any airplane. Indeed, I sometimes thought you must have had one at your service, for I found you before me with moves that checkmated my own quite successfully."

Going back to the heat of the campaign, someone likened it to the chase in the hills of Scotland, when James Fitz-James outdistanced all riders in the heat of the pursuit and ended his adventurous ride on the banks of lovely Loch Katrine, there to find fair Ellen on her secret isle and to brave the mortal enmity of Roderick Dhu, the master of the highland hills and self-appointed guardian of the passes of the Grampian Mountains.

Indeed, the race waxed hot and furious, for in Kentucky a nomination practically meant an election, as the state had gone Republican only three times in its history, and that because of unusual conditions and under the leadership of men especially suited to the time. First, under the extremely popular Governor W.O. Bradley; second, under Augustus E. Wilson who had the strength of Louisville behind him; and third, under Governor Bradley's nephew, Edwin Morrow of the silver tongue and gracious manner. Any ticket put out by the Democrats had to be alive to all possibilities and keep always on the firing line with plenty of reserves well in hand and ready to come up when needed.

The excitement of the primary centered largely in the race between Honorable J.C.W. Beckham, who had been both Governor and United States Senator, and Honorable Robert Crowe of La Grange, popular Speaker of the House. The former had made enemies as well as friends in such a long and distinguished public career, and all had to be reckoned with when opposed by an active and able opponent. Such a situation always results in talk of trading, which was disregarded in my own case, because it has been my settled conviction that the most potent appeal to voters comes to the individual and that the people of the smaller towns and rural sections like to make up their own minds, and that once set, nothing short of an earthquake can change them. They do not take much to swapping and trading among candidates. It is in these sections that the traditions of our forefathers linger, and it is there that liberty takes its final stand. No wonder they are jealous of their honor when approached with suggestions that they change from their settled loyalties.

However, as talk of "slates" grew on every hand, it did create some uneasiness, for where would a woman without a slated place be in the final count? As usual, the relief was given by good friends, who warned me to stand alone and not desert my principles. These began with counsel and assurance that they could be depended upon, and in county after county they rallied and reported their loyalty. Judge Bradbury of Shepherdsville is due lasting honor and shall always receive it for the firm stand he took which resulted in a fine majority in Bullitt County. He said to the manipulators, "All hands off in the Treasurer's race. If you attempt to slate against Mrs. Cromwell, who is going to carry this county, I will turn the table on you, and that quickly." Other friends in many counties took the same courageous stand with victorious results. What would life be without such good and loyal friends? Speculation was rife as to combinations in the race for Treasurer, but all came to naught.

So far, my dependence was on my faith in my own purposes, determination to work hard and to believe in final triumph as had proved so happily a success in my first race. This time there were two women on the ticket. Miss Ella Lewis of Leitchfield was running for Secretary of State to succeed me. The road to this office had been made comparatively smooth by this time. We both felt yet that the womanhood of the state was on trial and much depended on our efforts. In the Treasurer's race it seemed to narrow down to one question, "What did the women of the Democratic Party think of a woman as financier?"

The day of the primary was hectic, as always. Again friends rallied everywhere. In my own precinct and town they came in numbers early and wanted to know what they could do. Many rushed to cast a vote and then to work all day. One good friend came with a car to a certain difficult precinct and said, "Don't give a thought to this place. I am taking care of your interests and determined to see you carry it. I have never forgotten your kindness to my boy." Here was another example of the long arm of gratitude which reaches down through the years to give help when most needed.

Later in the day an excited group came in a hurry to the polls saying they had a puncture and other delays but were happy to get there in time to vote for a woman Treasurer.

That night I went to Louisville to headquarters and by midnight heard the news that flashed over the wires giving the complete ticket that would represent the party at the November election. For Governor, Honorable J.C.W. Beckham; Lieutenant Governor, James Breathitt, Jr., of Hopkinsville; Secretary of State, Miss Ella Lewis, Leitchfield; Attorney General, Honorable James Cammack, Owenton; Treasurer, Mrs. Emma Guy Cromwell, Frankfort; Auditor, Clell Coleman, Harrodsburg; Commissioner of Agriculture, Newton Bright, Eminence; Superintendent of Public Instruction, W.C. Bell, Owensboro; Clerk of the Court of Appeals, William O'Connell, Sr., Louisville.

This final decision of the primary had resulted in what was considered a strong ticket to carry the banner of the Democratic Party to a victory in the coming November election. It was opposed by a strong Republican ticket of high class men and a woman. That party sensed a possible return to power and girded its loins for a conflict worthy of the best battling days of the old Commonwealth.

The Republican candidate for Governor was Judge Flem D. Sampson of Barbourville, then a member of the Kentucky Court of Appeals; Lieutenant Governor, E.E. Nelson, Williamsburg; Secretary of State, Mrs. F.D. Quisenberry, Elizabethtown; Attorney General, Miller Hughes, Wickliffe; Auditor, John M. Perkins, Frankfort, an able businessman and party leader of prominence; Treasurer, John Rogers, Frankfort, a native of the Bluegrass, a businessman of great ability and withal possessed of charm and the aptitude for making and keeping friends; Superintendent of Public Instruction, Warren Peyton, Beaver Dam; Commissioner of Agriculture, Tate Bird, Shelbyville; Clerk of the Court of Appeals, W.A. Dicken, Albany.

While this ticket was a strong one, it had a weakness in having on it two men from the Capital City, for no matter how able and suited to an office, such a situation was bound to cause comment out in the state where it has sometimes been said that Frankfort gets more than its share of offices and perquisites. In my own case, for the third time the opposition was right at home and of a kind that could not be "whistled down the wind." As Librarian, my opponent of Frankfort had been Mrs. Mary Brown Day; for Secretary of State, Ben Marshall; and now Mr. Rogers, for all of whom I had only the warmest personal regard.

However, there was little time for reflection. Headquarters for our ticket had to be opened and this was done at the Seelbach Hotel in Louisville, where organization and a program of speaking were planned. As there were several on the opposing ticket of undoubted power and prestige, it was determined to hew to the party line, as far as possible, and let the chips fall where they might.

A meeting of the candidates and the leaders was called to attend to all the details, particularly to raise enough money to properly finance the campaign. Just why so much adverse criticism is given to the necessary use of money in a campaign remains a mystery. Putting aside the idea of the wrong use of money and the wrong ways of raising the funds, there is no more reason why anyone should think that a political campaign can be waged without sufficient money than there is to think that any other business in life can be so run. Perhaps if we consider what the Bible really says about money it will help to clarify our thoughts here. It is not money in itself, but specifically "the love of money" that is said in the Scriptures to be "the root of all evil." Let us realize that this improper love of money may be the love of a comparatively small amount and not necessarily the millions of a rich man.

Carrying on the likeness, it is not the use of money in a campaign that is any worse than the use of money to promote any other cause. It is only the wrong use of money and, believe it or not, that is up to the average citizen and voter rather than to the candidate. It is the duty of the candidate to help provide the funds that will be used for his or her benefit. It is up to the citizen who should value his suffrage as he does his life to be ever vigilant, to see that none is wrongly collected or wrongly expended. And, in the words of Edgar Guest's poem, "It can be done." To paraphrase Goldsmith's oft-quoted lines,

"A free enfranchised people is a country's pride,
'When once destroyed can never be supplied.' "

And nowhere can this free suffrage be safeguarded except by

Mr. and Mrs. Average Voter at the polls. If we believe otherwise and leave manipulation and the use of money to some far-off headship of which we know nothing; if we allow money to be improperly used without calling for an accounting, then we, the average citizens, are to blame. There is a double duty here, duty to the party of our choice to keep it above such things, and, higher yet, duty to our state to keep her skirts clean as she moves with uplifted head among her sister states as one of a mighty galaxy of lovely matrons, each proud of her sons and daughters.

During the campaign for the election some of the talk about a woman not being able to handle finances still cropped up, but it had been fully threshed out in the primary.

Back to the practical side of the campaign. One of the largest meetings planned was to be at Jackson, in Breathitt County, and it was understood that every candidate was to be there to take part in one grand rally. Monday, County Court Day, was set. The day arrived and the candidate for Treasurer arrived the night before, attended church on Sunday evening and started out bright and early among the women to organize and plan for the speaking. It may be remembered that the radio had not then been perfected so that it could be enlisted as it is now to influence and reach the voters; roads were not as good, and above all, we women of the Democratic Party had not established our Democratic Woman's Journal so firmly as now, to which we owe much of the interest that prevails today. The work during this race for State Treasurer was still hard going, owing to the difficulty of communication by roads more or less everywhere. This was then especially true in the mountainous and hilly sections of the state.

Mrs. Ethel Connif, Mrs. Margaret Bishop, Mrs. Martha Bach, of Jackson; Mrs. James Tuttle, of Barbourville; and Mrs. Emma Joliffe, of Louisa, told me of the hardships of getting women together in the days when the best roads were up and down the creek beds, while mountains could only be crossed on the back of a patient and sure-footed mule. It is to the everlasting credit of these workers that the way was never too hard, the roads never too slippery, the rain never too wet, nor the sun too hot for them to get out their workers in the precincts for election, and before that for these meetings that were so important in keeping up the morale of the women. Our roads in the level country in Kentucky have been good roads only very recently, and the good roads through the mountains are the product of even more modern times.

One incident told by a precinct worker is impressive and illustrates the loyalty and adaptability of our women workers. A faithful worker went to see a woman and bring her to the polls. The prospective voter did not have shoes that looked well enough, or so she thought when she saw the new footwear of the precinct worker. So she said, "If I had a pair of shoes as good as yours, I would not mind going to the polls." "All right," was the ready response, "I will exchange with you," and right then and there the exchange was made, and again that one vote — that may be so all important — was polled.

On that particular Monday, by ten o'clock only one candidate had shown up, and it was very disturbing to think we might have a flat failure when the people had come so far and under such difficulties to the Court Day meeting when they had been told they would hear some good speakers. In every part of Kentucky we find that the prospect of a good speech arouses the latent love of oratory that is inbred, and it is too bad to arouse such expectations and then have a fluke. The entire Republican ticket had spoken there very recently, and those of us who knew the value of such things felt that our meeting must be a success to offset the effect their efforts must have had.

Finally, just as we began to despair of results and to cudgel our brains for some adequate excuses, the day was saved by the appearance of the candidate for Lieutenant Governor, James Breathitt, Jr., and Honorable Fred Vinson, candidate for Congress. Mr. Breathitt was a virile young man, ardent, able, and patriotic. He came of a long line of men and women distinguished in culture, in public interest, and in faithful and efficient public service. Personally he had all these qualities and withal the ability to put over his ideas. Mr. Vinson was an able speaker, so we felt that all was well.

The enthusiasm of the crowd was great and both men waxed eloquent and rather long. This was not a bad thing in itself, for these people had come to hear speaking and that was what they wanted. But there came a pause in the proceedings when one of the precinct workers, she of the muleback adventures and the stout heart for work, arose and said in sweet clear voice, "We want to hear our woman candidate."

This provoked some laughter and good joking. The men protested they had not forgotten me, but had rather forgotten themselves in the heat of the discussion. It proved a good thing for the woman candidate, as it called attention in a better way than a formal introduction and created an aura of good feeling as the hearers "guyed" the men about forgetting their woman candidate, and they responded in a splendid way with wit and repartee, saying several complimentary things that might have been omitted in the regular course of events. The hearers had come on muleback, horseback, in wagons and buggies, and some in cars. This is remembered as one of the most successful meetings we ever had. Here in the mountains, we find as active, hardy, and intelligent people as any in the world. Here the Anglo-Saxon blood is pure and the loyalties are fierce and lasting.

On one occasion when campaigning up one of the creeks with a friend, we came to a neat cabin home. My friend called, "Hello." The man of the house came to the door with the homely welcome, "Light and come in." We alighted, hitched our horses, and went in. The wife was out milking, he said, and presently she came in with two foaming pails of milk. Her apology for her appearance was met with our excuses for coming in so late, and we told them we would not stay long or take up much time.

The gentleman said, "You are going to spend the night. Them clouds are too black for you to venture out again so late." He added, "We like company. We love to hear them talk about the settlements down there."

He promised that when Uriah came in our horses would be fed, and both he and his wife took it for granted that we would stay. Our talk was interesting, we telling them about life in the valleys and they giving us some useful pointers on the voters of their neighborhood.

As the weather was really too fierce for us to face, we were well content, especially when supper came on with country ham, red gravy, fried eggs, hot biscuits and cherry preserves, milk, and coffee. It was a better supper than was served once when Queen Marie of Rumania was entertained at a hotel where we paid eight dollars a plate, and we are not knocking on the hotel menu either.

The children came in after doing all the chores; we popped corn, cracked nuts, and talked until a late hour, for them. Then the father took up the family Bible and all joined in family prayers. Just such a home inspired Burns's "Cotter's Saturday Night," and the lines of that poem lulled us to sleep while the blazing log fire died down to embers and silence filled all the mountain coves with the peace of God that passeth understanding.

This is what we would call a model home, rather than one provided with all the modern conveniences where the Bible is missing and the children untrained in religious observance.

The other parts of the state were not neglected. From the Big Sandy to Mills' Point the battle raged and the speakers came and went from headquarters with their minds surcharged with the importance of the election. They spoke in every courthouse, schoolhouse, and other public place, many local speakers being engaged as well as the state candidates. On and on, while in my own case, the duties of the office of Secretary of State still engaged my time and attention, though I did not neglect my part of this campaign which meant so much to me and to the women of the state.

Perhaps more outsiders were called in than usual; it seemed so. One occasion is recalled when headquarters notified me to come to a speaking engagement where they wanted a woman as well as the distinguished Congressman, who would make the principal speech. Mindful of the fact that audiences like variety in persons as well as subjects, this time Mrs. Wiley Marshall of Frankfort was asked to be my companion. When the leading speaker saw that he was expected to allow two women to share his time, he "blew up."

A friend told me that this was his attitude, so he was disarmed by being told that the Secretary of State came to do the handshaking and that Mrs. Marshall would make a short talk, while we wanted him to have the center of the stage. I asked, therefore, that Mrs. Marshall be put forth, as I knew how well she could take care of herself in any situation. Possessed of a keen and intuitive wit and a compelling personality, she knew also just how brief to make a telling talk so that she could put over her points, yet leave plenty of time for oratory.

It fell to my lot then to introduce the speaker of the day. Very few words were used, but these were as complimentary as they could well be made, so all was well that ended well once again. One never knows when starting out when tact will be called for, or sledge-hammer tactics, so one always takes along in mind two whole and complete vocabularies — some words strong, some sweet as honey.

Finally, election day was just around the corner and each hurried to his or her post to get out as many votes as possible, for what candidate does not want to make a good showing at home? In Frankfort, as has been said, the lines were drawn close, and perhaps as nearly every vote was cast as has ever been the case, so hard were all the people working for their own friends and chosen candidates.

The polls closed at four. This time I went to headquarters with the others, as reports of the results concentrate there. Hour by hour the news came in, now one way, now another, but for the most part favorable to our side, until about midnight there arose great distress because it was seen that our chieftain, the leader of the ticket, was in great danger of defeat. Of course, this led to wild rumors of a great defeat for all of us, and wires in the state were kept so busy that it was hard to get any reliable news, or to know what to depend on as one rumor succeeded another. This might well be termed the Night of Rumor and Unrest. It was probably the same in the opposing camp where the Republicans were listening to the same reports.

Just after twelve o'clock, when it seemed that reports became more and more confusing, a young friend, Mr. Bauer, went with me and we slipped away to the offices of the Courier-Journal. There I found another personal friend who let us have every report he had, and from his experience he gave us valuable tips on which was likely to be more reliable. As the three of us tabulated these, it became clear that Governor Beckham had been defeated and that the others on the ticket had won.

We breathlessly rushed back to the hotel headquarters with this news, both talking at once, all this being so exciting that my usual calm was broken, and I entered into the spirit of the occasion. Some had already gone home to give up the fight; some had gone thinking it was won; a few stayed on through the night, and as morning came we all saw clearly that our Courier-Journal information from the night before was correct. Any settlement of the election returns meant that the Secretary of State must be back in Frankfort very early next morning, as her office was the clearinghouse of much election detail and was in closer communication with the individual precincts than any other.

Our ticket was in by a safe majority except for the unique fact that for the first time in history a Governor of one party had been elected with a complete ticket of the other party. How this would work out we did not know. Even the enemies of Governor Beckham could not say anything harsh at the downfall of an upright man who had made an efficient and hard-working Governor and an able United States Senator. But just such uncertainties as these are woven by the ever-moving loom of politics. The warp and woof of change, the texture of the cloth varies, one comes, another goes, and human destiny is woven.

As soon as the election officers had met and passed on the votes and issued certificates, all Frankfort again made ready for its quadrennial pageant of the Inauguration. All committees were named, and the town was a hive of activity; housewives polished silver; glass and crystal shone with renewed splendor; the homes were opened with good cheer that is only rivaled at Christmas; and throngs from out in the state prepared to come to one great house party, while the van of visitors began to arrive day by day. In my home again we had a large house party.

In the reception and the Inauguration parade, my place was now, as Treasurer, between the Auditor and the Superintendent of Public Instruction, while Miss Lewis took the place next to the Lieutenant Governor. This was the official line of elected officers in our state. This changed the line in the carriages, as the Treasurer-elect had to ride with the incoming Secretary of State. This time there was for me the triple duty of the former office with that of the new one and a large house party at home besides. As before, this hospitality had been planned, and good friends did the honors for me.[2]

One incident may be related which will explain itself to many who have attended Inaugural balls. My faithful porter on duty that night was all dressed and primed for the occasion. He was told that he was in charge to safeguard my office from any who wanted to indulge in surreptitious jollity in honor of the occasion. Again this was not only done through settled personal principles, but also to guard the good name of woman in office.

Sure enough, they began to come and were all politely and firmly refused admission if there was any indication they had intention of drinking. One very good friend came in with a party and said to the porter, "We want to go into Miss Emma's private office to mix up some toddies. It's all right. You know I am one of her best friends."

"I hate to disappoint you. I know you are one of Miss Emma's good friends, and she would do almost anything for you. But she put me here especially to keep out the toddy-izers, and I can't make any exception."

This friend was more than ever my friend afterward. There are but few who do not honor a firm stand for principle, regardless of whether they agree or not with the one who forbids indulgence.

The Inauguration again was a spectacle the like of which is only seen on such occasions, and Frankfort did itself proud, while the unique circumstance of a Republican Governor and a Democratic Lieutenant Governor being sworn in together on the stand again erected in front of the Capitol gave rise to much talk and many speculations as to the outcome. Many saw in it a prophecy that "the lion and the lamb" would lie down together in perfect peace, but alas, such was not always the case and we were in for some stormy times, during legislative sessions especially. There is no space here to go into the details of the political history of the administration as such.

My own time was quickly and effectively consumed in closing up the office of Secretary of State preparatory to handing it over to my successor, and in making myself familiar with the duties of State Treasurer, for indeed, that office did require more thought, planning, and a different sort of system from the one I was relinquishing. Again I was determined to make good for the sake of the women of Kentucky who had a large share in putting me into such an important place. To this end I bent all my efforts for the three weeks remaining before I took over this new responsibility.

Since the election was unique in the annals of Kentucky, the size of the vote and the majority by which the woman won the Treasurer's race may be of interest. I received 352,715 votes and John Rogers, my opponent on the Republican ticket, 348,248, making my majority 4,467.

Regardless of one vote or many, the duty of officials is to both the majority and the minority. In democracies the citizenship is all to be considered alike, and of equal importance, to be equally safeguarded in every right and privilege. Minorities have their inalienable rights as well as majorities. Thank God and our patriotic Revolutionary forefathers for this right which they handed down to us at such a staggering price to themselves.

After this inaugural season which ushered in the new Governor, there remained a month as Secretary of State, during which time we set our house in order and prepared to turn over the records and the work to Miss Ella Lewis. This was a busy time and when it ended we had all in such readiness that we were proud of the work that had been done, the files we had prepared day by day, and the efficient systems we had installed.

In doing all this we had been economical, had kept within our budget, even turning a little back to the state each year. Personally, I did not have much time for reflection on the past, for new and very different duties awaited me, to begin in the very hour these duties ended. For now, I was to succeed Ed Dishman as State Treasurer of the grand old Commonwealth of Kentucky.

A glorious victory had perched on the banner of a woman; an honor had been given her by the vote of the people. Great duties lay before her, and she could only trust that Providence would guide her footsteps along this path hitherto untrodden by a woman's feet, knowing "that the reward of one duty is the power to fulfill another."

Chapter V Notes

1. While Mrs. Cromwell might have started considering the Treasurer's race before any other state elected a woman to that position, she was not the first woman elected as a state Treasurer in the United States when she won her race in 1927. According to a history of the Indiana Treasurer's office contained in the office's 1995 annual report, Grace Banta Urbahns had won election in 1926 in that state after having served the remainder of her deceased husband's term in the preceding few months.
2. Those cited by the author were Mrs. Hattie Buchanan and her charming daughter, Elath, now Mrs. Mac Coy; Miss Margaret Parrish of Richmond; Mrs. J.W. Basket of Central City; Mrs. Robert Brown; Mr. and Mrs. Frank Connely and their two daughters, Mary Bell and Harold Brown Connelly of Warsaw; Miss Ida Hodges of Bowling Green; Mrs. Johnnie Cook of Guthrie; and Mrs. W.V. Eaton of Paducah.

Emma Guy Cromwell's father, Ashley Duncan Guy.

Alice Quisenberry Millikin Guy, Emma Guy Cromwell's mother.

Emma Guy Cromwell's alma mater.

Reverend John Guy.

Lieutenant William Foree Cromwell.

Emma Guy Cromwell, William, and their dog, Coley, photographed in front of her Frankfort home.

Executive Office
Frankfort, Ky September 5. 1845.

Sir

Your communication of the 28th.
ult advising me that General Taylor
Commandant of the Army of Occupation
in Texas, was authorised, in case he
should need them, to call on the Governor
of Kentucky for auxilliary troops, has been
received.

In reply. I have the honor to assure
you that the Citizens of my State have
lost none of that patriotic ardor which
has ever heretofore distinguished them, and
which has led them to be among the first
to defend our common Country from foreign aggression. I will hold myself in
constant readiness to comply with any requi-
sitions of the Government, at Washington. and
I beg leave to assure the Government that
any call upon the militia of Kentucky
will be promptly and gallantly responded to

To
Hon W. L. Marcy.
    Secretary of War.

                        Wm Owsley
                        Governor
                        of Kentucky.

Letter from Governor William Owsley to the Secretary of War W.L. Marcy (1845).

Letter from Kentucky Governor John Adair to Tennessee Governor McMinn (1821).

(Above and right) A two-page invitation to General Lafayette from Governor Joseph Desna.

Barnes School, Simpson County, where Emma Guy Cromwell first attended school.

Emma Guy Cromwell's sister, Mary Sidney Wilkins, photographed with her two grandchildren, Rose Mary and David Balch.

VI

Sitting on Top of Forty-five Million Dollars
State Treasurer of Kentucky, 1928-1932

God give us men! A time like this demands
Strong minds, great hearts, true faith and ready hands;
Men whom the lust of office does not kill;
Men whom the spoils of office cannot buy....
... who live above the fog
In public duty and in private thinking.

The times, our times, any times, demand men of courage, convictions, and honesty. In private duties this was always true of women as well as of men, and we believe that women lived up to the very highest ideals in private life, which had been their only sphere since time immemorial. In 1920, almost overnight, this sphere was doubled in size and more than doubled in responsibility. In the same measure the number of citizen voters was increased.

This change had been on the way since the turn of the nineteenth century, but many did not see it as a reality to be reckoned with until the die had been cast. And when the number of voters doubled, so likewise did the number of office seekers and place hunters in public affairs.

Up until the election of 1927, all had gone well with the women in office. We were in a period of prosperity, and in such a time not many questions are asked. There is little heart searching and the competition in all lines is less than in times of strain and stress.

Little as we suspected it then, we were traveling rapidly day by day into such a time as tried men's souls and broke the stoutest of hearts. We had heard of panics in 1837 and 1873; had listened to tales of the "hard times" of 1873-75, one of the most remarkable financial

124

panics in the history of American finance. They seemed far away and long ago, and we were all lulled into a feeling of security that had no basis in world conditions. We had not yet paid the price demanded by fate as the aftermath of the World War. We did not know that even as we rejoiced at the results of this state election of the fall of 1927, the wolf was already at the door.

We thought of a monetary crisis as something that concerned Wall Street, which was more or less confined to the East. We felt that our solid Kentucky institutions were unshakable. It is not necessary to detail any description of this time, so recent, as we may point to the scars of burns not yet healed. Without recounting any of this, we may well remember that during that precarious time the state of Kentucky did not lose one dollar of the taxpayers' money, indeed came out ahead, as we shall tell later.

That such precautions were taken by the first woman Treasurer of the state can be attributed to her natural caution in money matters, which had been cultivated by the necessities of her own almost unaided struggle to gain a small measure of financial independence. So through that four years the money of the taxpayers was so safeguarded that we weathered the storm that was even then rising on the Eastern horizon.

In the final analysis, if my case for public service must rest on any one point, it will be the record made as Treasurer of the State of Kentucky. For, if "the mind's the measure of the man" or woman — as it is — surely money is the measure of peace, security, and comfort for the individual, the community, and the state.

It was on January 7, 1928, at about ten o'clock in the morning that the first woman ever elected in the United States as a State Treasurer was sworn in. This ceremony was held in the beautiful mahogany-paneled room of the Court of Appeals, Judge William Rogers Clay officiating.

On that wintry morning the courtroom was crowded with friends of the newly elected state officials and many outsiders to witness an historic and interesting ceremony which included the installation of the first two women to be sworn in at the same time as members of the official family of any state. This news item brought many favorable comments in the press concerning women in office, all of which were duly appreciated by all Kentucky women, who felt they were really coming into their own.

After this ceremony the new duties of the officials claimed

their undivided attention, for there is no playtime between taking the oath of office and beginning the duties that await each one in his or her department. My assistant was M.E. Edwards of New Castle, who, as assistant auditor under William Shanks, had won approval for his work, while his experience as a banker made him eminently suited to continue his public service in another place of trust and responsibility under the new administration.

Just before entering on my duties as State Treasurer I asked Mr. Edwards if he would accept this place as Assistant Treasurer. He said, "Mrs. Cromwell, I did not vote for you as I was under obligation to Mr. Phillips."

My reply was, "No one knows that better than I, but your experience and your competence impel me to offer you this position. Your loyalty and integrity have been proved, and I must insist on your acceptance."

He said, "I will accept and will do my best to make your administration a success."

My judgment was rewarded and his devotion to his duties, which he performed with a high degree of efficiency, made his services most satisfactory.

It is due to him and also to the other members of my staff to say that they figured largely in the success of the office during the next four years. Another member was the late Miss Margaret Parrish of Richmond, an influential and experienced businesswoman whose lovable qualities added social prestige to efficiency. She was faithful and true to her friends and responded readily to every call of duty. Miss Mary Malloy had proved her worth as one of my loyal and efficient secretaries during the four years just past and now entered into another four years of similar value to the state as well as to the Treasurer personally. L.O. Taylor was an expert and painstaking bookkeeper, faithful and laborious. His work stood us all in good stead. We seldom got out of balance, and when we did there was no let-up at Mr. Taylor's desk until every possible discrepancy had been cleared away. Steadiness and reliability were his watchwords — and who could summon better ones?

Miss Dorothy Shackelford, the junior member of our staff, was a great favorite with all. She was not only capable and interested, but always willing to do her part. During summer vacations of the staff, our dependable supply was Miss Rose Mary Balch, now Mrs. Morris Scott, who met the varied demands that each position made of her with interest in the work and speed in its execution.

One important member of the force was George McElroy, the porter, who was faithful and skilled in handling the constant succession of callers in a typically courteous Southern manner that gave dignity to all occasions. For him we provided a new uniform and a cap with "Treasurer's Office" on it, which identified him with his service and added greatly to his pleasure and pride.

The offices needed some renovation, and it was our fortune to get new furniture; these with a little paint and the finishing touches given by the women of the staff soon had our quarters glowing with newness and with a feeling that we merited the compliments of those visitors who said that we had the most attractive office in the building.

A majority of the force were women, five to two. There was plenty of work, which necessitated long hours. The office was opened and everybody busy at eight in the morning and it never closed until five in the afternoon, with someone on duty at lunch time always. The staff was most cooperative, and all believed in working when they expected pay, in which dictum I fully agreed.

My way of thinking is this, that the head of a department should not depend altogether on the staff, but should be on the job in person and earn the salary drawn and really be a working member of the office force. The businessmen who pay taxes have found they cannot succeed unless they follow this formula, so why should elected or appointed officers feel that they can succeed with a different program of service?

It has been said that in almost every administration the heads of some departments never know what goes on in their offices and are never known to do a real day's work. If this is the truth, it is not fair to either the office force nor the taxpayers, who pay the salaries of head officials as well as of their employees. It pays to be conscientious in all dealings and some seemingly strange upsets have been caused by the taxpayers finding out that their money was wasted thus.

A policy requiring all banks which handled state funds to be bonded to the full amount was adopted when I was installed into this office. This gave the woman Treasurer at first the worst moments of her career, and later on, the very best hours she has ever experienced. It had been the custom to deposit the state's money in various banks without requiring such an iron-clad bond, trusting to the probity and honor of the bankers who were men of integrity. But, alas, even the proved personal and business integrity of these bankers did not avail in the financial debacle that was just over the horizon.

It seemed to the new Treasurer that this prevailing custom was a dangerous one, that we must have the state deposits covered with approved bonds acceptable to the Federal government and must insist that each deposit bank should pay the same interest regardless of size and location. Perhaps some of the criticism met in the campaign that a woman could not approve bonds, handle funds, and so on, had made her think rather deeply into the possibilities of failing banks or unsteady financing. Perhaps it was just intuition, or the personal experience of losing hard-earned money as a depositor and as an investor. Whatever the reason, this Treasurer did require the same bonds and the same rate of interest from all. In the general mind the prevailing prosperity had lessened caution, and the whole country was to learn in a bitter school the value of foresight.

No sooner was this policy announced than it seemed the very heavens were to fall on the head of the new Treasurer. Rather, it seemed that some lower region was to yield up its ghosts to come like the cloud.

"The ghost walks" is the slang of the actor, leading back perhaps to Hamlet's ghostly visitor. Be that as it may, there are some things I should like to know. One of these is whether men candidates after successful election — or before — are visited by such ghosts as haunted the footsteps of a woman elected to a responsible office where she was guardian of the people's money. Such information is, of course, held behind closed doors, and it is possible to draw only from personal experience.

On the day I was sworn in there came to my door two emissaries who approached the subject of state finances with all courtesy and kindliness. They were representatives of my best friends, they said, and while they knew my qualifications, they hoped that I realized the great responsibility involved. They were prepared to take a great load off my shoulders by designating the depositories of state funds with those who would see that every penny was well taken care of and would give a strict accounting.

This all sounded good, but on questioning they were a little vague and hazy as to just the legal steps necessary, and especially on collateral for the funds and other details that I had found bankers were extremely careful about when my own small funds were in question.

They seemed to think the word of those whom they represented would perhaps be sufficient bond. When I said that all moneys

128

belonging to the state would be safeguarded by all the powers possible to the financial world, they seemed to think that I was over-cautious. My insistence on bonding was the first intimation that had gone out on that subject and it was plain to be seen that the ghosts were "taking backwater." Finally, they became really angered and prophesied that my administration would go on the rocks if I put too many impossible obstacles in the way of those who were prepared to handle the immense sums belonging to the state. It was with reluctance that they gave up, and it was evident that they had not expected opposition to schemes already deeply laid.

The State Treasurer was under a bond of $300,000 and was sworn to take every precaution in handling the finances of the state. There were pitfalls to be seen, and her avoidance of some of these soon after being sworn in was rather a surprise to some of the setters of traps and placers of pits.

There was plenty of advice on all these matters, some of it entirely reasonable and given by real friends, that it was best not to disturb existing relations nor to change too many of the customs and habits of the state's former officials.

I was willing, despite adverse criticism or friendly advice, to take the full responsibility for making changes in methods of handling state money which would safeguard it as fully as possible. So it was not long until every penny for which the Treasurer was responsible was safely in vaults, or on credit accounts which were fully bonded and protected, with interest mounting in our favor day to day. There were a few bleeders ready and willing to relieve me of much of the responsibility, but my oath of office did not allow me to shift any of this. They came like the Greeks of old, "bearing gifts" of better methods and less work for me and my office force, but were mistrusted with good reason.

May it be said here with emphasis that my staff stood by my determination absolutely and by me when it was attempted to call me to account for my so-called stubbornness in improving the methods of guarding the finances to my keeping.

With the office in good working order and everything going smoothly, all seemed well, but the fight was not over. Soon came another call to appear before the Grand Jury for questioning. By this time I well knew what such a call meant. There was an effort to make the woman official the goat and she was more or less on trial.

The Treasurer knew that there were dire possibilities when

work against her had been carried on underground, but she had determined on her stand, knew she was in the right, and resolved to go down fighting to the last ditch.

On this occasion the questions were directed largely toward this bonding, and there was a hidden intimation that there might have been some personal profit in the necessary transactions, or something that could be used later politically by my enemies. The best defense for such attacks is to be free from any taint of the offense charged. Next to that comes the necessity of keeping a clear head and not growing confused under the anger that is felt at the underhanded methods being used to discredit one who is doing all in the line of duty.

Questions were asked on matters that I had never heard of, on other things that to my certain knowledge had never happened, and on perverse twisting of real happenings. Oh, well, battles are won sometimes with no weapons except the right, courage, and a controlled tongue and temper. This was one of those times.

Supported loyally by friends and my office force, the work began to move smoothly and swiftly. The office was cleared from top to bottom of any stigma. We all could enjoy the fruits of our efforts as well as the work which daily became more interesting. While quietly working away with everything under control, there came to our ears the rumbling of distant thunder.

The crisis came when on October 29, 1929, a great panic started when the Stock Exchange crashed amid such tumultuous scenes as have seldom been enacted anywhere on earth. "Coolidge Prosperity" vanished in the wild cries and shouts of ruined investors, and the swift decline of President Hoover's popularity started like a snow man melts before the sun. Even then we did not fully realize that a great depression was coming in like a tidal wave on some peaceful coast.

At first these sounds were far off and everybody said, "Oh, how bad, for some places will suffer greatly." Somehow, we always feel that we in Kentucky are protected. We soon heard that banks in sister states were closing or breaking up entirely, and we were glad to feel that all Kentucky's money was safely bonded and bringing in interest.

One unforgettable morning, I picked up the Courier-Journal and there in a headline saw in cold black type the unbelievable fact that the National Bank of Kentucky had closed, and well I knew that it had in its vaults $3.2 million of the state's money. This was such a shock that I forgot for the moment that it was all bonded while a great wave of such despair as I had never felt before rolled over me. Even when I had recovered a little from the first shock, it seemed that the very marble walls of the state Capitol rocked around me, for if that great bank had failed, what might not happen to bonding companies?

It may be said here that only one other bank went under that had any of the state's money in it, and that was $10,000, all bonded. The distress of the time as it swept over Kentucky like a cloud does not need description here for it is only too well remembered by businesses and individuals who have not yet recovered from the shock.

On the failure of the Kentucky bank, the Treasurer finally collected every dollar with the interest, which was the legal six per cent, amounting to $26,000 on the $3.2 million, and $600 on the $10,000. Before this final consummation there were many dark and trying days when suspense hung like a cloud over the whole country. Kentucky was more fortunate than most, because the Treasurer had insisted that all the state's money must be bonded. Again, a woman's intuition and precaution had worked out for good and the results were highly satisfying to both conscience and reputation. In the joy of accomplishment one felt quite repaid for taking the abuse of ghostly visitors and the inconvenience of being called to task before the Grand Jury.

The bankers of the state deserve great credit. Those concerned worked hard along with the Treasurer to hold fast to the taxpayers' money. Many problems had to be worked out and much precaution was necessary. The problems were new ones to this generation and they were met with courage and determination. The banks of Frankfort were always alert and they had my perfect confidence. Eugene Hogue was one of the leading bankers of the whole state and a businessman of wide experience. Pat Sullivan and Leslie Morris of the Farmer's Bank and Trust Company, which had the state checking account, never faltered in a duty, were ready on all occasions, and were faithful during many trying hours.

George Hahlnhuber, then at the head of the People's State Bank, was another loyal and faithful adviser, on whose conservative outlook I could always depend. The late French Hogue also worked side by side with us, giving invaluable advice and always counseling caution and courage. These were blue days in the banking world and those responsible for the money of the people had to be alert and faithful to the last minute. These Frankfort banks which were guardians of a goodly sum of the state money were all heavily bonded, and they paid interest just as promptly as did the other banks. No favorites were played in giving out the money for deposit in the first place and, in the end, all worked out for the good of the state.

Nearly all our sister states suffered fearfully in state finances as well as in individual losses. The Treasurer was compelled to call in the state's money from some of the unfortunate banks, even though it was bonded. The bankers all over the state rallied to the situation and when my term ended were my friends, and I never failed to appreciate their loyalty and assistance during those dark days that are written so black on history's pages.

One bank deserves especial mention. In it the state had, when I came into office, about $300,000 of its money, and the depression did not miss Barbourville, where this institution is located. The citizens and bank officials are due untold praise, for they all joined and pulled together with the State Treasurer, saved the bank, and lost not one dollar of the taxpayers' money. This was a high point of the activities of my office. Such cooperation in the face of panic and threatened loss was almost a miracle. The stand taken by the people of Barbourville showed unusual courage and initiative and was duly appreciated by the Treasurer, who came through the experience with an abiding love for them and for their beautiful mountain town where such a test of real loyalty came to a successful conclusion.

James Kehoe of Maysville was a close friend on whose advice one could always rely. He never asked to have a penny of state money deposited in his bank, but was always ready with business advice of the greatest value, while the pleasant home where Mrs. Kehoe joined him in dispensing real hospitality was always open, and the Treasurer was a frequent guest.

Other confidential advisers in Frankfort were Sam Shackelford, a veteran in statecraft, and Sherman Goodpaster, who had served the people efficiently as State Treasurer. Many newspaper editors were valued friends during these strenuous times. In visiting my good friend, Mrs. Hattie Buchanan of Richmond, I often met and talked with Keen Johnson, editor of the Richmond Register, who already gave promise of the rapid rise he was to have in becoming Lieutenant Governor of Kentucky, and whose activity and alertness are now statewide knowledge through his service in that capacity and as Governor pro tem.[1]

Again recourse was had to the good will and friendship of the late Judge Robert Worth Bingham, publisher of The Courier-Journal and Times. At this time a few disappointed individuals were besieging the Treasurer in an effort to gain some control over state finances. The columns of this paper had been used in an effort to reflect on my work. My whole story was recited, my plans laid before him with a resume of what had already been achieved, and my determination to resign rather than take any chance with the money of the taxpayers. His encouraging reception of my plea opened a new world to me and made me more determined than ever to continue to stand for the people whose interests I had to protect.

Judge Bingham was a man of high integrity, always ready to right a wrong, and to him I owe a debt of gratitude for helping me to make good as Treasurer of Kentucky. His son, Barry Bingham, is following in his footsteps today in the great newspaper world.[2]

It took about six weeks to collect the sleeping $3 million, but every day the six per cent interest mounted and the $26,000 interest was paid along with the other. James B. Brown of the National Bank of Kentucky during that trying time was always found to be just, cooperative, and pleasant in all the necessary dealings with the office of the Treasurer.

It was a thrilling moment when Marshall Bullitt, the legal representative of the Aetna Life Insurance Company, handed to the State Treasurer the check for $3,226,000, saying as he did so, "This is the largest check ever paid out by an insurance company, and Mrs. Cromwell, it gives me pleasure, as the law directs, to hand it to a woman for our beloved State of Kentucky."

Percy Johnston, formerly of Lebanon, now head of the Chemical Bank in New York, said, "I never heard of money being made off a bank failure before."

The good ending to such a distressing story was brought about by not taking a chance and by staying on the safe side. The responsibility for all this rested on the Treasurer, but she had a strong right arm in the late Honorable James Cammach, Attorney General of the state, whose integrity and honor could be trusted, while his ability was equal to any emergency. He had always the interest of the state at heart. Aiding him was a brilliant young lawyer, Clifford Smith, always steady at the helm of the legal department where he was an assistant.

At this time I remember another friend who in the darkest days came into the office with words of cheer. This was Emmet O'Neal, who came in especially to assure me that I had done all in my power to serve the state, and that Kentucky's finances were probably in the best shape of any state in the Union. He told me that these same things were happening everywhere, with many much worse conditions than prevailed in Kentucky. He was one of my main supporters and advisers during the Depression and is now deservedly in Congress from Louisville, where he is representing his district with great credit.

Another Louisville citizen, Dr. Charles Welch, Presbyterian minister, originally from my home county of Simpson, was a tower of strength spiritually to his city and state. He made frequent visits to our office and his wise advice and counsel kept up my personal morale when the world seemed to be falling to pieces around us.

Kentucky in general was spared many of the worst aspects of the Depression. Being largely rural, with no extremely large cities, we did not see the heartrending sights that were always before the eyes of those who lived in great metropolitan areas. Each bank that failed brought many to the breadlines, cast many a woman who had lived in luxury down to the other extreme and left her penniless, with nowhere to go and no one to turn to in her distress.

The Treasurer thought she was in the midst of it with the worries of the finances of Kentucky, but a necessary trip to New York revealed situations that beggar description. From the entrance of the hotel I watched the breadlines of men, women, and children as they stood for hours to get soup and bread and a cup of coffee or tea, with a little milk for the children. The patience of these forlorn people would make one weep. And the pity of it all was that many of them were used to far better days and were willing to work if only given a chance. Many were half clothed as well as half fed. So it was a Godsend to the whole country when President Roosevelt and Congress gave relief to suffering humanity later.

Money and credit are mysterious things. They both are great and braggart soldiers in prosperity. In adversity and depression they hide away where no one can find them. There must be some medium of exchange. Bright beads or cowry shells did very well in their time and place. Systems of trade and barter have been tried many times in many places. Our modern system of currency and credit has evolved through trial and error until it suits our present complex civilization. In our system the banks are all-important. And with our present splendid chain of banks and modern banking methods, we hope that there was been built up financial strength that cannot be shaken in any depression to come.

"Old Kentucky Entries and Deeds" speaks of values in "current money of Virginia," "current money of Kentucky," and the pounds, shillings, and pence of English currency, while the Spanish "bit" was in common use for many years. In considering money in America, no one can overlook tobacco, which was currency for two centuries and more in Virginia and parts of the South.

It was upon the recommendation of Thomas Jefferson that the government, during Washington's administration, broke away from the use of English money and adopted a decimal system, part of the French tradition which Jefferson absorbed in his years spent abroad in his country's service. Gold, silver, and copper were chosen as the metals for making coins, and no paper money was issued between the years 1831 and 1863.

The first bank organized in this country was the Bank of North America. It was started by Robert Morris and others in Philadelphia in 1781. In 1790 three other banks had been established, the Bank of Massachusetts at Boston, the Bank of New York in New York City, and the Bank of Maryland in Baltimore. The story of banks, including the Biddle Bank in Philadelphia and the long fight of Andrew Johnson to break its power, would fill many books, whose pages would tell of the suffering of millions of people.

On September 2, 1787, an act was passed by Congress establishing the Treasury Department. This was under the Old Confederation and before the adoption of the present Constitution of the United States. The finances of the country were at a low ebb due to the cost of the Revolutionary War, the loss of British trade, and the loss in manpower and time by the colonists who had formed their new government. Alexander Hamilton was the first Secretary of the Treasury and it was said of him, "He smote the rock of the national resources and abundant streams of revenue gushed forth. He touched the dead corpse of Public Credit, and it sprang upon its feet."

The present Treasury Building in Washington was erected during the presidency of Andrew Jackson. The first reform made in the routine of the Treasury Department was in 1853 by James Guthrie, Secretary of the Treasury under President Franklin Pierce. At the time he entered the Treasury the unsettled accounts and balances amounted to $132,000,000, which by his economy and judicious methods was reduced within the four years to $24,000,000. Guthrie was a Kentuckian, born in Nelson County. This reminds us that in Kentucky today we have another man from Nelson County at the head of finances, Dan Talbott of Bardstown, appointed by Governor A.B. Chandler.

In Kentucky in 1792, the first Constitution of the state provided that the State Treasurer be elected annually by joint ballot of both houses of the Legislature, with an annual salary of $333.33. John Logan was the first Treasurer of the state, elected June 18, 1792, and held office for fifteen years until July, 1897, being elected annually. In 1798, his salary was raised to $600 per year. Later the Treasurer was elected by the qualified voters and the salary fixed at $933.75. Under the present Constitution that officer is elected by the people for four years at a salary of $3,600 per year.[3]

The responsibility of the office of State Treasurer cannot be exaggerated. That the people of the state realize this is shown by the fact that those who tour the Capitol building seldom miss seeing "where the money is kept" and how such large sums are managed. Among the visitors are always many teachers who bring groups of school children. During my regime we were never too busy to take time to show them around and explain every detail. These children of today are the citizens of tomorrow and the welfare of the whole country depends on what they learn and how they learn it. Teachers were always found to be firm friends who appreciated the information we could give them.

The Secretary of State and the Treasurer, both women, were on the Sinking Fund Commission, which at that time had responsibility for the disposition of the various funds belonging to the state. Other members were the Attorney General, Auditor, and Governor. In this capacity we learned there was a movement to take the State Highway Department from Frankfort to Lexington. The agitation came about because of a disastrous fire which had ravaged the offices of that department in the Old Capitol Building. It was necessary to have other quarters immediately, and Lexington had made what seemed a better proposition than was available in Frankfort.

Knowing the distress this would bring to my home city, I moved that the Commission recess until more information could be obtained on such a drastic change. Telephone calls were made to a number of leading citizens, and the response was instantaneous with meetings and emergency calls.[4] Several of us scarcely ate or slept for the ensuing twenty-four hours in which such a momentous question was to be settled. When the Commission reconvened we had plenty of propositions, and with much suggestion and a great deal of diplomacy the question was settled. Not all the citizens of Frankfort know of this today. Others remember all too well the strenuous fight that was necessary to hold such a valuable asset to the town.

During this time it became necessary to borrow money in New York in order to finance some very important bridge building. The

Secretary of State, Treasurer, Ben Johnson, Chairman of the Highway Commission, and A.B. Plumber, journeyed to that city in order to close the deal. Miss Ella Lewis, Secretary of State, carried with her the seal of Kentucky, which until then had never been out of the state. Mr. Plumber took charge of it and became our official "Seal Toter." The sum of nine million dollars was contracted for, the seal used to bind the bridge bonds, and this money brought back, deposited with other state money, and safeguarded in the same way until paid out to the contractors who built the fine bridges of which the state is very proud.[5]

H.R. Creel, the Bridge Engineer, deserves great credit for the wonderful work he and the staff have done in bridge building in Kentucky. You can say what you please about your engineers, but no state in the Union excels Kentucky in her engineering field. This strong corps of competent engineers was for the most part trained under Dean Paul Anderson of the University of Kentucky.

It was during this term of office that the great Democratic Convention was held in Houston, Texas, when Al Smith was nominated on the ticket for President of the United States. Among the Kentucky delegation were Judge James Garnett of Louisville; Urey Woodson of Owensboro; Roscoe Dalton of Monticello; Honorable A.O. Stanley and Mrs. Stanley; Senator Alben W. Barkley; Mrs. Dan Moore of Harrodsburg; Mrs. John L. Woodbury of Louisville; Mrs. H.K. Bourne of New Castle; Mrs. John Mayo, our national committeewoman, besides myself and many others. The Kentucky delegation was royally entertained by the Houstonians, who all seemed to be Kentuckians or descendants of Kentuckians.

Will Neal, a leading banker of Houston who was originally from Monroe County, Kentucky, gave a beautiful breakfast in honor of the Kentucky delegation and visitors, with several hundred people as guests. It will be remembered that the Governor of Kentucky was a Republican, so that the mantle of authority fell on the shoulders of several leaders of the party, who did the honors in a manner befitting the occasion.

This reminds us that sometimes there were rather amusing incidents connected with this anomalous condition. Among the survivals of a past day was the regulation that the Treasurer could not leave the state without permission from the Governor so, when it was necessary to leave the state, the Treasurer would write the Governor asking a permit, keeping a copy of the letters on file. The fact that they were of different political faiths made this seem more of a joke than it would have been otherwise.

Again as in the case of the Secretaries of State, it was found that the Treasurers of the forty-eight states were well organized and held annual conventions. The first I attended was in New Orleans, glamour city of the South. A great program was put over, and the citizens of the Crescent City welcomed us with grace and charm. There being only one woman Treasurer was the occasion of sly humor. Those addressing the Convention would say, "Gentlemen of the Convention and" — with a smile — "our Lady member." Several important committee assignments were given me, of which the most powerful one was chairman of the Nominating Committee.

My address came second on the program and was entitled, "The Treasury and the Treasurer." Needless to say that Kentucky's representative did the best she possibly could and only hoped it would be good enough, for those assembled were highly qualified to judge.

Many of the club women of New Orleans attended the sessions, interested in one of their own, and the president of the Business and Professional Women's Club graciously asked me to address her group that evening. This is remembered as a high point in the extensive entertainment we had during the convention. No compliment can be too great for the women who have the initiative and the progressive spirit to carry on this highly useful organization known as the Business and Professional Women's Club.

But journeys and conventions have been but a small part in the life of a State Treasurer. There are checks to be signed and endless documents to be read, examined, and signed. In my regime economy was necessary and the department had not yet bought many of the machines that make life easier now in that office. Every check was signed by me personally, and not one was ever signed on Sunday. Each was signed as soon as the voucher came from the office of the Auditor, and no one was ever kept waiting.[6] A much appreciated compliment was given us by Judge Charles Marshall of Shelbyville, who said he knew that his check would always be there on time if not a few minutes ahead, adding that many others had so expressed themselves as appreciative of promptness in the business of the state.

Every possible economy was practiced and we always kept within our budget and turned a little back into the treasury each year. Even our faithful porter was trained to save sheets of paper and especially uncanceled stamps. I learned to look for this waste in the office of Secretary of State, where I found good stamps to the amount of thirty dollars scattered here and there on the way to the wastebasket when I went into office.

"Pay as you go" has ever been my ideal, and for some six months of my term as Treasurer we were on a strict cash basis, but the big program of road and bridge building made it impossible to continue on the cash basis. The interest-bearing warrants then in use added greatly to the burden of the Treasurer's office. Our present Governor A.B. Chandler has reorganized the government, and the system is working in a truly businesslike way. It has been a Herculean task, and the full force of the reorganization will be felt in the future when the citizens appreciate all the labor that has gone into it and the cooperation that exists between the present efficient Treasurer, John Buckingham, and the Commissioner of Finance, Dan Talbott, who cooperated with Governor Chandler to the fullest degree.

Just here we may mention another constructive piece of work that has been done quietly and effectively by Nat Sewell, State Inspector, who looks on the state as a big corporation, with the taxpayers as the stockholders, whose interest he has at heart.

Not long after taking charge of the Treasurer's office we began a work similar to that done in the office of Secretary of State in classifying, filing, and cataloguing all the checks of former State Treasurers in numerical order, from the first State Treasurer down through 1931, so that any check or voucher could be located in a moment's time. We also classified and catalogued all securities then deposited by the various insurance companies doing business in the state; this latter amounting to about twenty million dollars. As formerly, the staff gave their time and effort to do this gigantic task, working gladly in order that the regime might have a constructive piece of work to view with pride.

As a piece of historical work this stands beside that done on the records of the Governors during my term as Secretary of State. Those not historically minded may not appreciate that task, but we believe that all taxpayers do appreciate the work of properly filing and cataloguing the checks and vouchers of the state from the beginning. For when it comes right down to the people's money, the precious dollars garnered from the taxpayers, which they have earned by the sweat of the brow or the activity of busy brain and strained nerves, ah, there is a vital point of contact. No excuses avail in the final count if the politicians lose or waste the people's money. Each man and woman may not be able to audit the account, column by column, but the taxpayers do keep a close audit that becomes quite effective, and as long as they have ballots to cast, candidates may well fear when the voter on election day adds, subtracts, multiplies, and divides the praise or blame for budgets balanced or unbalanced.

Our annual budget for the Treasurer's office at that time was only $17,000 for running expenses, and out of that we paid the firm of Cotton and Eskew, public accountants, for a complete yearly audit of the books. Great changes have been made in the work of the Treasurer's office since then. Better equipment, for one thing, has been added as needed. The amount of business has increased as the state has expanded and developed resources. During my four-year term the business doubled in volume and value. Much of this was due to road and bridge building and the care of the funds voted by various counties to meet state funds for these purposes. The details of bonding and depositing and withdrawing the state funds was a huge task.

During that four years we rode the stormy waves of a depression that threatened to engulf all that we held dear. Our department weathered the storm and came out into the sunlight of a new day with more money than the taxpayers had put in, with all accounts balanced, consciences clear, and many valuable lessons well learned.

In treasuries and banks and all the places that have the care and keeping of the money of the people, we sometimes mistakenly feel there is not room for high ideals. The fact is that nowhere can we find a better place to develop the highest ideals of which humans are capable. We do recognize that the handling of money develops character and honesty. We should go further and know that nowhere is there a better school in which to learn plain living and high thinking which were the ideals of our ancestors.

"Ideals are like stars; you will not succeed in touching them with your hands. But, like the wayfaring man on the desert of waters, you choose them as your guides, and following them you will reach your destiny."

As the term of office drew to a close, the darkest clouds of depression began to lift and we could see their silver edges followed by the rosy glow of coming prosperity. The greatest encouragement came through the banks whose officers had been tried as in a fiery furnace. As the burden of hard times lightened somewhat, all these good financial friends continued their duties with hearts that were much lighter. Be it said to the everlasting credit of the bankers of the state that they always bore the added burden of the times cheerfully and never once failed in loyal support to the state and to the Treasurer. The appreciation she felt and still feels for their courage, persistence, and unfailing support cannot be put into words.

The State Treasurer had about $45 million a year of the people's money to guard. These bankers had the responsibility of all the financing for business, homes, schools, and churches, added to this state money. All citizens owe to the bankers a debt of gratitude for the steadfast stand they took and held throughout this trying time. The State Treasurer realized more than most people the burdens borne at that time by our financial advisers and guardians.

The last six months in this office had been the happiest in all my experience in public service. This was due first to the lifting of the general financial burden that had weighed us down with anxiety; and second, to the absolute loyalty and cooperation of the staff who had weathered the storm with me. The hard days and anxieties of the time which they had all shared so uncomplainingly made a personal bond that can never be broken. Nothing could be said that would pay sufficient tribute to their fine loyalty.

Such being the case, there was more than the usual tinge of sadness as we said good-bye to one another and made ready to turn over the work of four years to the incoming Treasurer, Elam Huddleston, and his efficient staff, who entered with enthusiasm on the great task of collecting, guarding, and dispensing the money of the state in January, 1932, with the good wishes of the retiring Treasurer and her staff.

We felt in giving up this task that hard work had brought it to a successful close, that courage had sustained us, and that we could with a clear conscience turn over the records that represented handling four times $45 million without a penny's loss to the taxpayers of Kentucky, but a gain of $26,000 of interest collected from the Aetna Life Insurance Company on the bond of the National Bank of Kentucky.

The record then made by the office of the State Treasurer of Kentucky has been highly complimented by other states, none of which came through that troubled period as well as did Kentucky. When the term was ended, the state was better off instead of worse in its financial status. This was due to team work of the staff, cooperation of the banks, and wise counsel of advisers who helped us to weather the storms that threatened to engulf us. The foundation of our good fortune was laid in insuring the money. The depression was the most widespread ever known to history. This was due to the means of constant communication and transportation and the fact that the world had grown so interdependent; all countries were like one, so linked were they in interest. A shudder on Threadneedle Street in London, or the Bourse in Paris, was registered as if by electric needle on the markets of New York and Chicago. Any development of the markets of the world influenced Kentucky's finances, and as shock after shock hit the financial structure of the world, our own finances trembled in the balance time and again. In the providence of God we were able to think and plan and to keep out of the worst of the Slough of Despond and to come through our term with flags flying and all funds intact, and even augmented.

Chapter VI Notes

1. Keen Johnson served as Kentucky Governor from 1939-1943.
2. The Courier-Journal was owned by the Bingham family until being sold to the Gannett conglomerate in 1986.
3. The salaries of Kentucky's constitutional officers, now adjusted annually for inflation, are approximately $80,000.
4. Those listed by the author as assisting in the effort were Admiral Edmund Taylor, Cecil Farmer, David Davis, Judge T.B. McGregor, Charles Morris, Orval Harrod, Frank Dutton, John Perkins, and H.A. Gretter.
5. Mrs. Cromwell listed the following as bridges that were built during her term as Treasurer, with the amounts paid in "checks issued bearing my signature...."

The Ohio River Bridge, Ashland, $776,231.96; the Ohio River Bridge, Maysville, $1,520,548.02; the Ohio River Bridge, Henderson — Indiana paid half and Kentucky half — $1,399,996.24 each; Kentucky River Bridge, Tyrone; Kentucky River Bridge, Boonesboro; Green River Bridge, Spottsville; Cumberland River Bridge, Smithland; Cumberland River Bridge, Burnside; Cumberland River Bridge, Canton; Tennessee River Bridge, Paducah; Tennessee River Bridge, Eggner's Ferry ($4,057,832.77 for the last eight).

6. A signature machine is now used to affix the Treasurer's signature on state checks, one of numerous changes made affecting the office over the decades since Mrs. Cromwell's term. The Treasurer no longer has responsibility for or oversight of state funds; this authority now resides in the state Finance and Administration Cabinet, which is headed by a gubernatorial appointee. The elimination of duties from the Treasurer's office has prompted efforts to eliminate the office entirely; these have failed to win the approval of Kentucky voters, however.

VII

Kentucky's Glorious Parks Are Made More Glorious

Nature is the art of God.

On May 6, 1932, Governor Ruby Laffoon appointed me as State Park Director to succeed Mrs. James Darnell of Frankfort, who as the appointee of Governor Flem D. Sampson had been most successful in this position. Personally, I felt and still feel that this position should not be subject to changing politics, but it goes along with others and is classed with the "spoils" that belong to the victor. Dealing, as the park system does, with the very heart of conservation of natural resources, it had always been of paramount interest to me as an individual and a club woman. Still, there was a natural hesitancy in undertaking a job of such magnitude as this one.

Mrs. Darnell had made a splendid Director, painstaking, economical, and always on the job. She had developed the parks with all the means at her command and had great visions of more work to be done. There was a feeling among our citizens that this was work which a woman could do, that it was a place that called for a love of beauty, an interest in recreation, and a development of natural resources for their highest uses.

Governor Laffoon sent for me and after a few words said, "I want to appoint you as Park Director. It has been suggested as a suitable position for a woman, and your friends recommend you. Mrs. Darnell has made good in this place and our folks feel that the party should have a woman representative as Park Director. I know that you can fill the place."

In one moment there flashed across my mind, "What a difference in the attitude toward women in public office has come about in the past ten years!"

Aloud, I replied, "Governor, I am an ardent conservationist. Do not think, however, that I have studied the question in a scientific way, for I have not, but will inform myself and do the very best I can for the people and for your administration."

"You made good as State Treasurer and handled the finances of the state to the satisfaction of everybody. That is another point in your favor. This requires management of finances and I know that you can make fifty cents go as far as a dollar, and that you will account for every penny of the taxpayers' money."

"You can depend on me to do that," was my reply.

"This will be your whole responsibility," the Governor then said. "I am too busy to give the parks any attention, much as I should like to do so. It is all up to you."

It was plain from his attitude that he was most friendly to the state parks and duly impressed with the importance of conservation; also that he delegated the work and planning to his Park Director with whatever aid the commission and interested officials and citizens could give.

The growth of the park systems in the United States and in the state was slow in the beginning. Nature had been so prodigal with beauty and charm that the people seemed to feel that there would always be large areas that would remain open for pleasure seekers. Then the people wasted the resources in a wanton manner, taking little thought for a future when woods and waters would be scarce; when the deforestation would cause floods, when the fallowing of the prairies would add to droughts and cause dust storms.

Less than seventy years ago the first state park was established in America. California was the first state to have a state-controlled park. Even this and the opening of Yellowstone Park did not fully arouse the people to the fact that every state possessed unique features that would serve as the nuclei of parks. Even then we in Kentucky needed prodding by conservationists to make us realize the necessity of setting aside parks and park lands. Perhaps the natural beauty of the state, its rolling bluegrass pastures, its wooded hills and grand mountains, its clear streams and its waterfalls, were so much a part of everyday life that it was hard to realize that some of these magnificent views needed to be set apart so that the beauties could be preserved as the population grew and more and more of the areas became commercialized in one way or another.

It is now about twenty-one years since the first state park was established in Kentucky. Interested citizens have given land, and in every community where parks or shrines have been established they have given time and means to the development of the park idea. The ideal is that the parks should not only be areas to be enjoyed, but that they should be so developed and the funds handled in such a way that they would not be a drain on the taxpayers. Indeed, it is quite possible to make them a source of income to the state and nation, and absolutely self-supporting.

In ancient times parks and playgrounds were the private property of kings and nobles and were kept inviolate from the presence or use of the average family. The average man, woman, or child was not allowed to set foot within the precincts of the noble woodlands kept for hunting, or the princely estates reserved for royal pleasures. The severest penalties were inflicted for poaching on these preserves and punishment was swift and sure.

What a contrast in human values is provided by the public park of today, owned and operated by the state or the nation for the benefit of all citizens, young or old, rich or poor, on wheels or afoot. It is needless to emphasize the fact that we should deeply appreciate this, our national and state park development, as one of the privileges of a free country that takes care of the pleasure and health of all who will take advantage of the opportunities.

We have a pardonable pride in our well-known national parks that occupy such large areas of land noted for great scenic beauty, all kept for public pleasure and enjoyment. These, however, are too far removed from the average family and not so accessible as parks should be to all our people.

Our Kentucky, by situation, climate, and environment, is admirably adapted for park uses. For countless years it was the hunting ground and play park of the American Indians from the north and from the south; and what race was ever healthier, more hardy, or possessed of sounder bodies along with the quiet strength of character developed within the natural parks and hunting grounds of our Kentucky land.

Our own ancestors came into this "wilderness beside the western waters" and found here such hunting, such adventure, such communion with nature as had not been seen since their forefathers, centuries before, enjoyed them in the dense forests of central Europe in days almost pre-historic. The years have been swift, and we have changed rapidly from a race of out-of-doors pioneers to a rural people who still loved the land and derived pleasure and health from close contact with nature. Then we changed almost overnight — many of us — from a rural to an urban, or semi-urban, people, and we must needs look for new ways and means to preserve mental balance and physical health. And this health does not mean that of the individual alone; it extends to the family and to the community at large, and consequently to the health and strength of the nation.

In our larger state parks we have vast areas of forest lands open for the benefit of the public, where we may find peace, quiet, freedom, relaxation, elbow-room, recreation, or more properly re-creation, which the latter has come to mean — re-creation of body, mind, and spirit. There is no power like that of the great open spaces to lift loads from the mind, to lift burdens from the heart — and when these are lifted, bodily health improves as by a miracle. The eye clears, the step becomes more elastic, as the blood, newly purified, courses through the veins and revives energy for familiar tasks, renews the vision of half-forgotten goals still worth striving for; animates the ambition for all the fine things that make life worth the living. Not the least of benefits is old friendships cemented and new friendships formed through delightful companionships.

What we need for health is pure food, pure water, pure air. Shelter, so necessary in winter, becomes of secondary importance in summer. Food and water we can do without for short periods, but pure air is the one great necessity of every minute, and nowhere is there so much pure air as in the parks. Would that we had many more of these health-giving centers! All our parks are so situated that good food and pure water are either within their environs or very near, so that we can conveniently enjoy all the needs of life that make for health and strength. How many lives have already been rebuilt — lives that seemed sometimes to totter on their foundations.

Go into any city in the evening; visit the parks; view the crowds gathered there; note the happy romping children; see the grown people playing games or looking on; peer into the faces of those coming in, marked with lines of worry and care; glance at them as they leave and compare the change, in the rested and refreshed appearance, the contented look, the softened demeanor. We may repeat this experience in parks where they beckon with refreshing mountain breezes, where they woo with woodland zephyrs; they entice with cool waters, sun and shade.

In our love of parks and of woods, our lure of crystal streams, our call to solitude, we have the example of our Savior who retired to

146

the mountains, to the gardens and the solitary places when the people thronged about him too closely and the strength went out of him at their eager touch.

Our parks have to offer rest for tired nerves, health supplied by outdoor life, recreation for the drooping spirits, and above all that variety that banishes monotony. This variety, this one element of change, has always been recognized as a prime factor in health. Travel and change are stimulating in the extreme; now, travel and change do not necessarily mean that we must cross the ocean or span the continent to attain them. A journey of a few miles may bring the healthful change and exercise we need.

What has Kentucky to offer in her state parks? All that nature anywhere can gather together of rest or peace and healing influence of outdoor life. That is the answer — and Kentucky has more than this, for every inch of her ground is historic. America is on wheels, and summertime sees the tourist pilgrims rolling along our history-haunted highways. In addition to our larger parks where we find vast acreage of forest and mountain and valley, Kentucky has a number of smaller parks devoted to the preservation of history and historic shrines. In these the student, the laborer, the professional man, the farmer, all may renew their courage and gain vigorous purpose of mind and spirit and body in the contemplation of the reminders of the lives and careers of those hardy, heroic, pioneer ancestors of ours, who seem to come closer to us within these hallowed precincts. The relics and memorials grouped there say to us in no uncertain tones: "Thus and so we lived and labored, without the comforts that are yours. Use your comforts and conveniences for mankind and posterity as we did....See what our hardships were; go home and lift your burdens again with a lighter heart."

There is nothing better than a true perspective of history to focus the eyes on life's realities; nothing surer than the breezes of historic fact to sweep the cobwebs from worried brains; and when worry and fear are gone away, health returns surely and certainly, and it is thus that our historic shrines give us new vim and deepened determination to live worthily and well and leave the world a little better than we found it.

The time is surely coming when a sojourn in the open and a tour of our parks will be a component part of the program of each family, provided for in the annual recreation budget. There, as nowhere else, the health-seekers and the health-giving agencies make connection and meet on a common ground of health and happiness. What has already been done to build up health will be multiplied many times in the future as we learn more of hygienic living and understand better that health and strength are to be found in the open; this will be when there are more parks and people take more advantage of the opportunities afforded.

Those who love Kentucky and her many-sided beauty, her highways and byways, her parks and her playgrounds, history and romance, whether inside or outside of the grand old Commonwealth today should do their part to build up and protect every inch of this God-given spot of ours.

Parks properly developed and handled appeal to every citizen of the state. They possess social possibilities of high value. To the young they appeal as places of pleasure; to older people they mean rest and quiet; to the nature lover and student they bring opportunities for study of flora and fauna, of rocks and earth and waters. Here the artist finds beauty; here the historian fits together the landscape, the geography, and the human actor. In all citizens they awaken civic pride because of the richness of nature's heritage open for all regardless of poverty or riches.

Following the trend of park development everywhere, our slogan for Kentucky parks was "Keep to Nature." It was our aim to do nothing to destroy primitive beauty while striving to make the original areas accessible and convenient for every visitor. Our ideal was to make the parks seem like an individual possession to each one who came to enjoy the peace, beauty, and solitude, or the association with others, as their wish might be.

My commission as Park Director was issued; I was sworn in by the distinguished jurist Chief Justice William Reese of the Court of Appeals, and immediately assumed the duties of my new office. It was Maytime and the natural beauty of the parks was at its height. They were widely scattered, but it was a pleasure to go from one to another, looking over the ground, dreaming of their possibilities and wondering what ways and means could be found to develop the available areas, with all their natural beauty and charm, into recreation centers for the people.

There was little money appropriated for either maintenance, development, or office equipment. Indeed, the latter was so lacking that it was necessary to make arrangements with the Progress Commission to share a corner in their room. We began with one chair, a

148

desk, and a filing cabinet — rather a slim outlook for an office that was expected to build up and develop Kentucky's twelve parks, which then consisted of about 8,000 acres of land in various stages of development.

The Park Director was assigned a secretary, Miss Agnes Schroff, who proved to be both efficient and painstaking. Together, we worked hard in our small corner, always keeping our promise not to disturb the Progress Commission. The efficient secretary of that body was Mrs. Frances Lester, who always made us feel at ease, being kind, cordial, and considerate.

My first visit as Director was to Harrodsburg, the Pioneer Memorial Park.[1] There was method in this, for their work was known far and wide and has served as inspiration for others. The Historical Society there had done valiant work in planning the park, in getting citizens interested, and in making every detail of their park perfect in reproducing the pioneer fort and surroundings. Those who composed this organization met with me, told their plans, showed what had been done and what they yet hoped to do. It was a fortunate visit for the new Park Director, for it was just what she needed to inspire and further enthuse her for the big job that lay ahead.

This park as a museum of pioneer life has many unique features and is rated by competent critics second only to the Early American Wing of the Metropolitan Art Museum of New York. In the replica of the original fort one gets the "feel" of the vast wilderness in which the first fort built was at once a home and a shelter from the wilderness and a protection from the Indians. One feels that here was really, as Lafayette said, "the Revolution on the western frontier." The builders of this memorial park are worthy successors of their pioneer ancestors. Here they have built with imagination and reconstructed with fidelity a half-forgotten glorious past.

Passing from this inspiring spot, there were travels over many miles as the new Park Director familiarized herself with the situation and conditions of the various parks, the acreage, topography, and natural landscaping. Reading of the development of parks in other states and growing more familiar with the federal plans for park development, a vision rose above the horizon and a dream took shape and form. Why could not Kentucky obtain aid from the federal government and use some of the funds and get the benefit of the work planned by the Department of the Interior for our state parks? Why not, indeed?

No sooner thought than an effort was made to gain the attention of Washington authorities. It seemed the wise thing to write to the Department at Washington, tell them what Kentucky had to offer in the way of park situations where the work of government agencies would make a fine show and where much good could be accomplished in developing the natural scenery of the parks while giving employment to the hundreds of unemployed, whom the government wanted to set to work at some useful occupation.

With all the eloquence at our command, we pictured the situation in Kentucky and asked that inspectors be sent to view our parks and see the possibilities and the desirability of placing workers where they could make the most show and do the most good. Our sincerity counted for much, it seemed. We did have much to offer, and in a very short time it was a real pleasure but hardly a surprise that two park inspectors appeared in our office. Paul Brown and Harry Curtis were the gentlemen, and it was plain to see they meant business. They had been trained under Colonel Richard Lieber of Indianapolis, a noted park authority. Arriving about three in the afternoon, they wished to go immediately to look over some of the park sites.

Butler Park was the nearest one to us that had the acreage required, and the only one that could be visited that afternoon.[2] Excusing myself for a moment, I sought a phone and called Frank Adcock at Carrollton, an interested member of my Advisory Board. I asked him to call together our local Board of Park Directors, both men and women, and be ready to receive us in an hour and a half and to show the park to best advantage, adding that we could all have dinner in Carrollton before returning to Frankfort. I had every confidence in this group and, without one doubt as to the wisdom and good judgment they would show, put on my hat and wrap, gave a few instructions to my secretary, and in less than half an hour after these inspectors came into the office we were bowling along the historic highway through Defoe, New Castle, and past some of the finest farm lands in Kentucky.

Former political campaigns over this and other parts of the state had made me familiar with the history and romance of the localities we were passing so rapidly, and I made the most of the time in pointing out every place of interest and recounting the life stories of some of Kentucky's great men and women who had homes along the route. The beauty and charm of the whole countryside made its own impression.

If it were possible to sell them the park idea, the Director was determined to do it. To this end, she recounted the parks, shrines, and sanctuaries that were strung like pearls along the threads of Kentucky's picturesque highways, emphasized the fact that the state is one big park and needed only cash and work to open up its beauties to tourists from all over the country, who would bless the government for helping in so laudable a project. Tourists had already found Kentucky a Mecca because nature had made magnificent and varied scenery, while her sons and daughters had provided history and romance.

Providence had placed Kentucky near the center of population of the United States, had provided natural parklands with waterfalls and terraced green mountains, as well as undulating pasture lands and peaceful, meandering streams.

As we were speeding on, in the lull of conversation I told them of our wonderful Mammoth Cave, that words cannot describe the natural beauty of one of the world's great natural wonders, the Mammoth Cave in Kentucky. It goes back to the year 1797 as shown in the records of Warren County at Bowling Green, designated as a corner of a tract of land. In 1812 a deed of the Mammoth Cave tract from Flatt to McLean again appears in those county records.

Owing to a lack of exploration, it seemed parts of the cavern had been used for generations by the Indians. The importance of the cave at this time was not realized. Local tradition goes back to the hunter, Houchins, and his wounded bear. If this story is correct, and if by seeking refuge in the cave the bear caused it to be discovered, he did more for Kentucky than any other bear either before or since his time.

In 1812 it was used for the production of saltpeter for gunpowder manufacture to aid in the war against the British. It is better known throughout the world than any other single thing in Kentucky. A register now kept at the cave shows names of tourists from all parts of the world.

It was hoped to impress the park inspectors when they were told that the 10,000 acres for parks already acquired and in prospect were the gift of generous people interested in conservation and development. They replied that they had always heard more about Kentucky than any other one state and were fully prepared to believe all that could be told them, judging from the samples that were gliding before their eyes as we rapidly neared Carrollton.

Here where the Kentucky and Ohio rivers meet is a scene of surpassing beauty. Here was Port William, as early as 1792. Here General William W. Butler wrote his poems while resting from his strenuous campaigns of the War of 1812. He had the unique distinction of being a hero of both the River Raisin and the Battle of New Orleans. Here he lived in the low, sturdy brick house overlooking the Ohio River and, listening to the song of each boatman who rowed down the wide expanse of shining water, wrote those rhythmic lines:

"O, boatman, blow that horn again,
For never did the listening air
Upon its lambent bosom bear
So wild, so soft, so sweet a strain."

Here at the confluence of the Kentucky and Ohio rivers, where the "bright waters meet," we looked upward and onward to the sweep of the glorious hills that finally hem in the wide view of river and valley where nestled many homes, chief of which were those of the "gallant Butlers" whose deeds adorned the pages of Revolutionary history.

Much as they had seemed to respond to my rhapsodies on the bluegrass pastures, I soon saw that the hills and the rugged picturesque breaks of the river bluffs, with the possibility of a lake and bird sanctuary, made by far the deeper impression. Here the possibilities of a real park burst upon them and I thought that this view and location had sold itself to them at once. Or was it only their innate politeness that made them praise the location of Butler Park? For, in the last analysis, these inspectors must "sign on the dotted line" before the government would send workers to develop our sites.

As we were approaching the town, I knew all the board would be waiting for us, for one thing we need never doubt and that is Kentucky hospitality. I was reminded of one summer in Switzerland when my boy and I were exercising our memory of Latin, by holding our hands in the icy waters of the River Arr to see which had the more endurance. We were just starting to climb to the Mer de Glace, the marvelous glacier at the foot of Mt. Blanc, and met two ladies who were just returning from there. They stopped and one said, "I know you all are from the States." We said, "Yes, and you are from the South by the way you use 'you all.'" Thus do Kentuckians and Southerners foregather the world over.

Meanwhile we crossed the Kentucky River over the new bridge of stone and steel, one of those built out of the nine million dollars secured in New York by me when State Treasurer, as told in a previous chapter. As surmised, my local advisory board was waiting for us at the Gypsy Grill, where every courtesy was shown the visitors who were impatient to be viewing the grounds.[3] The board members suggested that we women stay while the men went over the ground. I took occasion to tell Mr. Adcock privately that the points to be stressed were the hills, the river, and the view.

The men did their part well, and right here we may say that the women in this, as in all other park matters, did their full share in bringing about the many improvements we were able to make in the parks in the months following this.

Our dinner was wholly satisfying in every way, and there our inspectors told us exactly what had to be done if we were to have federal aid for Butler Park. Their attitude was such that we felt we had made the opening wedge, and the local members of the Advisory Board sprang to the pen like soldiers springing to their arms, and began to fill in blanks and make applications ready for filing.

Soon after my appointment it had been my care to appoint a State Advisory Board, which grew to the proportion of 1,000 interested citizens. A strong group was appointed in every locality where we had a park, to which were added many other conservationists here and there throughout the state. These proved to be a bulwark of strength whenever they were needed to push any local project. This gradually built up a great park movement unequaled in any state. Indeed, it was the pioneer, and other states copied its organization with good results. It was a means of much publicity as well as a focal point for work when needed. Commissioner Frederick A. Wallis of Paris was elected chairman; Mrs. Ruby Laffoon of Frankfort, vice-chairman; Robert Blair of Corbin, secretary; J.D. Brown of London, treasurer. The first meeting was held at Cumberland Falls, with about 200 people present. One of the first activities was organizing a State Park Advisory Board, as related.[4]

From the Carrollton trip we returned to Frankfort about eleven at night. The hotels were crowded and the inspectors spent the night in my home, where the butler ushered them to their rooms, from which they were called by five o'clock next morning to start on a long day. At Lexington we met John G. Cramer, manager of the Phoenix Hotel, a great worker for conservation, and he painted for them a fine picture of the possibilities of Kentucky as a park center. They told Mr. Cramer they had always heard of Kentucky hospitality and that it had not been exaggerated, that they were having an enjoyable trip where they had expected merely business connections. From their sincere expression we felt that we had sold them on our land of scenic beauty and hospitable charm.

My Advisory Board at Natural Bridge had been phoned to meet us at eight o'clock. With no time to lose we traveled out toward the mountains, where the woodlands and the picturesque setting of Kentucky's Natural Bridge spoke for itself, although we were not lacking in fine local members of the board to press its claims. From there we went by the way of the Old Wilderness Road, almost in sight of Pine Mountain, to Cumberland Falls, which we reached by noon, having stopped at Wilbur Hotel in Corbin where we were met by Robert Blair and Colonel Robert Heath, the mayor, and other members of the local advisory board, and had lunch. Again all details of applications were explained and they got busy in meeting the requirements. I took the papers, all signed, back to Frankfort, where the Governor added his signature and they were in the mail for Washington by the time the inspectors arrived in Nashville, their next destination.

The mere mention of Cumberland Falls brings to mind the valiant soldier of the pen whose blows for conservation in Kentucky have equaled any ever struck by the sword of doughty knight of old. Cumberland Falls and the pen of Tom Wallace fought the battle for conservation until many citizens were enlisted under his banner and the fight became general. He worked by day and night for every cause connected with saving the beauties of roadsides and of Kentucky's scenery in general and of Cumberland Falls in particular. One of the two moonbows to be seen in the whole world appears here on nights when the moon is full; and as long as the moon beams and the waters flow and the sixty-eight foot plunge of silvery water flashes, Cumberland Falls will be a silent memorial to the work done by Mr. Wallace in arousing the people of Kentucky to preserve the priceless heritage of beauty and charm.

The principal projects developed during the administration of Governor Ruby Laffoon and during my term as Park Commissioner were, at Butler Park, open shelter house, enclosed shelter house, custodian's lodge, thirty-acre lake with bird sanctuary and historic Butler mansion restored as a museum; at Pine Mountain Park, entrance landscaping on a large scale and beautiful development of the grounds where the Mountain Laurel Festival is held each year, custodian's lodge, a shelter house, and one mile of trails; at Natural Bridge, Hemlock Lodge remodeled and bridge built over the river and ravine, also custodian's lodge and shelter house; at Cumberland Falls, building cabins and furnishing them, remodeling Moonbow Inn, building duPont Lodge, and the highway completed leading from Corbin to the Falls;

at Levi Jackson Park, establishment of Early American Museum, road, gatehouse, lookout tower, trailside shelter, cabins, and custodian's house; at Blue Licks, digging well for Blue Licks water, building of new museum, remodeling of old museum, a custodian's bungalow, open-air auditorium capable of seating five hundred people, and the building of a road known as Buffalo Trail through the park; at Harrodsburg, the Cenotaph to Kentucky's unknown pioneers, the original idea of Governor Ruby Laffoon, two brick cottages at entrance and Mansion Museum remodeled and brought up to date with modern conveniences; at Columbus-Belmont, remodeling of dispensary and restoration of trenches and earth fortifications, two stone lookout houses on the bluff and extensive parking places, with a two-room log house approximating old-time slave quarters; at Audubon Memorial Park, the land secured, buildings erected, a lookout tower, shelter house, replica of Audubon mill planned, and one of the most ambitious projects in the park system — the Audubon Museum — planned, contracts made, and partly constructed; at Dawson Springs, land acquired, cleaned off, camp established, plans made for a lake, and a vitally interested group selected for local Advisory Board. At Mulkey Meetinghouse and Thomas Walker Park little was done at this time. At all the others wherever building was done, all modern conveniences such as lights, heat, pure drinking water, and sewerage, were installed. In landscaping at all places there were miles of trails made, parking places and roads built, in fact all the necessary details of progressive park systems were installed. Many trees and much shrubbery were planted in all the areas developed.

After the visit of the inspectors from the Department of Interior and their bird's-eye view of some of the sites where we wished aid for development, there followed a period of great suspense while we waited with what patience we could muster for a reply to our applications. Finally a telegram came saying that Kentucky parks had been accepted and that an inspector would be sent to make plans for Civilian Conservation Corps (C.C.C.) Camps that would supply the labor necessary to open up certain parks that met the requirements of acreage and situation.

Upon receipt of this, the good news was conveyed to the park advisory boards immediately, and there was great rejoicing throughout the state when it was known that our parks would soon be under development, and that this would be supervised by experts. While awaiting further orders from the Department, we consulted with the late Dean Paul Anderson of the Engineering Department of the University of Kentucky in regard to placing some of his best engineering pupils on these jobs, while we turned to Colonel Richard Lieber of Indianapolis and to Major William Welch, an ex-Kentuckian now in charge of the Palisades of the Hudson, New York, who are noted authorities on park work, to assist us in getting trained park superintendents.

By making these arrangements ahead of time, as soon as we had orders from Washington we were ready to start the wheels of park development rolling with no lost motion. Our park advisory boards at every park were all alert and ready for action at any moment. By this time we had secured an office in the Old Capitol Building in North Frankfort with furniture enough to be comfortable, and all was ready for conferences and orders. And then a long telegram came announcing plans. This was followed by a National Park Inspector, who assisted the State Park Director in putting the machinery for park development into running gear and getting it into operation. We were determined to carry out all the orders from the government to the letter, and in this we had constant cooperation from the State Board and the local groups. All were determined to use the means at our disposal to make Kentucky and her parks a Mecca for tourists. In this there was much friendly emulation, for each locality naturally pushed its own interests.

All preparations were completed for the C.C.C. Camps in the parks to which they had been assigned. At the head of this great caravan of youth was Robert Fechner of the Department of Interior, to whom the state owes a debt of gratitude for his program of using young men to assist our park authorities to develop Kentucky's state parks, as part of the great progressive program planned by President Franklin D. Roosevelt to hasten general recovery from the Depression. Colonel Conrad Wirth, assistant National Park Director, and Colonel Herbert Everson of the Department of Interior, were at the head of the projects in Kentucky, and they told us that our interest, enthusiasm, and organization made them a little partial to Kentucky.

The work done by these C.C.C. boys was directed by superintendents and foremen appointed for that purpose. The camp enrollees were turned over to them each morning by the army officers in charge and turned back by them each evening. Strict discipline was maintained but ample provision was made for recreation and wholesome pleasure.

It was early in 1933 that the national government inaugurated the Emergency Conservation Work program with the Civilian Conservation Corps, and at the same time appropriated funds necessary to operate all the seven camps needed at that time by Kentucky parks to be developed under the Department of Interior. Whatever may be thought of the various relief agencies, those established for the boys and for transients were God-given, for both were directly benefited; and for communities whose citizens were thus furnished with work and training in all useful activities, especially those carried on out of doors.

Depression had shadowed many families where the main dependence was on the growing children to whom there was no avenue of usefulness or training open. One was reminded of the hard times of the Middle Ages. Boys were roaming from place to place, without employment and rapidly deteriorating in morale, when not actively getting entangled in more or less criminal activities. Here in camps they were put under discipline, given good food, furnished with good clothing, and trained to various forms of useful labor. They had abundance of fresh aid and sunshine, work that did not tax them too much, and employment for mind and body during the formative years of their lives. There is no arithmetic adequate to calculate the immense amount of good accomplished by this agency. In addition to material benefits there is no doubt that thousands of boys had their eyes opened to the beauties of nature and were convinced of the dignity of labor.

One of the very first camps installed was at Natural Bridge in Powell and Wolfe counties, where 1,127 acres of rugged hills, clothed with magnificent forest, awaited development. Just in these wilds the three branches of the Kentucky River start on their winding, tortuous course, the hills gradually giving way to grand cliffs as imposing as the far-famed Palisades of the Hudson, making altogether a scene of grandeur unsurpassed. The central formation from which this park area takes its name is the great stone bridge or reddish rock, relic of Paleozoic times, known as Natural Bridge.

This park area was presented to the state by the Louisville and Nashville Railroad Company. Improvements include a water and sewerage system, custodian's lodge, picnic areas, three beautiful shelter houses, while trails that lead up and around the mountain sides have been improved so that ascent and exploration of the grounds is comparatively easy. The bridge built from the highway to the entrance of the park makes the rustic hotel easy to approach.

The advantage to the C.C.C. boys from trained work and regu-

lar discipline in a park of such surpassing beauty cannot be overesti-
mated. Perhaps the great gain to the state through this development is
far overbalanced by the gain in manhood and civic pride fostered by
this work so conducted.

Two C.C.C. Camps were stationed at Cumberland Falls Park,
which lies in Whitley and McCreary counties about eighteen miles
from Corbin and Williamsburg. This park is a veritable paradise of
over five hundred acres of virgin forests, with mountains, rushing
streams, and the mighty cataract that gives its names to the area and is
known wherever nature lovers foregather as "Kentucky's Niagara."
Besides this central feature there are other points of scarcely less interest and beauty: Lover's Leap, Natural Bridge, the High Bluffs, and
Little Eagle Falls.

This virgin forest with its famous waterfall was a generous
gift of Senator Coleman F. duPont, a native of Muhlenberg County.
His family had owned some thousands of acres of granted land in Kentucky as early as 1785. The mere statement of this fact brings to mind
how all native Kentuckians love Kentucky and how eager they are
when it is possible to give to their own state the best.

The interest of the family did not cease with the gift of the
grounds. Mrs. duPont later invited me when in Washington, D.C., to
visit her in Wilmington to discuss some of the park plans. At the time
we had the lodge at Cumberland Falls about ready for furnishing and it
was suggested that the board name it duPont Lodge. Mrs. duPont told
me that she and all the family appreciated very much the honor that
had been given to the name. My reply was that Kentucky was honored
by the gift of the park and could do no less than to express some small
measure of appreciation by naming the lodge for the princely donor of
this great park domain.

All that the development at Cumberland Falls at that time cost
the state of Kentucky was about $8,000, which was saved from the
park budget; and in addition the army gave us the lumber used in two
buildings that had housed the camps. The army was repaid by the labor
of Works Progress Administration (W.P.A.) workers under the state
contractor in removing other buildings. Every penny allotted by the
federal government was well spent in the park improvements (at that
time this amounted to about $81,000), which will remain for many
years an asset to the state and its citizens, well worth all the money
spent.

National Park authorities held annual conventions each year, and among these conservationists were the park directors of the various states. I found that as Secretary of State and Treasurer such conventions had been very helpful. Those held by park-minded people proved to be even more so, as in this office there was added to method of work and detail of systems an impetus to thought and action that passed from one to another of those interested in preserving nature and in making nature in the fullest sense serve mankind through ages to come. There was inspiration in the thought that destruction of great natural resources could be halted and these resources harnessed to serve the purposes of millions yet unborn instead of being regularly and ruthlessly destroyed by ignorant exploitation of one generation.

The first of these conventions attended was in Washington, D.C., soon after the forces sent out under the direction of the Department of Interior had been set to work to develop the parks of Kentucky. It was fine that one could meet with the heads of departments who were directly interested in doing the work that was so vital to one's own state. Exchange of thoughts, ideas, and plans proved profitable in the extreme. One learned that practical work was being developed through the application of ideals and dreams. One gained a new conception of what government could be when all its forces might be devoted to building up instead of tearing down. It was well worth being an active member and paying dues out of one's own pocket to gain the wide vision and the applied knowledge that was displayed by the speakers and workers who had gathered in convention. This has always been found to be true.

At that time no state made a stronger appeal for development than Kentucky, and its appeals were heard and the ideas we were working out seemed to be popular with all the various states and their representatives.

The parks around the Capital City of the United States were visited, and we saw there evidence of the great desirability of parks close to any city. A vision came to us that in the growth of our great nation, cities would come closer together, would fill up with people, would need breathing space, and the feeling grew that wisdom would be shown if we were prepared with wide open spaces as our country became more populated, so that our people would not lose contact with nature.

Another thrilling convention was held at Minneapolis, Minnesota. Here forty states were represented and Kentucky had four delegates: the Park Director; Tom Wallace, Editor of the Louisville Times;

and two of the park superintendents. Minnesota is a land of parks and lakes, beautiful in the extreme and a contrast to Kentucky in many ways.

When the business sessions ended and we had determined to do all in our power to serve our various states through park development and the conservation of our God-given natural resources, we had other treats in store. It was announced that we would visit the great Douglas Park near the Canadian border, where we would see the real source of the mighty Mississippi River. Lake Itasca! Was there really a lake of that name, and did it flow on into a mighty river that gathered force and power as it swept along through miles of lowlands into the great state of Louisiana where it was swept into the Gulf of Mexico?

In Douglas Park, where many thousand acres have been set aside, is Lake Itasca, nestled in a forest of white birch. We landed there after dark, but in time for dinner. We found a delightful Northern meal awaiting us and spent the evening around a fire of birch logs, talking, telling jokes, exchanging ideas, while now and then one could stroll out under the moon to view the lake as it gleamed like silver. Here was the home of the beaver who cuts his house from the fallen timbers and weaves his hut unlike that of any other animal.

Next day it was a treat to row on the bosom of the lake, travel the short distance to the spring that is the source of the great body of water, a spring that one might leap across, which gathers force until at St. Paul it has enlarged to a lovely stream and as it hurries on through the Southland carries on its broad bosom the fat of an empire. One recalled all the early history of Kentucky, when the fate of the new state depended on the commerce carried on the Mississippi River, and the destiny that made its length the possession of the United States, through the statesmanship of Jefferson and his co-workers.

Soon we broke camp at Douglas Lodge and made for Duluth, leaving that lovely city shortly thereafter and boarding a fast train for Chicago and back to Frankfort, where the C.C.C. and transient camps were fully in operation and forests were being conquered, buildings erected, and parks turned into playgrounds for the nation.

Back at my office, with fresh inspiration, I turned to the great task again with renewed energy. There were other conventions during my term, but none of them as inspiring as this one had been. Work was the order of every day and visits daily to the parks were necessary. Many conferences with contractors, builders, and superintendents took up every available moment. One day was like another, yet each brought

new problems and each added its small quota of achievement as our plans took visible shape and form.

A C.C.C. Camp was pitched at Pine Mountain, overlooking Pineville in Bell County, where 2,500 acres had been donated by the citizens of that county in 1928. Here history and romance vie with sheer beauty and variety of landscape for interest. Clear Creek winds through sixty acres of lowland. The crest of Pine Mountain towers more than 2,200 feet above sea level. Ravines and springs abound and the forested hills call to the hardy hiker. This was the first park set aside in Kentucky. Originally called Cumberland, the name was changed to Pine Mountain because of the similarity to Cumberland Falls. It was here that Dr. Thomas Walker of Virginia established his first camp while exploring Kentucky, long before the days of Daniel Boone.

The boys who were in camp had all this glory of nature surrounding them as they cut out many miles of trails and made a road to the pinnacle, from which may be seen one of the most enchanting views in the whole Appalachian system. Here they landscaped, built ovens and seats for campers and picnickers. They constructed a suitable entrance, built three attractive shelter houses with large open fireplaces, also a custodian's lodge. The most useful and beautiful work done there was the arranging of the natural amphitheater for the Mountain Laurel Festival which is held annually in a perfect setting, with its background of rhododendron and mountain laurel, its winding brooks and carpet of green grass. Here in the center of the park the Governor of the Commonwealth crowns the college girl selected as the most beautiful, while the laurel is in full bloom.

At the same time, the Levi Jackson Wilderness Road State Park with 350 acres had a C.C.C. Camp with 200 enrollees. At one time their splendid work entitled them to be the blue-ribbon camp. This park is located about two miles from London. Levi Jackson, to whom this land was granted, was a Revolutionary soldier, and his body rests in a graveyard within the park. G.D. Jackson and Miss Ella Jackson, his grandchildren, gave part of the land, while citizens bought part of it. Besides the usual improvements of shelter houses, roads, and similar projects, a bridge across Laurel River was constructed and a fence built around most of the acreage.

Another park developed by the National Park Service was Butler Memorial State Park, where 200 enrollees were employed in projects which included the usual picnic grounds, two shelter houses,

modern conveniences, and the restoration of the historic Butler home as a museum. These grounds had been deforested, as they had long been under cultivation, so the tasks for the camp boys included planting some 30,000 native trees and many shrubs. The glory of this park is the thirty-acre lake, which called for expert planning by engineers. It extends on both sides of the road within the park and is a bird sanctuary of which the feathered songsters have taken early advantage.

Butler Park is the only state park in Northern Kentucky, and on the other extreme, to the west, is Columbus-Belmont Memorial State Park, which vies with Butler in its historic associations. Columbus-Belmont brings to mind memories of the War Between the States, and it is a memorial of that time. Within its 300 acres was fought the battle of Belmont, and the earth fortifications have been partially restored, while there are a number of relics directly connected with those days. In addition to the usual improvements, there is an old dispensary used in the 1860s, which we restored, the plan being then to use it as a Confederate museum. A blockhouse built here in 1780 and the selection of this spot in 1820-21 as a probable seat of national government add interest to its history. The development by C.C.C. boys links the earliest history of our country with the later.

The Blue Licks Battlefield State Park takes us back to the Revolutionary War, for it was here on this thirty-seven acres of hallowed ground that there was fought the last battle of the Revolution, August 19, 1782, after peace had been declared in the east, and here rest the bones of those heroes. The British and Indians made a last onslaught on the Kentucky settlers and, led by the impetuous Hugh McGary, "the flower of Kentucky manhood fell."

A book might be written on the historic value of this park and on the valiant work done in its development. The acreage was not sufficient to meet the requirements of the Department of Interior, and so we sought other means of financing the needed work. We could not get a C.C.C. Camp, but we had a friend who secured an appropriation from the state Legislature for the development of Blue Licks. This was William Curtis, custodian of the park, who has given his life-long service to its care and to the collection of relics connected with it. He resigned as custodian and was elected to the state Legislature, where he devoted his time and effort to the passage of a bill appropriating $22,500 for the purpose of improving Blue Licks.

Then Judge Samuel M. Wilson of Lexington, noted authority on Kentucky history, and Judge Ennis Ross of nearby Carlisle, with

Mr. Curtis, aided in securing the location of a transient camp which, for our purposes, was even better than a C.C. C. Camp. These transient camps sheltered many fine workmen who had been thrown out of jobs by the Depression, and Blue Licks received the aid of more of these than any other park or project.

It was almost a miracle that so much was done with this money, the enrollees of the camp, and the splendid contractor who was sent to us providentially, William Snyder of Louisville. Our architects, Messrs. Frankel and Curtis of Lexington, planned the new museum and the repairs to the old museum. The open-air auditorium seats 500 people; the modern bungalow constructed for the custodian is complete in every respect, and all the walks, trails, and parking spaces were constructed in record time. Competent critics have valued the museum at $50,000.[5]

We might mention the historic road that leads by the park. This is part of the old Zanesville, Lexington, Nashville, Florence Highway, and every step of it has been bathed in blood and watered with tears. It is said that it is the "Road that cost Henry Clay the Presidency," for he was responsible for its building and expected Andrew Jackson to see that it was extended through Nashville. Jackson was against all "internal improvements" and refused to do anything about it, fought Clay for his extravagance, with the result that Clay was defeated by a movement which he had expected to add to his popularity.[6]

Pioneer Memorial Park at Harrodsburg has had the benefit of wide interest far beyond the limits of the state. The first of those who helped to make the park a center of interest without peer was the Pioneer Memorial Association, organized by Harrodsburg citizens under the leadership of the late James L. Isenberg, Mac D. Hutton, editor of the Harrodsburg Herald, and Dr. C.B. Van Arsdall. These gentlemen were instant in season and out of season in everything that would advance the park project in any way. This organization reproduced the old fort with fidelity and painstaking care. It had gifts from many individuals and organizations.

While the park was not large enough in acreage to be included in the work of the C.C.C. Camps, it was possible to obtain relief workers under the supervision of the superintendent who was paid by the state. About $4,000 was saved in this way, as the state only paid for materials and furnished the superintendent.

To the Historical Society, aided by Mr. Isenberg, Mr. Hutton, and Mrs. James Darnell, belongs the distinction of soliciting and obtaining federal funds for the magnificent memorial designed and made by Ulric H. Ellerhusen, sculptor, with General George Rogers Clark as the central figure. Ground was broken for this memorial on June 16, 1932, and it was dedicated November 16, 1934, in the presence of 60,000 people, by President Franklin D. Roosevelt, and formally accepted by Governor Ruby Laffoon.

The Cenotaph to Kentucky's unknown pioneers, the thought of which had originated with Governor Laffoon and for which the Board of Public Property had appropriated $2,700, was dedicated at the same time as the memorial. It was unveiled by me, as Park Director, and Mrs. Ruby Laffoon placed a wreath in memory of those whom it was designed to honor. The Marriage Temple to the memory of Lincoln's parents was the gift of Mrs. Edmund Burke Ball of Muncie, Indiana. The National Society of Colonial Dames of America and the Society of Colonial Wars (Kentucky chapters) erected the artistic Colonial Gateway and planted trees and shrubbery. The Clark Marker was erected and dedicated by the Harrodsburg Woman's Club. The McAfee Stile into the pioneer cemetery was built by the McAfee Clan. Descendants of the four Bowman brothers of pioneer fame raised the stately Bowman Gateway as a north entrance. The Daughters of the American Revolution dedicated a sacred spot adjoining Old Fort Hill Cemetery as "Memorial Acre" and raised a bronze tablet there.

With all the work obtained from the Department of Interior going at full speed in the various parks, my thoughts turned again to Henderson, where some years before a vision had come to me that there on the rolling hills above the Ohio River, just before they widen out into the fertile valleys of Henderson County, was a wonderful location for a park, while ready to hand was the memory of one who was worthy of the honor of the name. Henderson had pointed with pride to the name of John James Audubon, who had made that city his home and from there had begun many of his trips into the wilderness to study the birds of America and revel in all the wild glory of nature in the wilderness.

For some time, western Kentucky had talked of having a park located within its confines, and some citizens of Henderson were alive to the possibilities there. Miss Susan Towles, librarian of the Carnegie Library, had given much time and attention to collecting all data connected with Audubon and especially to securing pictures of his birds. Her library was regarded as a fountainhead of information, and when this movement for Audubon Memorial State Park got under way we

164

had a source of accurate information and unflagging interest on which we could depend, as plans went forward, to make the memory of America's naturalist into a tangible thing.

After I had told my vision to Mrs. Ben Niles, she collected sufficient nerve and courage and appeared before the mayor of Henderson and the council with a proposition that steps be taken to obtain land and locate a park near the city which would appropriately bear the honored name of Audubon. Henderson people were always responsive to any mention of Audubon and had named a suburb for him, but the matter of buying land and putting out good money to develop it seemed to the practical minds of the men nothing more than an airy vision, the "fabric of a dream." As gallant Kentuckians, the men of the council were kind and polite, and with soft words and general interest in such beautiful thoughts of womankind, they turned from the subject to consideration of such practical matters as bonds, sewerage, street paving, and so on.

While they were either dismissing the thought or considering how visionary women are, the women themselves awoke and began to work. Mrs. N. Powell Taylor; Mrs. Leigh Harris, wife of the editor; and Mrs. Lee Hurley, wife of the mayor, were added to our coterie of park dreamers.

Having, so to speak, exploded a bomb in the City Council, these Henderson women turned to more feminine methods of attack. Some had called the whole thing a "wildcat" plan, some had even referred to the valiant band as "Amazonians." The only real enemy of this forward-looking plan was indifference, and these Amazonians determined to enter that camp by "dressing up and giving a party." This they proceeded to do, sent out invitations to a banquet at the hotel, stating that it was in the interest of a projected park for Henderson. Now, the enemy to whom we give the name of Indifference is never averse to "talking it over" or to eating a good dinner and listening to flowery speeches.

The invitations were accepted. The Park Director was invited, just as if the whole thing were a surprise to her. The First Lady of Kentucky, Mrs. Ruby Laffoon, accepted, and her expected presence swelled the number of acceptances. We from Frankfort were entertained in the hospitable home of Mr. and Mrs. Taylor. That night we all gathered at the banquet table at the hotel, where the viands were fully up to expectations. Dinner over, the speechmaking began. The mayor of the city was the toastmaster. He first presented Mrs. Laffoon, who in well chosen words spoke of the need of parks in western Kentucky and her own interest in the location, as she herself by birth and heritage was a native of the Pennyrile and the Purchase. She graciously emphasized the fact that now was the time to get aid from the Department of Interior and that those who first applied would be given preference, as had been shown by the developments going on at a rapid rate in northern and eastern Kentucky park areas.

Then the Park Director was presented, and she was ready with very practical ideas which she had gained by long hours of labor devoted to the very kind of development sought by the Henderson women. She stated that it was necessary to work fast if western Kentucky was to get any benefit from the workers being placed by the federal authorities. She stressed the beautiful location for a park at Henderson, the name of Audubon waiting to be used in the locality where he had spent much of his younger days, and so on.

Added to this was a strong appeal for some concerted action. This "down to business" attitude rather took the gentlemen present by storm. They had come prepared to listen to pretty speeches and to say nice things about this intangible dream.

Here they were asked to do something about a situation and do it quickly. Among the objections brought forward, a little timorously, were the bald facts that Henderson had not an acre of land nor a cent of money as a nucleus.

Mindful of Edgar Guest's little monitor, "It can be done," the Park Director proceeded to appoint committees just as if all had been decided upon. Some of the bolder gentlemen spoke up and repeated the well-known fact of no acreage, no money, and said, "Mrs. Cromwell, how can we get anywhere with nothing to start with?"

My reply was, "I hope that no citizen of Henderson will refuse to work on a committee to do what we can," adding, "The possibilities are here. I wish you might see what has been accomplished in other places with not as good locations nor as prosperous communities."

To this the reply was "depression," that hateful word we had heard so much. To that there was a potent reply that this was general and that it was due to this slump in business conditions that the government was furnishing workers and as much money as possible to develop various projects to help the unemployed and the communities.

In short, there was not so very much opposition, but what there was carried a threat of defeatism which was a challenge by the women interested.

The committees named really got busy next morning.[7] With such quick response by patriotic citizens it was possible very soon to have a C.C.C. Camp with a trained park superintendent and eight technically trained foremen. There was no better regulated camp under our supervision. The speed with which this was accomplished constitutes a record: three days for the deeds to be filed and application papers to be on the way to Washington. Ben Niles appealed to Senator Barkley, and as I had gone on to Warsaw, Kentucky, called me to be in Louisville by eight o'clock the next morning. Suffice it to say I was there on time, and within a few hours the air mail carried everything necessary to the Department of Interior.

Leigh Harris in his paper gave an account of the neighborly scene that was enacted when these two hundred boys came to their camp in the park to begin its development. That the camp was named "Camp Cromwell" gave an added spice, if any was needed, to heighten the deep satisfaction of seeing a dream come to life and begin to bless other lives by useful work provided, by beauty made a common possession of all citizens, by pride of name and place being built into the very soil of our beloved Kentucky.

These boys had the satisfaction of developing a spot naturally beautiful into a place of surpassing charm that combined the woodsy solitude of Audubon's wilderness with the sophistication of highly socialized French life. For it was decided that the central museum building would take the form of a French chateau, which was contracted for and begun before my term as Park Director ended. Audubon was a Frenchman, and so was the architect of this beautiful building, Mr. Corley of Washington. Something of the mystery that always surrounded the great naturalist survives in these woods where he was once so carefree and happy in his chosen work.

Among the improvements at Audubon Park were a water system, a sewerage system approved by the state Board of Health, a light plant, miles of foot and bridle paths, parking spaces, picnic areas, two beautiful shelter houses, all with modern conveniences. A lookout tower was built and replica of Audubon Mill, and a custodian's lodge and a lake were planned.

One of the most important memorials added to the state park system during Governor Laffoon's administration was the Dr. Ephraim McDowell and Jane Crawford Memorial at Danville, which was turned over to the state by the State Medical Association. Dr. Irvin Abell, then president of the association, worked with the Park Director, and we were successful in buying the home where Dr. McDowell performed one of the most outstanding operations in history.[8] It was through the generosity of the Misses Emma and Lucy Weisiger, the owners of the old homestead building, that we were able to buy it. They graciously donated $10,000 toward the purchase, and the medical association paid ten thousand. The deed was made to the state, an architect drew plans for the remodeling, the contract was let, and work was started. It is being restored as it was and will be furnished in keeping with Dr. McDowell's day.

Someone heard me speaking on the beauty and variety of the state parks about this time and asked the very pertinent question, "Mrs. Cromwell, which is your pet park?"

My reply was that this was not a fair question, but would answer it frankly with the statement: "My pet park is the one where I am working when the question is asked."

There was a great measure of truth in this, for at each place the beauty and utility of its location, the appeal of its charm, and the pride in seeing its development would override for the time thoughts of others. Always the one where I was working seemed to me the best.

Of the many Governors of Kentucky, only four have been Republicans.[9] All of the Governors have been native Kentuckians or Virginia-born in the early days, gallant, chivalrous, and hospitable. When the Republican Governors were in power, they, like our old friend Andrew Jackson, believed in dividing the political pie among their own workers. Likewise, the Democrats indulged in the same practice. Even within the party a change of Governors always brings changes in policy and in appointments.

Reorganization of Kentucky's government had been talked of for many years. When Governor A.B. Chandler succeeded Governor Laffoon, one of his first acts was to get through the Legislature a reorganization bill, designed to fit Kentucky into the picture of modern progress. This called for rearrangement in all departments, a Herculean task.

The state park system was one greatly affected by this reorganization. A new director was appointed, who immediately took charge. General Bailey P. Wootton of Hazard, who had just retired as Attorney General, was chosen to carry on the work of the parks and make it coordinate with the other departments of government.

It was a severe wrench to think of missing the visits to the camps, the day-by-day improvements that it had been my duty to note, and the separation from the many fine people who had worked with me and for me as the parks became more what we dreamed they should be.

But when that time came and Mr. Wootton was appointed, I could say this to him with a clear conscience, "I have enjoyed this work and turn it over to you as the fruit of my best effort. If at any time I can assist in any way in this great and worthy task of developing Kentucky's great heritage of state parks, do not hesitate to call on me for suggestions or for work. It will be a pleasure to continue my interest in such a worthwhile undertaking."

Chapter VII Notes

1. This is now known as Old Fort Harrod State Park.

2. This is now General Butler State Resort Park.

3. Members of the advisory board were listed as Frank Adcock, William Atkinson, William Fisher, Mayor H.R. Lorch, E.C. Lee, Miss Ann Gullion, Miss Fredrica Gier, and Miss Gene Howe.

4. The author continued:

"Some of these directors whose names occur to me as unusually enthusiastic workers and boosters were Mrs. Charles Marshall of Shelbyville, Mrs. Brutus Clay and Mrs. Hattie Buchanan of Richmond, Mrs. Samuel Wilson and Mrs. Preston Johnson of Lexington, and Mrs. Cassius Clay of Auvergne, Paris (Kentucky)."

5. The author continued:

"In addition to the fine and loyal friends mentioned, there was Reed Wilson, now mayor of Lexington, who cooperated in every way. Citizens of Maysville, Mt. Olivet, Flemingsburg, and Carlisle took the deepest interest in all the developments at Blue Licks. The late Judge A.M.J. Cochran was always a loyal and dependable friend. He had an ancestor buried on the hill with the others who fell there so long ago. The Daughters of the American Revolution have taken the greatest pride in all our achievements at this park. Just before the museum was finally finished, the state meeting of the Kentucky Chapter in session at Lexington adjourned to spend a day there as the guests of the citizens of Robertson, Nicholas, and Mason counties, and the Park Director. Among the distinguished visitors that day were Mrs. Ed Norris, widow of the late Governor of Montana, her sister, Mrs. Herbert McPherson of Hopkinsville, and Frank Dunn of Lexington, who is a great leader in all historical projects. This was one of the most pleasant and profitable days of my regime as Park Director."

6. The author reported that digging a well in an effort to find "the famous Blue Licks medicinal water" caused her great anxiety. The water originated from a spring that would disappear and reappear at different places and had been "lost" for several years. A contractor was paid $500 to dig the well, with no result, at which point Mrs. Cromwell felt compelled to report the situation to the Governor. She followed his advice to go a bit further and the water thus found was piped throughout the park grounds. She added: "While I was Park Director this water, as well as the drinking water in all the other

parks, was tested monthly by the State Board of Health."

7. Mrs. Cromwell continued:

"The first one on location was composed of Mr. and Mrs. N. Powell Taylor, Mr. and Mrs. Leigh Harris, Mayor and Mrs. Hurley, Mrs. Laffoon, and myself. We proceeded to start the survey at nine o'clock in the morning. The second committee was the Acreage Committee, composed of William Stites, Ben Niles, Leigh Harris, with N. Powell Taylor as legal adviser, for it was necessary to have three hundred acres in order to obtain federal benefits.

"These two committees spent the next morning exploring the Wolf Hills. Those visited by the committee in regard to the land were exceptionally generous. David Clark gave a hundred acres which he had already set apart as a bird sanctuary. Colonel Alex Major followed with another 100 acres which had been the pioneer home of the Majors. Henry P. Barrett and his sister, Mrs. Susan Gant, gave another splendid grant of wooded land, and deeds were soon forthcoming, all being completed by October 3, 1934."

8. Dr. McDowell performed an ovariotomy on Christmas Day, 1809, removing a large cystic ovarian tumor weighing more than 20 pounds from Mrs. Crawford's abdomen. The surgery was performed long before the use of anesthetics or aseptic techniques.

9. Kentucky has had seven Republican governors to date, the last being Louie Nunn, who won election in 1967.

VIII

Library and Archives

The world's a stage on which all parts are played.

Which would you rather not be: a person in the wilderness without ax or gun, or yourself today without education or any of the acquired intellectual tools for getting on? The pioneer virtues of courage and common sense are no longer enough; every day we are faced with problems which native intelligence alone cannot meet. That is why every rural community, village, town, and city in the land not only needs but must provide the means for both formal education and informal, continuing education — must have adequate schools and libraries.

A library is a collection of books, and it is much more than that. The books that people buy and read or place in libraries for public use reflect the taste and culture of the individuals and the people generally. In turn the library influences the young and old alike and molds public opinion.

In early times there were two types of libraries: one of a religious character in the temples, the other consisting of records of the governments, or archives. Records cut on stone or on burned brick or clay were kept by the early peoples of Asia. These now are uncovered by archeologists, and scholars may read and translate for us the daily records of governments that rose and fell long before the time of Christ. Many such records were concerned with tax reports and consist of lists of taxable property, so that we feel a kinship with these long-vanished races who had the same problems of property and government that we have today.

In ancient Egypt, the scribes wrote on clay tablets and later on papyrus, which was extremely durable. Still later the use of prepared sheepskin, or parchment, was common. These books were in rolls and the manuscripts were collected by scholars, cities, and states, just as books and manuscripts are still bought and used. Many of the ancient libraries were burned in the constant wars that raged. We have heard most about the wonderful library at Alexandria, Egypt, that met this fate.

During the Middle Ages great collections of books were common in the large monasteries and abbeys. Monks and nuns alike spent toilsome hours in transcribing records of the church and state and there grew up a great industry in beautifully illuminated and colored manuscripts. Some of these are treasured in great collections to this day.

At first books were kept in closed rooms and taken out to be read, but about the sixth century the monasteries began to have separate book rooms, or libraries. In these the books were chained to desks. Library furniture of that time differed materially from the splendidly arranged and lighted reading rooms of today. From triple desks the library advanced to shelves for the walls. It is only in very recent times that the book stacks and files have been placed away from walls, with proper lighting, reading tables, and all the improved methods that make reading a pleasure.

The British Museum claims to be the most important in the world, and its contents are well arranged and accessible. It has about fifty-five miles of shelves. Its growth has been rapid, for it was begun in 1753, only 186 years ago. Its manuscripts are as important as its printed books. These include the Codex Alexandrines of the Bible, many early charters, and numbers of illuminated manuscripts. The great universities of England also have notable collections of books, each college of Oxford having its separate library. Cathedrals and churches and learned societies have great collections of books, not only in England but in Scotland and Ireland as well.

In England, Andrew Carnegie gave a great impetus to library building, as he did in America. With all the interest in book collecting and in building great libraries for scholars, the use of libraries by the general public was not greatly encouraged until our own time. This is one of the great forward movements we have seen grow by leaps and bounds. It is a matter of pride that the women of the world, and particularly of our own country, have been instrumental in the spread of library interest and the practical side of building and equipping libraries large and small. It is the small library that reaches most people now, and the hope of our nation rests very largely on the reading centers that are near to the community groups of people.

Among the many improvements since 1882 are the decimal method of Melvil Dewey which was part of a real revolution in library methods, library catalogues, card index systems, and open shelf collections. The open shelf is much more common in America than in England.

The first school in the world established solely for the professional training of librarians was started at Columbia College, New York City, in 1887, by Dewey, who was then librarian of the college. Other university centers followed, and now there is a large and active Association of American Library Schools and the requirements are constantly being improved.

The growth of library interest in this country has been steady and for the past fifty years very rapid, especially since 1900; it is said that during this time the larger libraries of the Old World have doubled, and those of North America have trebled in content, and most of this rapid increase has been in the first quarter of the twentieth century, and we may add that this has continued with unabated interest and work during the past decade. There is no question that the number of "library-minded" citizens has trebled and quadrupled during recent years.

In the colonies, at first, the only libraries were private. England took great interest in sending books to the colonies, and Rev. Thomas Bray of London collected and sent libraries. These were religious books but were designed to be read by the general public as well as the clergy. We have always looked to Benjamin Franklin as the promoter of many "first" things, and this is true of subscription libraries as well as other matters. He projected the first one in the colonies in 1731 in Philadelphia. Many public libraries of today owe their beginning to these early subscription libraries.

The nucleus of all our colleges is found in collections of books. Book lovers are unselfish and it is history that they wish to widen the use of libraries, and many such private collections of books exist and are in daily use by students throughout the length and breadth of our land. In our own state the libraries of Transylvania College and the College of the Bible at Lexington are noted. Many rare books and prints there, particularly those relating to medical science, cannot be duplicated. They were brought from Europe at an early day and from the East. Transylvania was the first institution of higher learning west of the Allegheny Mountains, and Kentuckians are proud of the record it has made and the many great men who have studied within its walls. The influence of this fine library doubtless had a great deal to do with

173

shaping the careers of the men who were trained there. Mrs. Charles Norton is in charge of this library and carries on there the great traditions of the past.

Our own University of Kentucky is gathering together rapidly a fine collection of books and has now a splendidly equipped library building as well as a new law library building, and in method and service is second to none. It is reaching out to aid various other agencies that are interested in developing the state. Under the guidance of Mrs. W.T. Lafferty the university offers a unique service to the club women of the state in program making and in outlining work as well as in content of study and constant guidance along lines of local library development. This splendid cooperative movement is bearing fruit in every community.

The Carnegie Library of Lexington has many treasures, the greatest being the practically complete files of the (Kentucke) Gazette beginning about 1790. The Louisville Public Library under the able guidance of Harold Brigham is keeping pace with other libraries of its type in spite of the serious losses suffered in the flood of 1937.

Several mobile library projects are making headway in the state, that of Fayette County being the most prominent at this time.

Philanthropists have found the library field a fertile one for the use of their money to the best advantage. No other philanthropist has equaled Andrew Carnegie in the number and size of gifts to libraries. The total amount of his gifts to the United States and Canada was $43,665,000 between the years of 1890 and 1917, when the library gifts were discontinued. This Scot-born boy who made his fortune in America was the greatest promoter of libraries in the world and gave the greatest impetus to the movement which was just then ripe for development. It is pleasing to think, however, that even Carnegie's munificent gifts have been topped in the aggregate by the thousands of individuals who have given one book, a few books, or many books, to smaller libraries all over the country.

The Library of Congress we might call the national library of the United States. A visit to its many departments reminds one of a beehive, despite the quiet that prevails. This great library was established in 1800 by Congress as a legislative library and, until 1897, was housed in the Capitol. At that time it was moved to its own building, which now is the largest, the most ornate, and the most costly library building in the world. Its principal source of growth is deposits under the copyright law, exchanges of official publications with foreign governments, and Smithsonian exchanges. It extends a service to all other libraries in the country by lending to college, university, state, municipal, and other libraries books they do not possess and cannot obtain elsewhere.

The earliest tax-supported library is supposed to have been the town library established in Salisbury, Connecticut, in 1803. The modern public library has been developed largely since 1850 and, for the most part, has grown up since the formation of the American Library Association in 1876.

After my years of service as Secretary of State, State Treasurer of Kentucky, and Director of our State Park System, my steps were led back to my first love, the library division of government, when on September 1, 1937, Governor A.B. Chandler appointed me as head of those units which are now coordinated under the Reorganization Act, known altogether as State Librarian and Director of Archives, for which appointment I am very grateful. I was immediately sworn in by Chief Justice Alex Ratliff and entered upon my duties at once.

Soon after my appointment, one of my first interests was to try to locate and have returned to the state of Kentucky the original Constitution of Kentucky, the work started when Secretary of State in 1924. To this end correspondence was renewed with the Director of Archives, Mr. Raimey, of the University of Chicago, and he soon wrote that this was among the papers on file there. It was required that we establish the handwriting and signatures of the President of the Convention, Samuel McDowell, and the clerk, Thomas Todd. When this was done, they were more than willing to return the document to its rightful owner. Not a moment was lost until this requirement was met, and in a very short time the long-lost document was in the safe custody of the State Librarian and Director of Archives of Kentucky, where it now reposes and may be seen any time during office hours. Many have looked it over and have expressed themselves as surprised at their own reaction on seeing with their own eyes a document so old and so valuable to Kentuckians. It is quite a different feeling from that one has in reading the same document in print. All praise the beautiful and legible writing, though penned with the goose-quill pen, perhaps made by some schoolmaster, as was often the custom in ye olden days, though schoolmasters were scarce and schoolmarms unheard of at that time.

It is encouraging to research workers that efforts of more than a dozen years before to locate the first Constitution of Kentucky were at last rewarded by finding that priceless document in the library of the University of Chicago, as was suspected when the subject first came to my attention while Secretary of State. It was then, in 1924, that we discovered that this and many other documents, among them original copies of the other Constitutions of Kentucky, were missing from the papers of the Governors rescued from the basement, filed and catalogued, then placed in the Historical Society rooms in the Old Capitol Building.

With the cooperation of Governor Chandler, this precious document was restored to us. Its reclamation makes us all the more certain that the originals of the other three Constitutions — second, third, and fourth — will be found at some future time, and we only hope that it will be our good fortune to help in the discovery. One ponders over such subjects until they become almost an obsession that can only be satisfied by the fulfillment of such wishes and dreams.

The document in question is in the handwriting of Thomas Todd, who was clerk of all the early conventions that led to Kentucky's statehood, and signed by Samuel McDowell, president of the convention. The paper in question has about 100 pages and gives the proceedings of five of the nine conventions held in Danville. Most of these were held in the splendid old "Constitution Building" which is now being taken over as a state shrine. It is proved by this document that some of the meetings were held "at the Presbyterian Meetinghouse adjoining Danville."

A close study of the paper reveals many items of interest. Here at the very first we see the division regarding slavery. The six ministers, led by Father David Rice, together with ten others, voted to insert "gradual" emancipation of slaves. As an echo of this, just before the final vote on the Constitution was taken, George Nicholas had a clause inserted which prohibited any minister of any religious denomination from serving as a member of the Legislature.

The meetings included in the restored document were those of July, 1788; November, 1788; July, 1790, and of the Constitutional Convention which began April 2, 1792. The immense historical value of this original document is unquestioned.

The documents of that day were written on parchment or linen paper with significant watermarks of paper makers who were proud of their work, as they well might be, for this paper is better preserved than much that is ten years old now. The ink, too, was the best quality, albeit ofttimes homemade from oak ball. The goose-quill pens for which the quills were so carefully selected and the nibs so expertly cut by the sharpest of "pen-knives," wrote this and other documents. All these old-fashioned implements of desk use have passed into discard now, but the work of their hands survives who first set the sails for the ship of state that has sailed on and on among her sisters, not the largest nor the least, but to all Kentuckians the best.

After this Constitution of 1792, the state grew so fast and its trade down the Ohio and Mississippi rivers and across the Appalachian Mountains grew so rapidly that many changes were needed. The expanding financial needs of the state — money, credit, banks — all the machinery of modern business, had to be set up, and the rather short first Constitution, worded in general terms, was not sufficient for the growing state.

So on July 22, 1799, a convention to revise the Constitution met at Frankfort and was in session twenty-seven days. The new Constitution was reported August 17th. By its provisions, the Governor and Lieutenant Governor were to be chosen every four years directly by the voters. Before this, they had been chosen by the Legislature every two years. This Constitution went into effect in 1800 and continued to be the basic law of the state for fifty years, until 1849.

By this time, in the middle of the century, there were forty-two counties, and the state had expanded in its interests, commerce, and manufactories to a degree undreamed of by its founders. Railroads had come into their own. Canals were being built in many places, and interstate commerce was fully established. The Age of Steam was in full command of transportation by water and by land. However, there were dull gray clouds rising on the peaceful horizon. Ten years more and the deluge would break. Slavery was one of the important points that was to engage this convention , as it was in the first one nearly sixty years before.

On June 3, 1850, the new revision was given to the state and it remained in force until 1890. On May third of that year, a convention was called to meet in Frankfort, and it gave us the present Constitution. It has had nine amendments, and for some time there has been much agitation for another revision. So far nothing has come of this. The interests of our state have become so diversified, so tied up with those of other states and with the federal government, that our statesmen are rather shy of calling another Constitutional Convention.

In addition to the many references to constitutions, to the many court and legislative records, there is in the keeping of the Archives Department much relating to the various Capitol buildings that have served the state through the years. The temptation is great when one enters on such a subject to expand the interest to include all the great and near-great who have trod these halls, all the shadowy ghosts who have inhabited them for a season and passed on to the realms of shade. The state has outgrown some of its habitations; fire has ravaged others. It is due to give honor to the memory of those who had them in charge that we have yet by far the greater part of all the archives of Kentucky, despite the many forces of destruction that have threatened them. Not the least of the destroyers is the sharp tooth of Old Father Time, relentless, never satisfied, always gnawing. His depredations must be fought by all the modern methods at hand, cleanliness, sanitation, the proper distribution of heat and cold in our buildings, and modern methods of filing and handling historical materials.

The first Constitution, now restored to us, was a great document, but its adoption was only a first step. Setting up a new state government was a harder task. To say how is easy; to do the job in the right way is difficult. But these men were not daunted. They had received permission from Virginia and from the federal government at Philadelphia. Now it was up to them to set up a stable government west of the Alleghenies in the wilderness that then constituted the known West.

June 4, 1792, three days after the state was organized, the Legislature met in a two-story log house in Lexington, then a village with houses built of logs, only one brick house in six. This session lasted twelve days and its members were paid one dollar per day. Governor Isaac Shelby delivered his message orally on June sixth. It is a tradition that the Senate met upstairs and the House downstairs, hence originated the Upper House and the Lower House. On June 15th, the session adjourned to meet on November 5th. On that date it convened in Lexington and on December 22, 1792, adjourned to hold the third session in Frankfort, which had been chosen as the seat of government of the new state by five commissioners, as provided in the new Constitution.

The next session of the Legislature was held in a house interesting to all historians. It was a large frame house on Wapping Street, first owned by General James Wilkinson, then by Andrew Holmes, and afterwards by Major William Love. Aaron Burr stayed there when in Frankfort, and in it was preached the first sermon in Frankfort. The sessions did not meet there long, although the gift of this house was part of the consideration for moving the capital to Frankfort.

The third Capitol, the first permanent one, was occupied by the General Assembly in November, 1794, and was destroyed by fire on November 25, 1813. The fourth Capitol was a rented house while commissioners were seeking ways and means of erecting a new one, which burned in 1824, less than ten years after its completion. In the sixth statehouse, fire again routed the Legislature, which adjourned its sittings to the Methodist meetinghouse on December 12, 1825.

The next statehouse, built of Kentucky River marble, still stands. It was first occupied on December 7, 1829, and is in the form of a Greek temple with a lantern central dome. The outstanding feature of the building is the circular stairway which rises from the first floor to the balcony above on the second floor. Additions of an east and west wing were planned, but only the east wing was built. It is used for offices of various departments.[1] The Legislature and Court of Appeals continued to meet in this Capitol for eighty-one years until in 1910 the present Capitol was ready for occupancy. In 1904, the General Assembly appropriated $1,000,000 for the erection of the present Capitol building, making it the eighth State Capitol. The building was designed by Frank Andrews.

Because an act which was passed by the Legislature of 1936 changes the relationships of the agencies devoted to library development and preservation of records, a resume is here given of the sections relating to our department. The state has long realized the great responsibility that is entailed in furnishing means of culture to adults as well as to the youth. Closely connected with this is the safekeeping of the archives of the state government. Through this reorganization, it is planned to so coordinate all the public means of education that there will be less waste and no overlapping. At the same time, through this means, it is hoped that the scope of school libraries will be widened and that through other agencies the opportunities of education will cover all the period from childhood to extreme age, with every citizen of the Commonwealth having the use of all the means at the command of the state government.

The newly created department includes all the functions heretofore vested in the Kentucky Library Commission, the Library of the Commonwealth, and the State Law Library, and "shall have such charge and custody of all property of the State Historical Society as may be provided by agreement between the said Department and the said Society under the terms of this Act....The Department of Library and Archives shall be composed of a Library Extension Division, a Legislative and Law Library, and the Kentucky Historical Society."[2]

While the year 1829 marks the first establishment of a state library as a separate department, the duties of such office had been performed since 1792 when the state began to function as separate from Virginia, the mother state. For the first twenty-eight years of the Commonwealth, the Secretaries of State had charge of books, archives, and records.

The first State Librarian, therefore, may be said to have been James Brown, appointed by Governor Isaac Shelby on June 5, 1792, as Secretary of State.

By an act approved November 9, 1820, the state library became a separate department, but was kept in charge of the same official, who was at that time Oliver G. Waggoner, under the administration of Governor Gabriel Slaughter. The next custodian of records and librarian was Joseph Cabell Breckinridge, by virtue of his office as Secretary of State.

By an act approved January 2, 1833, the office of State Librarian was created as a separate office. The amount appropriated for the new department was five hundred dollars, and the Librarian was to be selected annually by the Legislature. George A. Robinson, who was the first so elected in 1833, made his first report on January 16, 1834, and was unanimously re-elected February 18, 1834.

Elections continued annually until 1849, when the sessions of the Legislature were made biennial. The State Librarian was then elected every two years until 1904, when the Legislature provided a four-year term which was continued until the Reorganization Act of 1936, at which time the office was made appointive by the Governor and many changes incorporated into the statues regarding the divisions that composed the new department.

The State Librarian is now custodian of all the Legislative Acts, Law Journals, and Reports; in short, all documents of law pertaining to the state government. The materials included in our state libraries contain a vast amount of data which is made available to research workers. The Librarian exchanges these with other states and many of their printed archives are on our shelves, as well as hundreds of volumes of federal archives and documents of various kinds.

The books owned by Kentucky are as varied as possible. There is a large law section which has been collected by the Law Library Committee, composed of the Chief Justice of the Court of appeals and his committee. No change was made in this purchasing committee by the Reorganization Act. There are also rare books, fiction, biography, history, encyclopedias, bound volumes of old newspapers, maps, almanacs, and pamphlets, constituting a variety as wide as the bounds of literature.

In the Law Library, one of the early books of interest to historians as well as to lawyers is the compilation of the first statutes by Littell, in five volumes, which is an abstract of the laws passed during the first years of Kentucky's statehood. This and Hening's Statutes of Virginia are the first source books for Kentucky research workers. Through these the Virginia laws were cited for many years by our courts. Through these Virginia statutes the laws of our state trace their lineage back to 1606, the settlement of Jamestown, and 1612, Virginia's first charter. The laws passed by Virginia Burgesses in 1619, the first elective assembly held in America, were current in Kentucky until each was superseded or replaced by laws passed by our own Legislature.

Added to these old volumes are the Acts passed by the Legislature every two years, together with the ever-increasing number of volumes of decisions of our Court of Appeals and state courts, besides the new laws of other states and of the federal government. Not the least valuable of the constant acquisitions are the Law Journals from the state universities which contain legal articles and essays that are up to the minute, the newest thought and practice of law students, professors, and eminent jurists.

The office of the Librarian and staff is kept in the spacious quarters of the Law Library on the second floor of the new Capitol building.[3] The efficient staff employed to assist me there is composed of Miss Linnie Lewis of Mayfield, Frank Kavanaugh of Frankfort, and Mrs. Sadie Hubbard of Hodgenville.

The director of the Division of Library Extension is Miss Lena Nofcier who is very efficient in this line of work. Of the value of the library movement as exemplified in the Library Extension Division, it is impossible to say too much. Kentucky recognized its state responsibility for library service to the people by the creation of this division on June 13, 1910. Up to that time it had been carried on by the Kentucky Federation of Women's Clubs. It was also sponsored by the Kentucky Library Association.

The movement at that time was more than fourteen years old. It had originated with the Federation as a traveling library project for rural and mountain districts. By 1900, Miss Fannie Rawson, of beloved memory, pioneer worker in this field, reported to that body for the fourth year with a resume of work done, the needs, and the field that awaited development. That year, without state aid, the traveling library had in active circulation fifty libraries, averaging fifty-five volumes to the box, nearly 3,000 volumes. It is due here to say that this worthy achievement was only one of the many started by the Kentucky Federation and afterward entrusted to the state for further development not possible to a volunteer group of women, such as composed the organization. It seems a pity that such forward-looking work as this is buried in minutes and reports and not readily available to the general public.

The members of this body continued their interest and labor until, in 1910, they were able to turn over to the state 5,000 books and 100 wooden traveling library cases.

The Division of Library Extension makes the widest appeal to the average citizen. The lending activities of the division present more tangible evidences of service than the field work, although the latter is more important in the promotion of a statewide program for library development. Reference questions are asked by library trustees, librarians, teachers, club women, P.T.A. members, homemakers' clubs, students, artists, ministers, lawyers, businessmen, and individuals from practically every walk of life.

The Kentucky Historical Society was established by incorporating act on February 19, 1880, to collect and preserve Kentucky history and historic relics and books, receive donations, and make known the state's advantages, and increase knowledge of its resources on behalf of the state. It was given designated quarters in the Old Capitol Building. Early in 1920, the Sinking Fund Commission assigned the Old Capitol to the society, and its expanding possessions have almost filled these quarters.

Back in the 1890s, when the society had almost ceased to exist, Miss Sally Jackson and her friend, Mrs. Jennie C. Morton, took up the work, and their zeal and knowledge saved it from oblivion. They both loved Kentucky history and revered those heroes and heroines who had made it. The organ of the society is the Register of the Kentucky State Historical Society, which compares favorably with the historical publications of any other state. Of this, H.V. McChesney, Sr., is editor and business manager and Mrs. Jouett T. Cannon associate editor.

The cooperation and service that the State Librarian and Director of Archives receives from the Historical Society, the Library Extension, and Dr. Harry Peters, Superintendent of Public Instruction, and their efficient staffs have made the work most interesting. Everyone is ready to do his part to put this great project over — the building and protection of libraries and the preservation of archives for the betterment of the state and people. In this connection we cannot fail to pay tribute to Dr. Frank L. McVey, the president of our State University, and his co-workers in that great institution.[4] Our other Kentucky educational institutions, the Eastern State Teachers College at Richmond, headed by Dr. H.L. Donovan; the Western State Teachers College at Bowling Green, headed by Dr. Paul Garrett; the Murray State Teachers College at Murray, headed by Dr. James Richmond; and the Morehead State Teachers College, headed by Dr. Harvey A. Babb, all with their splendid staffs of educators, have rendered valuable assistance in building up the libraries of our state and preserving our archives.[5]

Another institution that has given valuable aid in all the lines connected with library and archives is The Filson Club of Louisville. At all times its extensive collections have been made available to us. We have been free to call on its competent staff for advice and we can always depend on their understanding and cooperation. The liberal policy of its head, R.C. Ballard Thruston, is reflected in the splendid work of the staff, chief of those with whom we have had contact being Miss Ludie Kinkead and Otto Rothert, and Lucien Beckner, a member of the club who is an authority on Kentucky archives.

It has been said that most state officials, when they come to Frankfort, immediately become members of the "Why Not Club," which is another way of saying that as they view the Governor's Mansion and the executive offices and take the measure of the incoming and outgoing Chief Executives, the thought occurs to each, "If he can become Governor, why not I?"

So Frankfort through the years has been the burying ground of many dead hopes and vanished dreams. This is not generally true, however, for most officials do regain balance, become accustomed to their own status, and if they do have lofty ambitions and are defeated, take it like good sports, realizing that the race is not always to the swift nor the battle to the strong.

An unusually large number of officials do continue to make Frankfort their home after their terms of office are ended. It is truly one of the best places to live. There is a spirit of friendly interest and neighborliness that is hard to match, no matter where you go.

Frankfort is happy in its location, educational advantages, and the quality of its citizenship. It has always had a body of permanent citizens of solid background, people who are possessed of culture and social charm to a degree. Visitors to the city often remark on the high quality of citizenship, and especially on the charming women who entertain in their homes or make up the Woman's Club, the patriotic societies, and the clubs for business women. It has always been my pleasure on such occasions to state the truth, that the state capital has drawn to itself for 165 years the most alert, ambitious, and best equipped citizens from each county in the state. It is an advantage, too, that it has remained small enough that these individuals have not been swallowed up as might be the case if the state capital were a large city, especially a commercial city. As said before, many who have come for one administration have remained to become useful citizens of the community. Others who for various reasons have returned to their former homes or have settled elsewhere are almost certain to remain friends of Frankfort. These are some of the reasons why Frankfort is the friendliest capital city in the United States. There are few who have tasted the flavor of her hospitality, for either a long or short time, who will not agree with this.

This accounts, too, for the many titles heard on our streets. "General," "Governor," "Senator," and "Judge" remain when the term of service is ended and are worthily borne by those who have been elected or appointed to office at various times. The title of "Colonel" or "Kentucky Colonel" has been so well publicized that it need not be expanded here. Suffice it to say, however, that many times this honorary title has been bestowed in recognition of splendid service rendered to the state or country.[6] It is well to remember also that there have been literally hundreds of men in Kentucky and in and out of Frankfort who have honorably gained their titles in distinguished military, diplomatic, or governmental service.

As my mind reverts to history there arise before me — some of them in the rather remote past, others almost of today — such men as Judge William Lindsay, whom Theodore Roosevelt named as one of the few truly honest men he had met; Captain W.J. Stone, distinguished Confederate soldier and Confederate pension commissioner; Dr. John South, minister to Panama and Portugal; and many others, among them not the least distinguished, the retired officers of the United States Navy who have honored Frankfort in making it their home.

We cannot say too much for the lovely and gracious women who have graced Kentucky's new Executive Mansion in the past two decades as First Ladies. Mrs. A.O. Stanley, Mrs. James D. Black, Mrs. Ed Morrow, Mrs. William J. Fields, Mrs. Flem D. Sampson, Mrs. Ruby Laffoon — all these were women whose social ability and charm made them loved by all Kentuckians.

As one who has been entertained officially and socially at the

Mansion numerous times, it would be poor taste to make any comparisons; suffice it to say that no mistress of Kentucky's beautiful Mansion has been more gracious in proffering the spacious parlors for entertainments, nor in receptions and parties where she is hostess, than Mrs. A.B. Chandler, now Kentucky's First Lady. She is often assisted in entertaining by her mother, Mrs. M.L. Watkins of Virginia, and her charming young daughter, Marcella. Mrs. Keen Johnson, wife of the Lieutenant Governor, has also made a place for herself in the social life of Frankfort.

Following our First Ladies of Kentucky of the past decades, the women of the country are proud of our First Lady of the nation, the wife of the President of the United States, Mrs. Franklin Delano Roosevelt. Her loyalty to women, her broad thinking, independence, and feeling for her people, have endeared her to all Americans. The Victorian Age cannot surpass the Rooseveltian Age that will also make history for coming generations.

Patriotic societies have engaged the attention of our women for the past sixty years. These are devoted to history, genealogy, preservation of records and archives, and the promotion of a friendly spirit among those who inherit the same traditions and pride in the building of America by our forefathers. Various societies have chosen certain well-defined fields of research. Of these, the Daughters of the American Revolution lead in membership and maintain two splendid buildings as headquarters in Washington, D.C., Memorial Continental Hall and Constitutional Hall.[7] And the United Daughters of the Confederacy have come to Kentucky for two Presidents General.[8]

Let us review for a moment the position of women of yesterday and today. It is to be remembered that we were about seventy-two years securing the vote. Today there are under the last census 35,886,867 women over twenty-one years of age in the United States. We have had twenty-three women in Congress, one from Kentucky, Mrs. John Langley, who has proved herself to be a friend to women and made an outstanding Congresswoman. During 1937, 140 women Legislators served in thirty-five states. Since March 4, 1933, 7,900 women have been appointed postmasters. In our Capital City of Frankfort, we have Mrs. Maria Fish as postmaster, and she is making quite a record in her line of work.

We are sometimes apt to minimize the part played by women in olden days when we think of the many things they are doing now. But volumes could be written about the women of prominence and power in ancient times and the middle days. We are apt to forget that during the reign of most queens the age of their country has been called "Great," or named for the woman herself, as the "Elizabethan Age" or "Victorian Period." In all civilized countries women have always played an important part in the church and social life and have deeply influenced the governmental or political life. Women are leaders in church work, and it is a fact that no women took any part in the crucifixion of Christ. No woman touched the Cross; but, on the other hand, women were last at the Cross in sorrow and first at the Tomb in service and joy. In England, particularly, we are told women have always used their social prestige or the influence of their prominent positions to mold public opinion and to lobby for measures in which they are interested.

The missionary movements among modern women, as well as the woman's club movement, had their beginning with the early years of the nineteenth century, and by the middle of that hundred years both movements were well under way, although the general public did not get wise to this until about 1870, when women's clubs sprang up everywhere and the organizations of church women began to be powerful in all denominations. The whole century was one of great awakening in all lines, particularly humanitarian. The rights of the individual rose in the democracies to new heights. It was inevitable with such leaven in the social lump, that the hitherto neglected rights of women should be foremost in thought.

Added to this era of thinking in new terms was the fact that the Age of Invention so influenced the homes that one after another the ancient duties of women were uprooted from the hearthside and planted anew in factories, where machinery freed women from the daily drudgery of the past as it did the laborer in all fields. This was marvelous, but it quickly created new problems with which this generation is now wrestling.

It was in 1848 that the organized Woman's Rights movement began in the United States. It is significant that in a meeting in the East that was called for the purpose of agitating freedom for the slaves of the South, the women who attended sat in a gallery and were not allowed on the floor with the men. So blind are humans to the equal rights for all, even when considering the rights of a particular group. In 1869, women from nineteen states met in New York and formed a National Suffrage Association, headed by Elizabeth Cady Stanton and Susan B. Anthony, to work for an amendment to the federal Constitution which would enfranchise women. Later was formed the American Woman's Suffrage Association, led by Mrs. Henry Ward Beecher and Miss Lucy Stone, working to obtain suffrage through amendments to the Constitution. The two bodies united in 1890 to form a National Woman's Suffrage Association.

New Zealand was the first country in the world to grant women full suffrage, in 1893. Australia gave national suffrage in 1902. The first European country to give women full suffrage was Finland, in 1906. Norway followed in 1907. Many Central European countries granted woman suffrage before the present disturbance upset their governmental system.

In 1850, Clara Barton, later to found the Red Cross, was given a position in the patent office, the first woman to hold such a government place. Today there are more than 162,000 women in government work; we have twenty who have served in Congress, including two appointed and one elected Senator. Five women are in Congress at present and one in the Senate. Women have also held posts as Assistant Secretary of Treasury, Director of Mint, Assistant Public Printer, two federal judges, and one cabinet officer, while two women have been appointed as ministers to foreign countries. Judge Florence Allen of Cleveland, Ohio, was mentioned prominently for the place recently vacated on the Supreme Court.

In our own state, several women have been members of the welfare boards, where they have served faithfully and efficiently. Miss Linda Neville of Lexington was one of these, and in addition to her work on the state board, she devoted her whole life to philanthropic endeavor, most of this being in the interest of blind children and in the stamping out of trachoma, which is prevalent in many sections of the state. Dr. Lillian South is another who has devoted her life to the service of public health in every phase in Kentucky. She has been a living link between the health department and the federated women of the state.

Governor A.B. Chandler has not forgotten the women in giving out his appointments. Miss Marguerite Wohl is a recent appointee as head of the Welfare Board, while Mrs. Fanniebelle Sutherland, widely known for her work as police judge of Paris, is head of the Women's Division of the state prison, located in Shelby County. He has given me the honor of appointment as State Librarian and Director of Archives.

The woman of today values her vote and wants to use it where it will save and serve to build up the country. As officeholders, women ask only that their work stand on its own merits and be judged for conscientious effort and efficient achievement.

The changing times have brought changed ways. Can we not all go forward as fellow citizens, men and women, each "in honor preferring one another," each giving credit where credit is due, all together striving for the best and the highest? Each has a contribution to make to society and to government. Women have long been trained to look to men for leadership. They ask of men only recognition for their worth and for work in the sphere of their activities. Women have been led into a wider sphere and there they have wider opportunities. They ask that men who hold the destiny of nations in their hands act as statesmen.

Here in the library we meet the majority of all the lawyers of the state, who come here to consult the many volumes of law reports. We meet practically all our state legislators, when the General Assembly is in session biennially.

Many others come to see "the law." So many faces rise up from history — a great pageant of colorful characters, musical people, wise, talented, and witty people, who have been acquaintances and friends and loyal supporters of Frankfort, through these years of building upward and onward.[9]

There is a law on our statute books that allows counties to deposit archives with the state, where they are added to the treasures already assembled. Genealogists and research workers find more and more that such local records are the very lifeblood and sinews of history. Too often the writers of history in former years mentioned only a few leaders whose exploits are repeated over and over. Now we are adding the deeds and thoughts and lives of the great body of plain citizens who built up the country.

In this line a very outstanding work is being done by Walter M. Hoefelman of Louisville, head of the Archives Division of W.P.A., in cataloguing the documents of counties and localities. As rapidly as these are put in shape, copies of them are deposited in the State Library, the originals going to the counties. No more valuable work could be done in preserving our records and making them available. The state is fortunate in having at the head of this work a man of ability and discrimination.

The growth of the divisions at present included in the Department of Library and Archives has gone on with great rapidity during the past decade. The materials accumulated are increasing in bulk and in value constantly. Old documents are coming to light and being renovated. The extent, variety, and value of all the books and archives belonging to Kentucky can only be gauged by their titles as they appear in catalogues of the departments, on index cards, and in reports.

No one person can know all the details of such a vast assemblage of materials. Only by close organization of the various staffs, by lists and index cards, can we realize fully the immense amount of this valuable material. The old days when a librarian knew instantly by memory where to reach any book on a shelf are gone forever. System and efficiency require much mechanical skill on the part of the staff of modern libraries. The heads of such modern departments call for executive ability. Ripe scholarship with experience is an aid in appreciating all the historic and literary treasures of Kentucky. Those of us who work in the archives and the libraries realize there is a definite commercial value to the materials gathered here. This commercial value appeals to the taxpayers, especially in the last analysis; however, since the state does not sell or barter any of these literary and historic possessions, it comes back again to the sentimental and patriotic values involved.

We have, as a Commonwealth, treasures worth millions in our libraries and archives. They may be touched, handled, and used, yet we cannot "cash them" into actual money. So their values still remain largely intellectual and spiritual, since the priceless part of this heritage in books and laws and relics is intangible.

Our education as citizens should include appreciation of these precious possessions, knowledge of their value as inspiration for the youth, and pride in their possession as citizens of a state and nation so rich in resources that make history and encourage intellectual advancement.

It is just as much our duty to preserve the records of the past as it is the records of the present, for they are the source material in writing history. While it is true some have said that old records did not amount to anything and should be destroyed, when we hear remarks like these we are reminded of what Longfellow said,

> "Lives of great men all remind us
> We can make our lives sublime,
> And, departing, leave behind us
> Footprints on the sands of time."

Perhaps the poet had just such footprints in mind.

The importance of old records was not fully appreciated until they found the Rosetta Stone, a tablet of black basalt found in 1799 bearing inscriptions in hieroglyphic-demotic and Greek characters belonging to the period about 192 B.C. This furnished the key for deciphering the Egyptian hieroglyphics.

Really, a state cannot retain its self-respect or have the proper viewpoint about the future if it does not preserve the records of the past. The archives of our nation and state are gems that make history and build government. The foundation built by our ancestors will play a great part in building a firmer government for future generations.

Our country owes a debt of gratitude to the Daughters of the American Revolution and other historical organizations throughout the country for the great work they have done in preserving the archives of the past.

The world of tomorrow belongs to the youth of today. No age has ever presented such opportunity as the present. With the changing wheels of time, no one can visualize what is in the future. Traveling in air, under sea, on Mother Earth are some of the inventions far beyond the vision of our ancestors.

Then, should not all the records be well preserved for the benefit of future generations, so that they will have some material at least to build on. The future improves upon the past by opening up new avenues of usefulness.

Every kind of work that has been mine to do as a part of service to the public has been interesting and absorbing. Yet, had I the choice of any or all, it might be the department where my work now lies. Here the memory of school days has a chance to expand. Here, there are times when beloved books can be read and when one can add to them the experiences of time and change and enjoy the pleasures of youth enhanced and enlarged by the thoughts that have ripened with the years. Here some of the childhood ambitions of reading and thinking deeply really come to pass like dreams that become realities. Here dreams come out of the books around me and, in the language of the modern movie, they "walk and talk" and they surely do enlarge one's view of life and satisfy one's soul.

Again, one wishes mightily for friends, true friends, close friends, loving friends. Here in the library there are my friends, the books and those who have written them, friends who come when I open the pages and go back when other duties call me, there in the fast-locked pages to await my time to see them again. And, do not believe that only books are friends. Through these years of public duty, there have been "troops" of friends, real people, from all over the state, people from other states, friends who have been loyal and fine, on whom I could call at a moment's notice. They come and go in my memory; and happier than that, they come and go in reality, from day to day. There is no day that is not made more pleasant by visits from friends. Sometimes they have business to call them to the office, and it is always a pleasure to see them and render them every service possible.

I have learned that service in public office is not only an asset to success, but it enlarges your number of friends and makes you happier in your work.

In any case it is always an unmixed delight to have friends, and I realize, had my lot been cast in a sheltered home, I would have missed most of these delightful contacts. So there is always compensation. Which reminds me of Emerson and his, "For everything you have missed you have gained something else; and for everything you gain you lose something. Pray God that the scales will balance evenly when the last is said and all is done."

In the words of Bayard Taylor, it is well for all to remember that:

"Fame is what you have taken,
Character is what you give;
When to this truth you waken
Then you begin to live."

Then, why not live within our books with the "Book of Books" as a guide?

Chapter VIII Notes

1. This wing now houses a museum and the Kentucky Historical Society offices.
2. The Kentucky Historical Society is now part of the Education, Arts, and Humanities Cabinet.
3. The State Librarian's office is now in the Department of Libraries and Archives' Clark-Cooper Building on Coffee Tree Road in Frankfort.
4. Mrs. Cromwell continued:

"Chief among those who have aided the Department of Library and Archives are: Dr. Thomas D. Clark, Bart N. Peak, Ezra L. Gillis, Mrs. W.T. Lafferty, and Miss Margaret King."
5. These schools are now, respectively, Eastern Kentucky University; Western Kentucky University; Murray State University; and Morehead State University.
6. Kentucky Colonels have been issued more freely in recent decades, used to reward political friendships as well as meritorious service. The Kentucky Colonels organiza-

tion continues its support of worthy causes.

7. Cited by the author as past state regents and leaders were Mrs. Stanley Reed of Maysville and Washington, D.C.; Mrs. Eugene Ray of Louisville; Mrs. Mary Shackelford of Frankfort; Mrs. Grant Lilly of Richmond; Mrs. Graham Lawrence of Shelbyville; Mrs. William E. Rhodes of Lexington; Mrs. Keene Arnold of Versailles; and Mrs. Frederick A. Wallis of Paris (Kentucky). Among the "earnest workers" were Mrs. Charles Keith of Richmond; Mrs. Bright Hawes of Maceo; Mrs. William E. Richards of Owingsville; and Mrs. John Chenault of Louisville.

8. Those associated with the United Daughters of Confederacy were Mrs. Roy W. McKinney of Paducah and Mrs. John L. Woodbury of Louisville, both Presidents General; state president Miss Jessie L. Yager of Owensboro; and Mrs. Preston Johnston of Lexington; Mrs. Josephine M. Turner of Louisville; Mrs. Robert Price of Providence; Mrs. Harry McCarty of Nicholasville; Mrs. Mary Dowling Bond of Lawrenceburg; and Miss Annie Bell Fogg of Frankfort, who "rendered great service in preserving the records of the War Between the States."

9. Those listed by the author were Judge Thomas Hines, General Basil Duke, Attorney General Jack Hendricks, Marse Henry Watterson, General John B. Castleman, General Simon Bolivar Buckner, Senator Jo. Blackburn, Robert B. Franklin, Robert Burns Wilson, Paul Sawyier, Major Henry T. Stanton and Theodore O'Hara.

IX

Onward and Upward

Help thyself and God will help thee.

Sometimes I have felt the past is like an ever-shifting panorama, so swift have the years of my life sped on, but a sharp pain in my heart makes me realize all at once that this is not so; that the years have held realities that hurt the heart and seared the soul; when the memory of mother, husband, and son, and dearly beloved kin, friends who have gone before becomes so sharp that it is easy to see, or rather to feel, why there are some who seek solace in trying to rend the veil that hides our immortal ones from our earthly view. My father passed on before the days of my recollection and his high ideals were passed on to me by mother and near relatives.

The vain question, "Why?," keeps forever forming in the mind when I think back on the World War and why it had to come into the peaceful years of America's life, and my life, and that of the million mothers who were bereft through it and its results. For in the last analysis that cataclysm of horror changed the tenor of our lives so that other tragedies followed in course. The war and its effects caused the loss of my son long before his time — of that I am sure, according to nature. It changed the nerves of the boys who took part until in civilian life they could not respond to safety measures as they would have if the even tenor of their lives had not been interrupted by the ghastly days of 1917-1918.

Yet again, I think all is a part of a whole so large and so inclusive of all humanity that our own small part is but an atom in a great Sahara. Yet, with all the personal tragedies that have deeply touched me, I can say with unfaltering faith that there is an overruling Providence and that sometime, somewhere, we shall know all, and that all will be well.

193

While sitting here on Coronado Beach, Florida, the land of flowers and sunshine, gazing on the blue waters of the mighty Atlantic, watching the beautiful yachts as they ply so gracefully over the billows of rolling waters, each one pulling for its destiny with a mission to perform, I thought how like the restlessness of the mighty waters is the soul of man. Onward and upward we are traveling like the surging billow just before me with the whitecaps that come and go, with little time to linger on the shore. And so it is, the great human family sailing onward, each soul fired with ambition in some form, striving to reach its goal upward.

The restlessness of man may be compared with the mighty deep, rushing for the shore — not to linger long — but back and forth it continues its course, sometimes smooth, with its stormy hours, then peaceful; as in our lives some days are rough with sorrow and troubles that shut out sunshine until we muster up courage to pick up the thread of life and pull to the port of happiness and carry on with the great throng of humanity just as the ships from the sea make for the port of safety, their haven of rest.

Here, time, the great measurer of lives, is our guide as we journey along and it is up to each soul to keep step with Father Time and do his or her best as the moments pass. Today in this progressive age of action, vision, and meditation, a glimpse backward and a look forward show a pathway bright with the glory of a great heritage of womanhood through the ages, with guideposts along the way as one by one women gained the equal rights of citizenship; and another shining pathway of light leads on toward years when these privileges will grow greater and will be appreciated more and more by women everywhere.

Personally my thoughts run along the same road, keeping pace with my sister women, thinking with them on the problems we have solved and on the problems that will arise, praying that we all may be guided by the beacon lights of patriotism and Christian service as we fill our places of labor in the home, church, school, and state.

Many of my diversions might sound like work to those who follow more recreational lines. I have always found that a change of work meant a chance to rest. The few times I have felt the need of rest in the supine sense I have "hied" away to the ocean, especially the Floridian coast as today, listening to the sound of the rolling tides that comfort my soul as I contemplate the sea of life and think of the ceaseless, ever-surging activity of humanity and the Omnipotence that controls the tides and the seasons. One of the truly restful scenes of the earth is found near the surge of the ocean, another is the vastness of the mountains. To go in a car with congenial friends, leave the valleys far behind, and the plateaus, to rise imperceptibly by winding roads until one is in a mist of green where the forest reigns supreme, where one after another rounded peak rises towards skies of blue, this is enhanced when the elevation is high enough for little wisps of cloud to float around the green-clad mountains, or the rain clouds swoop down and darken all the day so that the soul withdraws within and the outer world is shut away, as if a veil were drawn across our very consciousness. It is so with the individual soul. When one attempts to tell the inmost secret of the heart, how difficult it is. One flees inward and looks upon the secret and sacred places, and there are no words to express the thoughts. All the glory and beauty of mountain scenery is enhanced when one's companions are in fully sympathy and the very raindrops patter in songs without words.

One recent motor trip to the mountains in the interest of my work as Librarian and Director of Archives has brought the same kind and degree of pleasure as those that were part of my duty as Park Director. I took this trip with some friends up to Highland School in the heart of Breathitt County. It is nine miles from Jackson, with the creek bed for our road, tall mountains towering on either side, banks and ravines closed in a dense thicket of mountain laurel, rhododendron, and holly, while ferns dip in graceful fringes from beneath the forest robes of the steep mountain sides.

Here the school has a God-given opportunity and the devoted workers are answering a challenge that appeals to all. The good people up and down the creek came in numbers, all alive with interest to see and hear visitors from the settlements.

On this particular day I was accompanied by Mrs. R.L. Northcutt of Lexington, Mrs. Ethel Cuniff, and Mrs. Martha Bach of Jackson. We spent a thrilling and interesting day among these good people who represent the purest Anglo-Saxon blood extant today.

In my home I have tried to be as hospitable as possible when my hours were governed by public duties, for I verily believe "the ornament of a house is the friends who frequent it." Hours of conversation with friends cannot be measured in pleasure or in profit.

It is the same with books. From girlhood days when much-loved skates were traded for books, it has been the same. The companionship of a good book is well bought even at a goodly price; and evenings spent in my library are well remembered.

Someone asked if I, who have had a political career, loved my home life. I looked in astonishment, for how could anyone think that any amount of laborious public service could ever dim the love of home latent in the heart of any woman? When the seasons come and go for cleaning and refurnishing the home, I feel the same urge as if I had never spent an hour in an office. Perhaps there is really more glamour to it, for had it been the monotonous duty, year after year, it might have palled. However, every picture on the wall has a meaning and history to me.

Things stand today as when the home circle was broken, and may I say to those who are so blessed with a happy home and their loved ones, enjoy your blessings for you know not how long they will last. There is not a spot where we roam that can fill the place of a happy home; be it in a mansion, a cottage, or a hut, it is home sweet home.

Early in life it came to me with overwhelming force that toil is everywhere. I remember a story of our childhood reading days, probably in the old McGuffy Readers. This story relates how the little boy ran away from Mr. Toil, who wanted him to study hard and then to work in his garden. This seemed such a hard lot that the boy started on a journey to get as far away from Mr. Toil as possible. He visited dances, music halls, playgrounds, and all the places where people gathered to play and forget work. Each time he was entranced with a life that promised all play and no work, until he would stay on a little longer and begin the play life with the others. He would find each time that Mr. Toil ruled all the world. That no one could run so far that he did not have to toil at some task, even if he called it play. It seems to me that this story could be told and heeded many times in this modern life, when we hear so much about recreation and leisure. In preaching against the goodness of hard work, we fall into the same dangers the little boy encountered.

I would not for a moment deny the pleasure, the necessity of recreation and leisure. It is a very desirable goal to see at the end of a hard task the playground of life. But just here we need to check up to see if we are overstepping the bounds of healthful play and leisure. It is in directed play we find the answer to the word fatigue. This is true whether it is the directed play of children under a recreation teacher, or the directed play of adults under the stimulus of their own determination to make the best of playtime as well as of work time. The right use of leisure is one of the greatly needed lessons of today. Just leisure with nothing to add is appalling to consider.

There is much beauty in everyday things, in the flowers by the roadside, the stars that begem the sky at night, the seasons, and the changing weather; there is so much to learn every day that we despair of ever learning much, but we do not despair of enjoying every minute of our time. The more we know, the less we think we know, and we begin to see what a great field is ahead for us to cultivate.

Nowhere on earth is there a greater joy in looking at scenery than in our own beloved Kentucky. We have the greatest variety of scenery, as of weather, and if we would make the most of it as those who live in lands where the climate if the principal source of income, as well as of conversation, we could all make our task as delightful as any other. A lovely place to live is largely a state of mind, but bluegrass, forest trees, fertile fields, fine farms, and in fact every section of our state filled with scenery, history, and romance, with its hospitable people sheltered in every nook, make it a real Mecca for tourists from every section of the globe.

Church going is another pleasure open to all, and we feel it not only a duty but a pleasure to attend service when roaming around, as well as when in the home town. It has always been a fetish of mine to see that my help in the home have their church life. It takes but little managing and planning for them to attend the church of their choice on the Sabbath, just as the family in the home. They should have the same opportunity to attend their church, for I am sure they feel as uplifted and helped as we do when they enter the sacred place where everything is designed to make one forget worldly cares and think of heavenly things. It is a pleasure to see that my household help always have the time to enjoy their religion.

For many years after the family circle was broken, I lived in the home with Aunt Winnie Thomas and Herbert Dodson, of whom I have already spoken, and Judge and Mrs. Ernest Clarke, General and Mrs. Tandy Ellis, Dr. Jaggers and wife, and Miss Anna Lou Deeds. These splendid people helped me to keep the home fires burning and to carry on during their stay in the Capital City. Today I have with me my sister, Mrs. Mary Sidney Wilkins, and her grandson, David Balch, Jr. There is nothing like the companionship of your family, those who have the same recollections, the same congenialities. "God set the solitary in families" for a purpose, and a deep purpose.

My only other close kin surviving are two nieces, Rose Mary Balch Scott of Frankfort and Ann Wilkins of Cairo, Illinois, and my nephew Guy Wilkins of Vicksburg, Mississippi.

A political worker, or any woman who has a career, sometimes seems to herself to be something less than a woman when she sees about her those who have been so fortunate as to be placed in a family that had few changes as the years went by, a quiet place where all the virtues and the pleasures of companionship had time to flower and bring forth fruit. Yet, there comes again the thought that if one does her very best where fate seems to have prepared the way for her to live and cleared the path in which she is to walk, that she has also merited the praise of "She hath done what she could."

A friend once said to me, "You don't have any fun; you take life so seriously, with the whole world on your shoulders. You are not modern at all. My advice is to be up to date and do the things that others do." While she was sincere in her advice, I replied, "We all have equal rights and privileges in thought, action, and deeds, and if we do not want to do certain things they say are modern we have the same right to do our way as you have yours." So each one has a right to be independent in thought and action. We shall never go astray if we take for our guide a Higher Power who always directs the destiny of man. This, after all, I have found to be the key to success, not only in the church, but in business and politics. Experience has taught many of us that one can be as clean in business and politics as in church and home, the two sacred spots of life.

In the library where my duties now lie, in the various extension and historical divisions, and in the archives lie the olden, golden dreams of girlhood, when I came as a timid tyro into the library of the state, hoping and praying for guidance and teaching that would develop my personality and ability so that I might do an acceptable piece of work and that the friends who had brought me this opportunity would be proud of my labors, at least would not be ashamed of my efforts.

Now, as the years have rolled on, so many prayers have been answered, so many golden dreams have come true, that sometimes it seems the many blessings that have been mine far overshadow the troubles that have come. So far health and strength have been mine to do the given task at the right time, and I trust it will always be so, and that success will measure up to every effort in all my undertakings. I fully realize with the help of God all things will work out for good for those who trust Him.

Every year one learns to do things in a better way and looks ever eagerly forward to a continuance of opportunity to work and to do one's part in a world that needs all the work and thought that earnest people can give to it. If in a few words I could give guidance, to the young people especially, it would be to say, "Find work, fit yourself for it, carry it on" as unto the Lord; never forget the hand that feeds you, then feel that no matter how small a duty it is, you have in it success. Cultivate the feeling of success; fight defeatism and failure.

My leisure time and vacation days are usually taken up with parliamentary law, out of which I get a real joy and thrill. No other study gives quite the poise and preparedness as this subject, and everyone before the public today should know something about it in this progressive age. How well I remember when girls were twitted because they did not know how to conduct a meeting or even put a motion; boys knew about as little, but it was said girls knew less. My advice to all young people, especially those who expect to be in public life, is to have a broad knowledge of this science which directs successfully all organizations. In reviewing my pleasures, it seems to me that in my parliamentary law lies one of my greatest. It has brought me into pleasant contact with the leading women of my state and other states. It has deepened the bonds of affection for the fine women who comprise the Federation of Women's Clubs, Daughters of American Resolution, Daughters of the Confederacy, the Professional and Business Women's Club, the Garden Club, the Pen Woman's Club, and many other groups, including thousands of men and women, boys and girls, who have been in my classes in parliamentary law all over the state.

In parliamentary law there is a sense of system and order to be gained in no other study. It is to be recommended highly among the many studies that women take up, to give them a sense of balance and confidence. This science that I have worked hard on has been the greatest help to me of any in my public career, and I can honestly advise our women to study it. When we talk of culture and study art and literature, it sometimes happens that we emerge from our profuse baths in them with rather confused concepts, rather vague ideas, it seems; but when we test our knowledge of proper procedure by the set of principles of parliamentary law it sets a definite bound to our mental activities and gives symmetry and form to our thoughts, so that of necessity it is not dry. One friend laughed when I spoke of parliamentary law as a real relaxation for the mind, but it truly is. It sets a pattern to which we must cut our cloth; it eliminates vagueness and sharpens the outlines of what we may learn.

In my present position there is a glorious opportunity to live among books, to absorb their ideals, to treasure the golden memories they inspire, and to preserve the priceless archives of our state. The books on these shelves and the documents in the files silently tell a wonderful story. It is a pleasure to be situated where these sublime thoughts prevail, and where the deep thinkers of our state come to consult with the wisdom of the ages that is imprisoned here. Truly, the Librarian keeps the key to a vast storehouse of knowledge and history.

And so it is that the first woman to seek and to be elected to state office in Kentucky, who has passed through all the various stages of elective and appointive achievements, now finds herself again State Librarian of Kentucky, first an elective office by the State Legislature, and today an appointive office by the Governor. She spends her time among precious documents, garnering more, caring for these, trying to interest others in such a useful and sentimental hobby. Here she spends her time at work in the historical archives of golden days gone by, for in these books are imprisoned the gleam of the knightly valor of the Kentuckians, the soul of their daring adventures, the story of their achievements.

Again I must say that such success as I have attained as Librarian, Secretary of state, Treasurer of Kentucky, and Park Director is due not only to my own efforts, but to the help of the women of Kentucky who were anxious to see one of their own make good. We have worked together to secure the confidence and support of the men, which we now feel has been accomplished. Women have come into their own kingdom, and now they must not abdicate the ideals of our women that hold the fate of our country.

One aim in my life which is bound up with ambition to succeed is to continue to carry on the great work started by our leaders in suffrage, paving the way for women of the state and nation to travel beside the men, assuming our full share of the burdens and responsibilities involved, to do my work so it will be a credit to womanhood. Then the men will realize that women can be a help in building up government. Together we can make this country the greatest in the world.

America has a great destiny and it is up to the women to help in its fulfillment. Thus I have chosen to quote from "America the Beautiful" and to apply it to Kentucky, my beloved.

"O beautiful for spacious skies,
 For amber waves of grain,
 For purple mountain majesties

200

Above the fruited plain!

"O beautiful for patriot dream
That sees beyond the years
Thine alabaster cities gleam
Undimmed by human tears!

"America! America!
God shed his grace on thee
And crown they good with brotherhood
From sea to shining sea!"

To those who read this book I cannot refrain from passing on the key that unlocks the door to success as far as the writer has attained it, not only as a public servant in politics and business, but from a woman's viewpoint and experience. God first in every action; love of work; service; preparedness; energy; promptness; personality. These with high ideals and a smile will unlock any door into the great chamber of life for which all are striving — Success. And so brings up to date the story of my public service, which I hope to continue by helping carry on the great work ahead with the high ideals that befit the womanhood of America.